Praise for
. . . Almost Della

"Della Barbato is a living testimony to the fact that the truth indeed sets us free. Her story is powerful. Her telling is authentic and clear-eyed. This message of healing and empowerment is needed in our world now more than ever."

—**REV. MICHAEL GOTT**, Senior Minister, Unity of Houston

"Painstaking truth; heartfelt reflection; powerful prose."

—**NORA FIRESTONE**, Author and Journalist

". . . *Almost Della* is the story of a courageous woman who, more than anything, wants to help others through their darkest moments. To relieve the shame, guilt, blame and remorse and to help others recover as she has. It is truly a story of courage."

—**DIANE ST. YVES**, Family Law Attorney

"Della shares her life experiences to let young women know that they are not alone, their life has value, and they are not their circumstances! Raw truth written by a survivor."

—**KATHLEEN F. LEONARD**, EdD, Family and Life Coach

"My heart felt for Della and for myself. I too am a victim of abuse and although our paths and recovery may have differed, . . . *Almost Della* is able to touch upon wounds with compassion, vulnerability, and love. Her bravery and courage to 'tell all' will no doubt help to heal so many women worldwide."

—**AMY O'BRIEN**, Artist, amyobrienart.com

"... *Almost Della* is an amazing journey and discovery of self-worth. To know Della is to know of her love and compassion for all living things. To read her story is to see incredible bravery as she confronts her past with brutal honesty to help us see that transformation can free our spirit to soar to a new awareness of self-love."

—**JON VAUGHAN**

"Courage is the first word that came to mind when I met Della and learned of her book. For decades, my work as a psychotherapist has involved adults, men and women alike, who suffered with the trauma of childhood sexual abuse. Della's story recounts the tragic experience of thousands and her book is a brilliant and inspiring account and example of a way forward to healing. I salute Della's authenticity and honesty and know that this book offers hope and guidance for all its' readers."

—**SANDRA C. ZBOYAN**, M.S., L.M.F.T.

"I was absorbed as one might be with a suspense novel, where the heroine unbeknownst to her, but not to us, is being drawn ever deeper into an evil web. At times almost unreadable, Della Barbato grippingly describes the state of the vulnerable adolescent psyche tortured and distorted by a pedophile's manipulations. While horrifying and heartbreaking, these accounts may prove important and perhaps even consoling ultimately to others similarly victimized."

—**EILEEN**, Sister Survivor

"This book is a brutally honest story of one young woman's journey through childhood and adolescence that will help others in its telling."

—**LEIGH PAGE**, Dad with a daughter

"... *Almost Della* is an honest, emotionally charged autobiography by a fresh new author. Her story, some told in diary excerpts, is that of a teenager who, at the most vulnerable time in her life, is a victim of sexual abuse. Instead of the love and acceptance that she so desperately needs, she is thrust into a relationship that will have repercussions in her life for decades to come. This is also a story of redemption. Della shares her journey, her experience, strength and hope, as she navigates her way back to herself."

—**CINDY WYLIE**, CASA Guardian Ad Litem

"The author details her journey involving sexual abuse as a teenager that no young woman should have to endure. Unfortunately, it is an all too common occurrence that stays hidden due to denial and shame and an unsupportive society at large. The harmful impacts continue long after the abuse ends. But the author demonstrates with warmth and compassion that help is available and that recovery and healing are attainable. . . . *Almost Della* is a story written with courage that offers encouragement."

—**WES SCHULZ**, A Grandfather

"Della has such an honest voice. I have a great deal of respect for her to share her story with the world. I know women will be able to relate to her and become empowered through her voice."

—**ASHA JOHN**, Supporter & Survivor

"Della doesn't just survive—she thrives—and this book is a testament to how one can stand in her own strength, overcome abuse and reach far beyond the adversity that comes with the longstanding trauma of being victimized. Through her story she provides inspiration and hope for so many."

—**JENNIFER J.**

Almost Della:
From Sexual Abuse to Survivor
by Della Barbato

© Copyright 2017 Della Barbato

ISBN 978-1-63393-541-9

All rights reserved. No part of this publication may be reproduced, stored in a retrieval system, or transmitted in any form or by any means—electronic, mechanical, photocopy, recording, or any other—except for brief quotations in printed reviews, without the prior written permission of the author.

AFTERMATH
Words and Music By ADAM LAMBERT, FERRAS ALGAISI,
ELY WEISFELD and ALISAN L PORTER
© 2009 UNSUB PUB, LLC (ASCAP) and CROWN AND
SCEPTER MUSIC PUBLISHING (ASCAP).
All rights on behalf of UNSUB PUB, LLC and
CROWN AND SCEPTER MUSIC PUBLISHING
Administered by WB MUSIC CORP.
All Rights Reserved
Used by Permission of ALFRED PUBLISHING, LLC

Published by

www.dellabarbato.com

...Almost Della

from sexual abuse
to survivor

Della Barbato

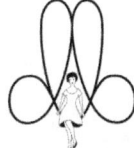

For the love of my sister

Preface

WRITING THIS BOOK was often quite painful. I suspect it will also be tender for many of you, my readers, who have traveled a similar path. Although some names have been changed to protect the innocent, the stories are real.

It is my sincere hope that in sharing the suffering of different periods of my personal journey, I will somehow empower others who are hurting. In this sense, I am sharing a gift that others have bestowed upon me. After all is said and done, it is the power of our stories that bless us with the courage to heal and move forward. I pray you find this strength as well. Life is a work in progress. I encourage you to explore your own life as you read through the story of mine. Writing this book was a labor of love. As you will come to know, I am . . . *Almost Della*, and that is magnificent enough.

Table of Contents

INTRODUCTION 1
KNOW MY TRUTH. 4
GROWING UP. 9
THE FRED DIARIES 37
OFF TO COLLEGE. 85
FORBIDDEN FRUIT 120
OFF TO EUROPE, BACK TO MYSELF . . 167
CALIFORNIA 234
HOME TO TEXAS 245
DADDY 249
MORE TRAVEL, MORE MEN 262
INDIA CALLS AGAIN 274
THE VIOLATION 295
MY JOURNEY TO SURVIVOR 303
THE BIG REVEAL 315
THE LETTER OF MY TRUTH 342
LOVE YOU ALL 352
EPLIOGUE 368
ACKNOWLEDGMENTS 374

Introduction

DO YOU FEEL that you are good enough? Are you important? Do you matter in this world? Do you make a positive impact on others? For the majority of my life so far, the answer to these questions was "no."

Since childhood, I have spent much of my time and my heart seeking acceptance and approval from my family and peers. My parents separated and got a divorce when my older sister and I were only five and four. Then, a year later, Daddy moved out of state. Neither of my parents ever found true love from a life partner, so I was not able to witness a healthy relationship.

My mother raised us on her own, earning a minimum wage for many years. My father and I had a strong, albeit long-distance, relationship throughout my childhood and teenage years. Undoubtedly, however, his absence was a factor in my "never good enough" stigma. I especially sought acceptance from my older sister, who threw criticism and meanness at me on a daily basis until I was sixteen and she moved out. I was cast aside and shunned all throughout my school years, even by my supposed "best friends." I will never forget the despair and loneliness I experienced as those "friends" sped away from me in the high school parking lot on the one day seniors could leave campus for lunch. I'm guessing you have felt a similar experience of "not good enough." Most of us have.

I am a survivor of father abandonment, teenage sexual abuse, psychological abuse, self-blame, depression and addiction. It has been a long and difficult journey, but entering my fifth decade of life, I am finally in the process of finding unconditional love for the magnificent being that is me. And I am ultimately learning to trust myself, to pause and listen to that gut feeling that says, *this does not feel right.* I no longer shove my feelings down deep inside me, thinking that they are wrong or feeling guilty for even having them. I have learned that my feelings are real, and that they are important. In essence, they are data. A window to what is happening deep within me.

I no longer seek approval from anyone. I have found that needing approval from others for my life choices shifts my power to them. I also try to surround myself with people who uplift me. Negative energy only goes in one direction.

Throughout my lifetime of pain, I have been very fortunate to have traveled to twenty-six countries—and counting—on this great planet. I don't just visit the tourist attractions, I get off the beaten path. I make a point to get to know some of the locals. I experience the culture. Immersion in other cultures has opened my mind to all the possibilities life has to offer. It allows me to know that every human being is on this Earth for a reason. And that no one has more basic intrinsic, human rights than anyone else. Not even the pope.

Through a lot of hard work, recovery, and therapy, I am tapping my inner strength. Through realizing and embracing a love for myself, I have rediscovered and nurtured a compassion for all human beings, especially those who have been sexually, emotionally and/or physically abused. I have devoted my life to increasing awareness of those who mean harm. If you feel that you have been harmed or violated, talk about it with someone. And if that person does not listen, go to the next person. Do not stop until your voice is heard and your feelings validated.

I am humbled and honored that you have decided to join me on this journey. I am dedicating my book to the women of the world. Why? Because I believe that our future hinges on women finding and nurturing a love for ourselves. So that we can then reach our highest potential and use our God-given talents to make this world a better place. Through my suffering, I have learned that it is really all about rethinking the way that I have treated myself in the past. Which stemmed from the way that I thought about myself. We must change our behavior towards ourselves. But change cannot happen unless awareness happens first.

Chapter One

KNOW MY TRUTH

SILENT FOR SO LONG

Truth has many meanings. What is truth to one is a lie to another. My "truth" was kidnapped by a series of events during those fragile, formative teenage years. Over time, a deep and abiding fear arose within me that warped my thoughts and emotions. Desperately afraid of losing their love, I kept my secrets from those dearest to my heart, my sister and my mother. I kept them from everyone. I lived for decades within a dungeon of my own making, a dungeon built of shame and pain. My carefully created illusion became my bitter reality, one I would foolishly endure for decades. It was an ugly truth.

The abnormal became normal for me. I clung to it for so long that I gradually grew numb to how my shame was tearing me apart from the inside out. At some point in my teenage years, I innocently decided that if I just ignored my truth long enough, eventually the pain would fade away. The opposite proved to be true. But as Paul Simon writes, "silence, like a cancer, grows."

Over the years, my self-imposed silence and solitude slowly ate away at me. It gave birth to depression, suicidal thoughts, and addiction, unwanted offspring of my persistent denial. Still, I clung to the misguided belief that it was the price I had to pay to protect my loved ones. Until I no longer could.

After thirty-plus years of this insanity, my life unraveled. I was left, finally, with only two choices: confront my demons, or die denying them. Through the grace of my Higher Power, whom I choose to call God, and the helpful souls in my tortured path, I was finally blessed with the courage to do battle with my twisted torment. Come hell or high water, it was time to face the truth. *The real truth.*

I faced tremendous fear sharing my truth with my mom and sister. Their love and acceptance was critical to me. I felt that I could not risk losing my relationship with them. Through three and a half years of intensive therapy, I finally came to realize how my absolute dependence on the need to share my truth with them fueled the fear of my self-imprisonment. It is incredibly difficult to come to grips with the truth I had fled from for so long. Be that as it may, I was out of options. I only hoped our shared love would be strong enough to conquer those evil twins of pain and shame.

From a young age, I found great comfort in capturing my feelings on paper. I now know that I did so to relieve some of the ever-present pressure, my self-imposed fear of telling another human being my dirty secrets. As will become apparent, and indicated by entry dates, words I put to paper throughout my life have documented my traumatic past—warts and all. Sometimes chronological, other times retrospective, I trust they will provide an accurate glimpse into my psyche, reflective of thoughts and feelings at the time they were written. I encourage you to keep a journal of your own, because with awareness and time come change, but truth never changes.

There is a quote from the movie *The Help* that I feel we could all benefit from if we recited it daily to ourselves and to our children: "I is kind, I is smart, I is important." Through experience, I have found that before I could truly love another, I must first love myself. I did not truly believe this until I experienced suffering as a result of blaming, shaming and hating myself. I now see how crucial it is to begin building self-worth at a young age. Somehow I missed that. This book will portray the story of my life. *Almost Della* chronicles a path to become aware of the shame we carry, and teaches us to transform it into an abiding love of self.

March 2016—A Sign from God

So much healing, light, and love has happened to me over the past few years. I had written a four-page letter, my pages of truth, to share with Mom and my only sister, Marissa. The date was set for February 13th, 2016. Finally, after thirty-four years, my sister and my mother would know what happened to me! But I had to cancel, because on February 9th, my heart had raced, and it felt wrong as I practiced reading the letter to my therapist of two-plus years, Jasmine. Reading it aloud, I realized that I had to face more and more buried guilt before I could reveal my truth to them. And I was terrified of the pain my truth would bring to them. I was even more terrified of losing the love of my only sister and my mother. I was also certain that my niece and nephew, the only children I helped to raise and loved as my own, could never know my truth. It would hurt them severely. I held the protection of my sister's family in my mind as I hid my truth for three decades. And so, I dropped the idea of revealing my truth to Mom and Marissa. Or at least postponed it, until . . . I don't know what. A sign from God?

Well, I got the sign! On March 11th, my niece, Alexa (she goes by Alex), was coming into town for a cousin's wedding. Marissa had planned a lunch for her with family that Sunday after the wedding. On March 9th, I called Marissa to ask her if she would move the lunch time forward one hour, because daylight savings was happening that weekend. She told me that she couldn't, because she had invited others to our family lunch with Alex. I had not been aware of this. She said that she didn't want to call Fred, their father, to move the lunch time. I froze in terror. Of course, she immediately noticed. I sensed that she could feel my fear through the phone. But I could not say a word. I could not even move.

"That was a long time ago, Della," Marissa said after a pause.

I panicked because I didn't know what to say. And I also knew that my silence was evidence of my fear. I could not tell her that I could NOT GO, and I could not tell her *why* I could not go! I could not face my abuser. Not now! I could not face Fred!

Marissa finally said, "I'm sorry. What's wrong?"

Continued silence followed. The adrenalin was rising in my body. I thought, *No, no, no! Not like this! Whatever I say next will be the beginning of the end of our relationship!* I could not speak. I could not find words. The silence consumed me. I was sweating profusely. *This is it*, I thought. I was keenly aware that my continued silence was speaking volumes. I was terrified, and I didn't know what to say!

"Well, I can't uninvite him," Marissa finally said.

And suddenly, I was somehow able to spill the words that seemed appropriate and yet not too revealing, "No. But I can uninvite myself."

And there it was! The cat was finally out of the bag! Those few words marked the first time that I had been true to myself in over three decades. Marissa knew that I could not see Fred. In that moment, by telling my sister my truth, I had finally found my voice and become authentic. The sincerity with which I was finally able to speak my truth felt like a dam of lies breaking through my soul to release the flow of reality that I had kept hidden for so long.

But at what cost? I froze in terror. What would she think of me? Would she judge me for my terrible act at the age of sixteen? Was I going to lose my sister forever now that she knew the truth? And what about my mother? And my niece and nephew?

We finished the conversation with small talk and hung up. Then I broke down in panic. Sheer terror tore throughout my entire body. I sobbed uncontrollably. I did not know how to handle this alone. Then, a light bulb: I had to speak to my therapist! She was the only one who could help me. She is a family counselor, in addition to being my individual therapist. She is trained in helping all family members with substance abuse and trauma. And she was the only person in the world who knew my story. Who knew *my truth*.

I quickly texted Jasmine and begged her for an immediate session. Could she squeeze me in today? I would not ask if it were not important. I had never done that before. She texted back that she had no openings today, but that she could talk with me on the phone for fifteen minutes later in the afternoon.

When we finally got to talk on the phone, I explained the conversation that I had had with Marissa. She was amazing, as always. She told me that I was in a state of panic because I was taking on the emotions of Marissa and Mom. YES! That was exactly it! I was reacting to my silence, because my decades-old truth was never talked about! She said that I could acknowledge my truth to Marissa without revealing the extent of the abuse. I could speak to this without violating any boundaries. She told me to own this changed approach to the truth, that it was not denying my truth. She told me that this was finally my opportunity to pit respect and integrity against the culture of silence that me and my family had been nurturing for so long. She told me that I had prepared for this. She was so amazing. By the end of the conversation, I felt confident, clear, and calm.

I wrote a one-page letter for this new conversation I would have with Marissa, one on one. As it turns out, she was coming over the next day to color my hair for our cousin's wedding. Our appointment had been postponed one day due to bad weather. Coincidence? I think not. It was perfect! The opportunity had risen by itself, or perhaps it was a sign from God, but it did not come from me. It was not me who was in control of the timing of this revealing of my truth. I felt a bit nervous about the confrontation with my only sister, but I knew that this was right. The time had come. That sense of knowing was strong. Perhaps it was another gift from the universe.

TODAY

After suffering for so long, I was more than ready to face my past, and hoped I could now begin to move forward. *Not so fast, Della,* the spirit whispered in my ear, *you still have much work to do!* Patience has never been one of my strong suits, but

I knew the advice should be heeded. So bear with me, and join me on my journey. The destination can wait, and will always be there . . . waiting.

Chapter Two

GROWING UP

THE OLD HOUSE—1967

Marissa and I were born to Sicilian parents. We are third-generation Italian, full-blooded. We are only thirteen months apart. In the beginning, our family lived in a small, two-bedroom house in a suburb north of Houston, Texas. Marissa and I shared a double bed in the second bedroom, first door on the left from our sunken living room. Our bed was covered with a lumpy, old, light blue bedspread. It wasn't lumpy because it was old: it had those little fluffy balls made from the same material somehow sewn into the fabric. Those were popular in those days.

Mom was a stay-at-home mom. When she heard Daddy drive up in our attached garage after work, she would yell, "Daddy's home!" My sister and I would run to the door leading to the garage to hug him. I remember him picking me up and hugging me at the front of our light-yellow Volkswagen van. When he put me down to pick up Marissa, I marveled at all the poor squashed bugs on the grill of the van. They were at my eye level. I also remember the little potty seat that we kept in the van for our "emergencies." Funny, the things you remember. I remember holding Daddy so tight around his neck. I also remember riding on his shoulders around the age of three. I was scared of falling, but I knew he wouldn't let me fall. That feeling of ultimate love and adoration that I got when I was with him was matched by nothing. I was Daddy's girl.

While we were still in high chairs, dinner time was a messy event. After spaghetti dinner every Friday (fed to us out of the ugly, olive-colored plastic bowls), spaghetti sauce would cover not only our faces, but our bodies, the high chairs, and Mom. Daddy would simply pick up the high chairs with us still in them, take us to the back yard, and hose down everything, including Mom and us.

Marissa is thirteen months older than me. Thirteen is only four months more than the nine to make a baby. Mom later said I was "a mistake," as she and my dad were not trying to have another baby so soon after their first one. In fact, I doubt that they would have planned another baby at all, as they would separate and divorce just a few short years after I was born. So I guess I am happy about this mistake. Otherwise, I would not exist. You see, back in the sixties, there was an old wives' tale that a woman could not get pregnant if she was actively breastfeeding. I am living proof otherwise.

This is not to say that Mom loved me any less. She told me that I was her little angel, and that as a baby I only slept, ate, and laughed. Marissa, on the other hand, would cry and fuss often. She tells me today that my beautiful sweet smile reflects the beauty within me, and that it is the same sweet smile I have had since I was a little girl. But perhaps the story of me being "a mistake" somehow got infused into my self-worth, or lack thereof. But more about that later.

As toddlers learning our words, neither of us could pronounce each other's name. When Marissa tried to pronounce *Della*, it came out *Bea*. And *Marissa* became *Bossy*. So we became *Bea* and *Bossy*. Although I didn't know it then, Marissa would hold true to her nickname. Daddy used to tell a story about us when we were just toddlers. He had taken us to get ice cream at a local parlor. As we were looking in the big glass display, deciding what flavor we wanted, I spotted a bug trapped on the inside of the glass facing us. I decided to share my finding.

"Ooh, look Daddy, there's a bug," I exclaimed as I pointed to it.

Marissa, quick to correct me, retorted, "That IS NOT a bug! That's a fly!"

Not to be outdone by my older (but barely older) sister, I blurted out my truth, "Well, bug is his last name!"

Of course his name was Fly Bug, sitting in there with the ice cream. It made so much sense. I was right, wasn't I? Most children group crawly things in the "bug" category. I guess saying the word "bug" is kind of fun, and complements the creepy-crawliness that they exhibit. It is more fun than saying "insect," which also houses "bugs." Whenever that started with parents and their toddlers, it stuck. Hence, that crawly thing was a bug to me.

When I was around four, Marissa and I were arguing as usual. Apparently, I grew tired of arguing with her. I think my angel must have sent me a message in the form of a thought, because I just stopped talking to her. This made Marissa even more angry, as she tried to get me to continue the argument. She finally told Dad, "Daddy, Della is ignoring me."

Daddy looked at me.

I lifted my chin and announced, "I am not talking to Marissa. God said I didn't have to." And that was the end of that.

But for all our arguing, Marissa and I loved each other, and we played together every day. And we laughed together, at least for a short while. We built forts with blankets, and played with the kids next door who were our age. We played hopscotch and threw rocks at passing cars with our new friends. If we saw the brake lights of an angry driver, we would run into the house squealing. This idea must have originated with our neighbors!

One time we were playing in the front yard. Marissa went inside the house and came back out claiming that Mom loved her more because she had given her the pretty pink liquid that makes tummies feel better. She even breathed some in my face to prove her point. Of course, I had to go get some too! We swung on our backyard swing set, and we played with our dog Sandy and her new puppies. That was the best!

Daddy Leaves Us

Unfortunately, that daily love that I got from Daddy was very short-lived. Daddy left us when my sister and I were only five and four. We saw him regularly for a short while after that, but then he moved out of state to New Orleans, when I was only five. Forever after that, we only got to see him three or four times per year: summer, Thanksgiving, Christmas, and sometimes Easter. Some years he made an extra trip to see us. Even though at the time I did not know the weight of its impact, Daddy leaving home was my first experience of abandonment.

Daddy and his sister were also abandoned by their father at a very young age. My grandfather left my grandmother, whom we called Nana, then married Nana's first cousin and had another family. After that, Nana did now allow him to even see the children he'd had with her. Ever. She used her children as revenge instead of thinking about their welfare and emotional growth. My father and aunt did not have a relationship with their father until they were eighteen and moved out of the house.

Mom was devastated, hurt, and confused that my father had left her. She did not know for a decade that he left because he was homosexual. He never told her. She, of course, thought that she was the reason that he left. She must have done something terribly wrong for Daddy to leave her and their very young children. No doubt, this tore at her own self-worth. She pleaded with him to stay and work it out, and told him that she loved him so very much. But all he could tell her was, "I don't know what love is."

Mom was in the dark and in pain, but so was I. As a very young girl, I had lost the most important male figure in my life. Father abandonment can have a huge impact on children. I had no idea at the time that this would be the foundation of my emotional insecurity and vulnerability that would stay with me for decades.

I don't blame my father for leaving us. He and my mother had a very difficult seven-year marriage, and Mom tells me that they argued a lot. As a homosexual, he had married my mom only to seek acceptance from his own family and peers. Both sides of my family were devout Catholics. When I became an adult, Daddy told me that as a young man, he could not understand why he would get an erection in the men's locker room. He thought there was something very wrong with him. Can you imagine? Society at the time told him that *he* was the problem. Through false medical and psychological science, it was believed that homosexuality was a disease that could be cured. He tried very hard to cure himself of this terrible sickness, which was neither a disease *nor* curable. At that time, marriage and a family were thought to be part of the cure for homosexuality. As Daddy judged himself for these unwanted and "sinful" feelings, he would then judge Mom for her eating habits, and being slightly overweight. And, in turn, my mom would starve herself for the weight that she strived to achieve to please him. Sadly, neither my father nor my mother ever found true love from a life partner. Was I doomed to the same fate? If Casey had her way, then yes. But more on her later.

Childhood Memories

Daddy left our home in the fall, right after the daylight jumped back an hour. I know this because it was still dark when we got out of bed. So we had that eerie feeling of being awake super early. Marissa and I would get ourselves ready for breakfast before Mom was awake. We could bring the cereal, bowls, spoons, and milk to the table. But neither of us could pour the milk onto our cereal from the gallon jug. It was just too heavy for our little arms to aim for the bowl without spilling it all over. So we would yell for Mom to please come and pour our milk into our cereal bowls. Then she would go back to bed. She was in a very sad state, and would yell at us often, even for spilled milk. When we spilled the milk at Daddy's, he would just calmly say, "And it will happen again." Mom got to where she would expect the somewhat loud request to pour our milk, and she must have started to dread it. One morning she got wise, and when we yelled, "Mommy," she stormed into the dining room, poured our milk, then said, "you don't have to yell so loud!" So the next morning, we got a huge giggle out of quietly singing "Mommy" in a very soft voice. Somehow, she heard us and would come and pour our milk.

Another time, when Mom was making us peanut butter and jelly sandwiches for lunch, a huge cockroach crawled up her leg. She screamed, and Marissa and I just laughed and laughed.

I remember being scared without Daddy's presence and protection, but I also remember feeling I knew everything would be all right. One night, for some reason, Marissa and I were trying to go to sleep on the floor in the dining room near the window facing the front driveway. In the distance, I heard a siren. It kept getting louder and louder. I thought for sure that the loud, scary siren was going to pass our neighborhood soon. But it just kept getting louder. And shriller. And then, it was on our street! And it was still getting closer. The sound was earsplitting. Then, to my horror, it pulled up in *our* driveway! It scared us half to death. Then, it backed out and went the other way. Mom came in and told us that everything was all right and to go back to sleep. You may as well have told a skydiver to forget the ground! I was awake for a long time.

Watching TV was sometimes an adventure for us, and Mom tried to protect us from "the bad stuff." She would allow us to watch her nightly television movies, but when a risqué scene began, or the man and woman started taking their clothes off, or if the man with a gun broke into the house, Mom would make us go in the other room until the scene was over.

One night, all three of us were watching a movie and a man had a heart attack in a phone booth. It upset me because I did not understand how the phone booth had caused this man's death. When the movie was over, me and Marissa went to bed. But I could not sleep thinking about why the man died so suddenly. After a while, I got up and went to Mother. She was in the kitchen emptying the dishwasher. I told her I was scared because the man died in the phone booth. She told me that there was nothing to be scared of. Then, just as I asked her why he died in the phone booth, I suddenly understood why. The notion that something went wrong inside his body became clear, and I was no longer scared. I went back to bed. Perhaps my angels put that little thought nugget into my head.

Of the two of us, Marissa misbehaved the most. We were mostly just grounded for it, but one time when she was six, she misbehaved enough that Mom decided she deserved the belt. Mom went to grab the belt and returned to find Marissa standing on the other side of the dining room table. As Mom walked toward her with the belt, Marissa went around the table in the same direction. As Mom stopped and started in the other direction, Marissa would follow suit. Mom's threats quickly turned into smirks because Marissa just kept keeping the table between them. About the third time around, I could not hold my laughter any longer. That was it, the tension was broken and we all started laughing. Needless to say, Marissa did not get belted that night. And in fact, Mom never threatened either of us with it again. Marissa's sentence was reduced to an hour in our bedroom.

The day Marissa, Mom, and I moved out of that beloved house where I began my life was very sad for all of us. I was five years old. It was the only home Marissa and I had ever known. Our family had broken apart, and now we were moving out of our home. Movers had already taken the furniture, so we had no table to eat our breakfast cereal on. Mom found a crate and placed it in front of the fireplace in the living room to place our bowls on, and we ate breakfast sitting on the fireplace. I can still see the empty home, the red and white bricks of the fireplace, and the grate that stood at its opening. Somehow, I knew that that was a moment to remember, sad as it was.

Then, just as we were walking out the door, the phone rang. The phone company had already disconnected it, but it still rang. When Mom picked up the receiver, the phone continued to ring. She kept saying, "Hello . . . hello," but it just kept on ringing. It finally stopped, but fifteen seconds later, it rang again. We guessed that they hung up and tried again. But when we picked it up, the phone just kept on ringing. We got a big laugh out of the whole thing and it helped to ease the pain of leaving our home forever.

To add to our grief, we had to give up our beloved dog, Sandy, because the 600+ unit apartment complex that we were moving to did not accept dogs . . . or so Marissa and I thought, but our neighbor did have a dog. Perhaps Mom told us that because she could not handle taking care of three beings after the pain she was going through. Or perhaps Sandy reminded her of Daddy.

I cried when we stopped at a local gas station and the attendant took our Sandy. I later found out that she asked him if he would please take her. That she could no longer care for her.

So my mother raised us on her own. She was a single parent for the rest of our childhood and adolescent years. I remember being baffled when people would express their condolences when I told them that my parents divorced when I was five, and that my sister and I were being raised by a single parent. I did not understand their sympathy until decades later, when I began to unravel the dysfunction that was my life. Funny thing about dysfunction, you don't know you are in it until you pull yourself out of it. To us, things were just normal. It was all we knew.

Single-Parent Life

After we left the house in the suburbs, we moved to the inner city to a small, two-bedroom apartment in a huge complex on the west side of town. Marissa and I still shared a bedroom, but now we each had our own twin bed. The frames, which used to be bunk beds, and box springs were rescued from the city dump. I was very happy that I got the bed by the window. I used to love looking outside from my bed through the opening in the curtain while falling asleep. To this day, I keep my blinds open so that I can see the trees outside while I fall asleep and first thing when I wake. But if Marissa was awake, she would yell to Mom watching TV in the living room, "Mom, Della's got the curtain open again." Mom would yell at me from the couch, and I would have to close the curtain. Then I tried leaving it just open enough to have a little sliver I could look out of. Sometimes this worked, but most of the time Marissa yelled at Mom again to yell at me again to shut the curtain completely. I mean, what harm was it doing Marissa that I was looking out of the curtain? Marissa yelled at me a lot during those days.

Mom earned a near-minimum wage salary as a secretary at the local public television station for her first eight years of single parenthood, and the monthly child support she received from Dad was quite small, so money was always very tight. She enrolled us both in a private Baptist elementary school. We were both too young to qualify for first and second grade in the public-school system, but Mom could no longer afford childcare. So we would spend our school years always a year younger than the rest of our class. This would add to my sense of not belonging in later years. We only spent a year in that private school before we went to the public school zoned to our apartments.

Mom could only afford to buy us each one new pair of jeans and two shirts at the beginning of each school year. I remember playing in the school yard during recess. One of my favorite things to do was to find a frog and pick it up. After frightened frogs peed on me several times, I would learn to hold the back end away from me as soon as I picked one up. Then I would pull it close and hug it gently. I would bring it to my teacher, Mrs. Max, who was supervising recess, and she let me sit next to her with my frog. I felt a strong attachment to most of my teachers, but especially Mrs. Max.

Mom found a teenage babysitter living in our apartment complex, Joy, to look after us after school until she got home from work. Joy was also our babysitter when Mom would go out for the evening. We had a lot of fun with Joy. She would play games and act out made-up skits with us. At bedtime, she would piggyback us from the living room to our beds. We abused this privilege: one of us would run back to the couch while she piggybacked the second, and she would have to start all over again. This brought much laughter. After school, she would sometimes take us for pizza at a nearby pizza parlor called Sunny's that we could walk to. I can still remember the red checkered tablecloths, the red glass candle holders, and the wonderful smell of baked pizza crust.

To my delight, Joy let me brush her long blonde hair. I loved brushing her hair, as mine was dark brown and so kinky curly that I couldn't even get my fingers through it. It was hard to know exactly what style to attempt with it. Each morning before school, Mom brushed and styled Marissa's hair, as it was soft and wavy. But I would go to school looking like I had just gotten out of bed. Because I had. School pictures were not a fun day for me. When questioned about my bed head years later, Mom always said, "I never knew what to do with your hair!"

For most of our childhood and adolescent years, Mom took out her anger and hurt about Daddy leaving her on us girls. Mostly every day. When she came home from work, it was not five minutes before she was yelling at us. "Did you clean the bathroom like I asked? Clean your room! Stop fighting with each other! I told you to get your purse off of the kitchen table! My dresser is still dusty. It would have taken you five minutes to dust this like I asked!" This was just about every day. We learned to expect the yelling as soon as she walked in the door from work. And we were often afraid of her reactions, even if what we had done was completely unintentional. Our friends would tell us they were scared of her. After we had gone to bed, she would often yell at us from the bathroom and make us go back in and clean up the mess we left from our nightly baths. Our wet towels were never placed exactly right. To this day, my bath towels are hung perfectly so that they can dry properly. Mildew is my enemy. Sometimes we would even get a spanking while in bed. We never talked about how awful that made us feel. We also never talked about Daddy. Or hurt feelings of any sort.

It wasn't all bad. Mom was affectionate with us, and filled us with as much love as she could. We adopted a gray and black striped tabby kitten. He was pretty rough with us, and could scratch us, breaking the skin. So we named him Killer. Whenever we came home, one of us would exclaim, "I get Killer," which would exclude the other from petting the cat upon arrival.

Mom took us on some really fun trips during the summers. Sometimes we went with my aunt and our two cousins. Marissa and I used to love to wake up early and go on long trips. One summer morning we woke up at 5:00 a.m. to get ready to leave. As Mom was finishing the packing in the hall with the hall light on, we both hopped out of bed and got dressed. We were too excited to be sleepy. We were on an adventure. By 6:00 a.m., we were on the road watching the sun rise. It was so much fun! But by 7:00 a.m., Marissa and I were both asleep in the car. When we woke up, we would get out the sweet rolls, like we always had on road trips, and eat breakfast. Mom had coffee in a thermos for herself.

She even took us to Mexico one time when we were tweens.

We stayed in an old, run-down hotel in Isla Mujeres. Marissa kissed a local boy on the lips on the roof. It seemed the only two English words he knew were, "One kiss." So Marissa obliged him.

I will never forget that Mom did not have enough cash at the airport to pay for the exit tax to leave the country. The man in line behind us at the airport thankfully paid it for us. I am proud of my Mom for being so relaxed. But at the time, I was horrified.

My aunt had also divorced her husband around the same time, so we spent a lot of time with our cousins, Josephine (Josie) and Georgeanna. We all loved each other so much and had so much fun together. Sleepovers were such a blast. We played games endlessly. Card games such as Canasta, Crazy Eights and our favorite, Spoons; board games; hide and seek; sardines; hand-clapping games for four to the song *Rockin' Robin*.

One of our favorite activities was telling ghost stories at bedtime. Josie, the oldest, would silently leave the room while Georgeanna continued with the story. Then, with no warning, Josie would slowly come toward the bedroom, banging her hand against the wall as she got closer and closer. The suspense was thrilling.

We would walk around the neighborhood, too. And at night, we would sometimes sneak out of the house. Georgeanna would bring her cigarettes and we would smoke them. She loved to be the rebel. She would often give her mother grief, and would sneak out of the house at night and get into trouble with friends. Sadly, she later developed a big problem with drugs and alcohol, and was forced into recovery programs in her teen years. She became an alcoholic, and would eventually die of complications from that when she was just forty-four. But back then I wanted to be just like her.

Christmas time was always very special. Mom would stay up late on Christmas Eve, lay out our presents from Santa, and fill our huge Christmas stockings. She would always let us wake up on our own to discover them. Plus, we knew that we would get to see Daddy and the other set of cousins. There was so much excitement every year around Christmastime. I remember wondering how Santa got into our apartment with no chimney. I don't remember the exact year I realized that Santa

Claus did not exist. But Mom continued to lay out our presents until we were teenagers! She took a lot of care to make sure that our Christmases were happy. She must have saved up for a long time. I still get that special feeling of Christmas deep inside of me when I see the first Christmas lights in December. I feel lucky about that.

We opened our presents from the family at Mom's parents' house on Christmas Eve. We loved our Maw Maw and Paw Paw very much. Except when it was time to kiss Paw Paw goodbye, his stiff facial stubble would always scratch my cheek! Sometimes Daddy would pick us up from Maw Maw's house on Christmas Eve and we would get to open another whole set of gifts with that set of cousins at my Aunt Beth's house. Sometimes Dad's mother Nana was in a good mood. But many times, she would gripe at all of the children and tell us that we were bad. One year she did not get any of her grandchildren a present. She was mean a lot.

After exchanging gifts with Mom and Marissa Christmas morning, we spent the day at Maw Maw's or my Aunt Jannie's house. Christmas meal was served around 2:00 p.m. and was always authentic Italian, two traditions that still live today. Spaghetti or tortellini with Italian sausage, bone-in pork and beef cooked all day in the suga (the Italian word for sauce, and what you would call marinara) was always cooked by Maw Maw. Frosha (vegetable pie) made with asparagus or broccoli, eggs, breadcrumbs, olive oil, and a ton of hand-grated parmesan cheese was always a must. Pecan pie, homemade cookies, and pignolatta (a hard, Italian candy made with dough drops, almonds and honey) were staples for dessert. So good. I feel lucky to have experienced authentic Italian food Maw Maw cooked. I learned a lot from her. She and Paw Paw were first-generation from Sicily, so she learned everything from her mother. Nana was also first-generation Sicilian. Their parents were from the same area of Sicily. Both of my grandmothers even went to the same grade school in Houston. Isn't that such a coincidence!

I will always remember our first bicycles that we got from Santa. Marissa could ride, but I was still mastering the art of getting started. Mom really wanted to get a picture of both of us riding our new bikes. So we bundled up and Mom helped us get them down the stairs. She stood on the balcony with the camera and said, "Okay, start at the end of the sidewalk and ride towards me so I can get a picture."

I don't know how many times I fell while trying to start riding. I just could not stay balanced long enough to catch up with my sister. She took a lot of pictures of Marissa alone, or with half of me cut out. Of course, this was in the 1970s, so we had to wait to get them developed to see them. We all had a good laugh.

Before I could ride confidently, Marissa would pump me on her bike. I would ride on the very back of her seat, and she would squeeze on the front part remaining, or ride standing. I don't know why it was called pumping. One time, I was being pumped and my foot dangled too close to the rear wheel. My left foot got caught in the spokes and a good-sized gash was torn into my left heel. I remember that I had hard, black dress shoes on, but the spoke went in right above the shoe. I screamed and Marissa stopped. And we were far from home. I don't remember how I got home, but Mom had to drive me to the emergency room. A neighbor was called to watch Marissa, and while we were waiting for her to arrive, Mom wrapped my ankle in a towel. I stopped crying and had a thought, "Am I going to be on the news tonight?" I asked. We all got a good laugh from that one.

Eventually, I did master the art of bike riding, and loved it. Biking was my escape from everything. I would wake up early on Saturday morning and sneak out of bed without waking anyone. I got on my bike and would be gone all day. I got myself a basket, and rode around to construction sites collecting empty glass soda bottles. I paid no attention to the danger signs. I would take the bottles back to the store for the refund and save my money. One Saturday, I made a sharp turn in a gravelly parking lot and fell on my face. I chipped a front tooth, but that did not even hinder my riding.

In fifth grade, I was old enough to be on patrol. We got to wear the orange body belts, and direct the traffic in the drop off line. It was a real honor, as only those with good grades could apply. We had to be at school extra early, so I rode my bike through the park to the school. This brings back such good memories.

Adjacent to our apartment complex was an empty lot filled with native plants. One of them was a thicket of wild Texas blackberry. In spring, the fruit would turn from white to red. And in early summer, they would turn a beautiful midnight black: huge, plump and delicious. Marissa and I would grab baskets and go berry picking. Since they had thorns, we would often return quite scratched up. But we soon got the hang of it. We brought our baskets home and washed the berries, then mixed milk with a bit of sugar and poured it over the bowls of berries. Mom was always proud that we brought dessert home. This was one summer activity that Marissa and I loved to do together.

Mom made some good girlfriends, Janice and Deonne, who were so nice to us. They would have adult parties and let us come! Janice would let me sit on the floor in front of her while she played with my curls. It felt so nice. They always paid attention to us girls.

One summer, Mom wanted to take an extended vacation by herself to Club Med in Mexico. So we got to stay with Janice and Deonne for one week each. Janice made us her favorite snack, Texas Trash, and played cards and board games with us. To this day, Marissa makes Texas Trash every Christmas, and I am reminded of that summer with Janice.

One day, Janice invited us to her Tupperware party. First, she showed and explained all the items. Then we sat around, looked at the items, and drank sodas. Mom ordered mustard and catsup bottles with the squeeze top. One person was very late, and the door did not get locked behind her. Suddenly, it opened and a naked man ran through the house and straight out the back door. Everyone screamed, laughed, and got a big kick out of it. Except Marissa. She was so scared that her teeth were chattering. That is when she started sleeping with Mom. They later explained to Marissa the man was called a streaker, and that it was all done for a joke. That was the seventies.

Music was a huge part of our childhood. Mom had an eight-track player and a turntable that Daddy had left us. Cat Stevens' *Tea for the Tillerman*, Simon and Garfunkel, the Beatles, the Carpenters, and Nadia's theme were favorites. We would put the headphones on for maximum listening pleasure, but we just could not hold back from singing to the music. Much laughter was to be had listening to us, because we were always off pitch and really low. We would put on concerts for Mom, singing to Donna Summer and Barbara Streisand in our best, flowy outfits. Serving spoons served as our microphones and our rectangular wooden kitchen table served as our stage. The entire soundtrack to *A Star is Born* was our favorite concert to perform.

Mom always got the best vinyl music albums to grow up to: Barry White, Stevie Wonder, The Temptations, The Carpenters, Al Green, and Earth, Wind, and Fire. We actually fought over who would get to hold the words that were printed on the vinyl sleeve of *Sergeant Pepper's Lonely Hearts Club Band.* Journey and Steve Perry became our first loves, and we went to many of their concerts as adolescents. In Houston, they would be applauded into six encores!

As a little girl, all I ever dreamed about was falling in love, getting married, and having babies of my own. I wondered where babies came from, so I made up that babies were the size of pin heads inside the bellies of all girls. And when the time was right, they grew bigger and popped out. I could not wait for my little baby to grow so that I could have children of my own! I just knew that I would be a great mommy. I would not let my children fight the way that Marissa and I fought. And I would never yell at my children. Well, only on rare occasions.

When we were eight and nine, Mom enrolled us into gymnastics at a nearby gym. I don't know how she afforded it, but we both loved it. Floor, vault, uneven bars, the dreaded balance beam, and our favorite, the trampoline. Coach Ed would belt the class one at a time to a pulley connected to the ceiling over the trampoline, and we had no fear doing front and back flips. It was so much fun! We took gymnastics for several years, and spent many weeknights and weekends there. I still remember the smell of the gym, and the dryness of the chalk that we put on our hands for the apparatuses. Izzy was the cutest gym coach, with his mustache and Italian looks, but Ed became a family friend. He spent days on family outings with us and even took some family portraits.

We finally entered the middle class and got to leave our huge apartment complex for a three-bedroom townhome the summer before my 6th grade year. In 1977, we finally got our own bedrooms! This was a huge deal. I remember that we celebrated by doing cartwheels in our empty rooms. Mom was still very angry and depressed, and still yelled at us every day. A friend of ours, Dawn, told us that she did not like to come to our townhome because of it. Dawn said that Mom scared her. That sometimes Mom was hateful and mean to us.

Mom had a bell near the couch. If she was all snuggled in watching TV, she would sometimes ring it and we would have to leave our friend in the bedroom to go get her a glass of ice water or throw something away. Dawn did not understand why Mom refused to buy Marissa nail polish, or even nail polish remover. She did not understand why Mom was emotionally unavailable to us. On the other hand, Mom was almost too lenient with us. She did not punish us for bad grades (well, she did not punish Marissa, I made all A's and B's). And we could mostly go wherever we wanted and spend the night with our girlfriends whenever we wanted. But our love for Mom was undisputable. She was, in our eyes, a good mom. We were lucky to have her.

Mom finally left the public television station and got a job as a headhunter. She was successful at this, and would often bring home the prize for salesperson of the month. Our favorite prize was four live lobster. We boiled them up and listened to them scream. We knew they were not actually screaming, but it was still eerie causing such a horrible death. I still remember Mom trying to explain the difference between computer software and computer hardware. Pretty funny, since she has never in her life owned a computer.

BULLYING SISTER

As the younger sibling, I constantly sought approval and acceptance from my older sister. But instead, she threw criticism and meanness at me daily. Her putdowns were constant, and I believed a lot of what she said. But as she was *only* thirteen months older than me, I refused to let her boss me around. As much as she tried to, she was not my boss. I made good grades in school, but she always had to be number one. Thus, there was a lot of arguing in our home. A lot.

Of course, we had a lot of good times too. We had the same thought at the same time often, just like twins.

But I barely remember a time when my sister and I didn't argue. Mostly, I remember arguing several times a day. It was exhausting and emotionally painful. But hey, she *always* started it. We argued every day until the day she moved out at seventeen. When I was in school, I wrote about the grief I was receiving from my sister, and that we argued 80 percent of the time that we were together. I do not believe this to be an exaggeration. Marissa seemed to have an endless supply of putdowns and retorts, thought of just for me. She let me know every time I did or said something wrong. To her, this was pretty much everything I did or said.

I remember being around six or seven, when one of Mom's friends told us that we argued so much because we were so close in age. At that time, I remember thinking that it was her telling us that put the thought of bullying me into Marissa's head. It was easier than accepting that she was always so mean to me on purpose. I mean, Mom says that I am so sweet! I didn't do anything to her to deserve such treatment.

When I was thirteen, I wrote this poem:

My big sister
Small but mean
Argues constantly
As loud as a baby
If only I were an only child

At one point after we moved into the apartment, we stopped sleeping in our twin beds. I think we were scared. So we slept with Mom in her king bed every night. Well, actually, Marissa was the one who was scared from that streaker at Janice's, but I did not want her to have Mom all to herself! I loved my bed. I loved the feel of the cool sheets against my skin, and would move my legs around to feel them. I still do that. Anyway, every night we would lightly scratch each other's back. I always wanted to be the last one scratched, so every night I would scratch Marissa's back first. Then, when it was my turn, Marissa would always pretend to be asleep. So I would get cheated. But the next night she would *promise* to scratch my back this time. She never did.

Marissa always insisted on sleeping next to Mom in her king bed. Since Mom refused to sleep in the middle, I always got stuck on the end. One time, I caught pneumonia (we used to call it "ammonia"), but Marissa still did not let me sleep next to Mom. I remember Mom setting the alarm clock to go off every four hours all through the night so that she could make me take an aspirin to reduce my fever. I felt so awful! I made Marissa an agreement that she could sleep next to Mom for the rest of that year, but then it was my turn. I never got to sleep next to Mom. Eventually, after a year or two, I went back to my own bed. I loved sleeping alone. It made me feel grown up.

One time, Marissa demanded that I follow her order to do something. When I refused, she said, "Okay, you asked for it," went to the bathroom, filled her hands with water from the faucet, and poured it on my bed! When I still refused, she did it a second and a third time. So I got a cup from the kitchen and poured water on her bed. She saw that my way was better, so she copied it. Dumb, huh?

Going clothes shopping with Mom was always boring for us, so Marissa thought it would be fun to play on the inside of the circular clothing rack. As we were in close quarters, Marissa told me for the millionth time, "Your breath stinks!" and the fun was over. To this day, I hold my breath or back off while I am speaking so that no one will smell my breath.

I remember another fight when we actually started hitting each other, which was not very often. As always, she took the first hit at me. After a while, I finally got fed up and hit her hard. I was scared, so I ran into the bathroom and locked the door. She was so mad that she could not get at me, so she tried to persuade me to come out. When that didn't work, she grabbed one of my framed school pictures and started hitting it against the bathroom door. "Della, I have your favorite picture!" When

I still didn't come out, she hit it real hard and cracked the glass. Frustrated but trapped, I kicked the door from the inside. Then, she had the nerve to tell Mom that I cracked the glass with my kick from the inside!

One time, Marissa announced that we were going to have a contest. She asked me to come up with a song and sing it, and she would do the same. I was to go first. I sang my song. When it was her turn, she loudly sang *"We Are the Champions"* by Queen. But she changed the lyrics of the song to "I Am the Champion" to pronounce her as the winner. I just walked away, announcing I was done with that game!

I don't know why, after the way that my sister treated me, that I kept going back to seeking her love and affection. One Sunday we had gotten into an especially vicious fight. I cannot remember what it was about, but I remember that Mom had to sit between us at church to keep us from killing each other. As the mass was nearing its completion, I got a bright idea. I'd send Marissa a message to put our fighting to rest, at least for that day. I opened Mom's purse and found a pen and a little piece of paper. I wrote three simple words on it, "I Love You," and passed it to Mom to give to Marissa. Mom read it as she passed it, and smiled warmly at me. I carefully watched for Marissa's reaction to the note. She read the note, put it down by her side, and pretended to continue listening to the priest. There was no reaction. I was crushed.

SUMMERTIME WITH DADDY

Daddy moved to New Orleans shortly after he moved out of the house. Every summer, Marissa and I would fly there to visit him. Mom took this opportunity to travel and have fun on her own. Because we barely saw him, we treasured our summer visits. We used to count down the days on the calendar with big X's for the big plane ride. He became my favorite parent, because our time with him was so infrequent and so very precious. And Daddy never yelled at us. It did not occur to me then that it was Mom who was actually there for us every day.

One of the first trips we made to New Orleans, Daddy took us to a donut shop for breakfast. I must have been around six. For some reason, I would always order the same kind of donut that Marissa ordered. This time, Daddy got smart and asked me what kind I wanted first.

Confused, I asked, "Well, what kind do they have?"

The clerk then went through the long list of toppings and filled jellies. She stopped and all eyes were on me. And then she added, "And we also have plain."

Because I had just gotten off of a plane, or maybe because it was the last thing she listed, I ordered the plain donut. Marissa and Daddy proceeded to order what they wanted. When we got back to the table and started eating, I was terribly disappointed with mine. I sat there staring at my donut until a huge tear came rolling down my cheek. Perplexed, Daddy asked me what was wrong. I looked up at him and said, "They forgot the plane."

This makes sense if you know that the airlines used to hand out metal pins of tiny little planes as a marketing ploy. We asked for them every time we flew, and they loved to give them to children. Especially children who were flying alone. Since I had just gotten off the plane, I had expected there to be a miniature plane sticking out of my donut! Funny, the things we remember.

Daddy planned such fun things to do with us during our summer stay. We always went to the amusement park at Ponchartrain Beach. Our favorite ride was the scary Haunted House, which had cars on a track. On the back of each car was a huge monster, whose arms became the car arms. So the car's rider felt surrounded by this monster. I stayed close to Daddy and would not touch those scary arms, even though I knew they were made of plastic. The cars would bang open the doors and take us into very cold, dark rooms with flashing lights and beasts and goblins that would jump from the eerie fog into view. Each room was separated by swinging doors the car would hit very loudly to open and enter. That was a thrill, and was one of our favorites.

We also rode the bumper cars, and Daddy would laugh and laugh as he bumped into us. I will never forget that laugh. He was not completely without fear, and would refuse to ride the Ferris Wheel. But he did take us on the roller coaster. To help us get over our fear, he would tell us, instead of screaming and tensing up, to just relax our bodies on the downhills and let our bodies float. This allowed us to see it as fun instead of fear. To this day, I still love roller coasters. Marissa, however, still hates them.

Our favorite summertime activity by far was crabbing on the fishing bridge over the shallow bayou. Daddy would buy raw chicken necks for crab bait and fried chicken for our lunch. We always looked forward to getting up before the sun on crabbing days. But it took Daddy a full pot of coffee and nearly an hour to wake up, and the sun was up by then.

He taught us to tie the chicken neck to the center of the basket and drop the net into the brown bayou water. To check the net for a crab, he taught us to pull up on the string hard and fast to make the net become a basket, trapping the dining crab inside. Since we could not see the net, we were thrilled when we pulled up a big blue crab. We would scream with delight and bring the net to Daddy. He would place the net on the bridge and lightly step on the crab to free it from the net. He taught us that to safely grab the crab, you must go from behind and tightly grab both of its swimmer legs in one hand. This was the way to avoid getting pinched with those big red pincers. I got the courage to do this way before Marissa did. He also taught us to release the little baby crabs and the pregnant ones back into the bayou. Pregnant crabs were evident by a large mass of orange eggs on her abdomen. We put the other crabs into the ice chest with the sodas and Daddy's beers. We were amazed that they would quickly "go to sleep" so that we could grab a soda can. One time, Marissa was standing at the bridge rail and dropped one of her flip flops into the flowing bayou. She would not go into the crab-infested water, and screamed that she her shoe was floating away. I proudly announced that I was not scared to enter the water, and quickly fetched her shoe. We came home with dozens of crabs that Daddy would boil with Zatarain's Crab Boil in the largest silver pot that I have ever seen. I can still smell the crabs boiling.

They say that the olfactory sense is nearest and strongest to memories. Anytime I sauté onions and garlic, I can remember the smell of Daddy cooking. He had to learn to cook for himself after he left Mom, and found he really enjoyed it. I still have the binder of recipes that he typed up and placed in sleeves. Daddy's cooking was so good. Better than Mom's. She never really found a love of cooking. But Daddy's cooking almost always started with peeling garlic and onions to sauté. And now, mine does too.

I also remember the smell of Daddy's rust-colored convertible with the white leather seats. We thought it was magic when he would push the button to make the top open to the sky. He had that car for over ten years, and got very depressed after it was stolen.

Anyway, back to crabbing. To eat the crabs we caught, Daddy spread layers of newspaper over the outdoor picnic table. He patiently taught us how to crack each of the crab parts to reveal every delicious morsel of meat. We would be at that table for hours. When the sun set, he lit his tiki torches so that we could see. The smaller crabs were saved, and the next day he would make the most delicious brown rue gumbo from scratch. We loved Daddy's gumbo.

Since Daddy had his own court-reporting firm, he could not take off the whole summer. So we would sometimes go to the house of his scopist, Jackie. We loved it over there. She had five kids of her own, and the younger two were our age. We also became members of their neighborhood pool, and would spend many summer days there with her kids. Marissa and I often reminisce about going to that private pool and chorus, "And the smell of the snack bar!"

Every "get out of pool" time or adult swim was a race to the snack bar. We would stand in the hot sun and burn our feet on the concrete to wait in line. When we finally got near the snack bar window, we could feel the cold air conditioning pouring out and smell the snacks.

Jackie's oldest son Mickey introduced us to a lot of music. I'd spend hours in his room listening to Elton John's *Goodbye Yellow Brick Road* and memorizing the words from the vinyl sleeve. So many good times at Jackie's house.

Eventually, we became old enough to go to Daddy's office with him. I remember he would hold hands with each of us on the way. He must have always been late, because he would walk through the downtown streets so fast that we had to run to keep up with him. He wore the same old nine suits for twenty years. When we finally got there, he would keep us busy by asking us to color the ice cream coupons that he gave to all his lawyer clients on their birthday. When we got older, he would trust us to take the city bus from his home on Canal Boulevard on our own. He would put us to work photocopying the exhibits and filing the invoices. We got to know all his staff, and they treated us with kindness and love.

We rarely saw Daddy angry. But when he was, and if we evoked "the look," we knew we were in big trouble. But Daddy was smart. He knew that we feared his disapproval. I needed Daddy's approval no less than I needed air and water. One time he caught me in a lie when I was eight or nine. I was mortified. I got a "talking to" from him: he knew I had lied to him and he would not stand for it. He never raised his voice, but I never forgot the lesson.

No Positive Male Figure

Absent Daddy, yelling Mother, and a bullying sister: all these factors really hammered home that I was never good enough. I yelled at myself in my head to continue the bullying I received from my sister and constant yelling from my mother, and to punish myself. Growing up, I never witnessed a healthy relationship, or what that might look like. Because of the way she viewed herself, most of Mom's dating relationships were emotionally abusive. Some of her boyfriends were liars. One of them, Joe, even had a secret wife and family. But he lied to Mom and told her that he was divorced. He was forever known "affectionately" as "Bastard Joe." Not a good ambassador for his gender.

Of course, Dad did not date women. At some point I cannot remember, I accepted freely that he was a homosexual. This did not change my love for him. But he never found a lifelong partner, either. We had no close uncles. My mom's only sister was a single parent as well, from a failed relationship with an alcoholic. And we hardly ever got to see our paternal uncle from Dad's one sister.

My maternal grandfather, Paw Paw, began suffering from dementia and confusion when I was a child, so we never really had full-on conversations with him. I do remember my grandmother yelling at him daily. It was easy to see how Mom picked that up. Paw Paw mostly talked about how his father had died from a falling tree while working the lumber yard in the Big Thicket of Texas.

I never knew my paternal grandfather; we met him only once.

So there were no consistent male figures in my life at all growing up, meaning I never had anyone to compare my potential boyfriends to. Plus, I had little to no encouragement for self-worth from anyone in my family. No one praised me, or told me that I was kind, smart or important. This and the absence of men while growing up may have contributed to the men I chose to get close to later in life.

Daddy and I had an extra-special, strong and loving, albeit long-distance relationship throughout my childhood, teenage, and adult years. Daddy was the saint, and he could do no wrong in my mind. Mom was the scapegoat, even though she was there for us every day, and she loved us very much. However, Daddy's absence in our household as a child growing up was undoubtedly a big factor in my self-inflicted inadequacies and "never good enough" stigma that I created for myself. He passed away at the young age of sixty-five from bladder cancer. I feel like I lost so much by not being able to spend more time with him. Thankfully, after he was diagnosed and in the year before his death, I was able to visit him from Texas nine times.

Introduction to Alcohol and Drugs

My father drank every day. He would make a joke of it. Around 5:30 p.m., he would glance at his watch and say, "I do believe it is Scotch:30." Around us girls, he would only drink one or two. I don't know if he was an alcoholic, but he sure was addicted to cigarettes. He smoked at least two packs every day. I remember that he would repeatedly light a cigarette when he had one burning in the ashtray in the other room. Maybe two or three. This happened both at the office and at home. He was also addicted to coffee, and he drank pots of the stuff all throughout the day and evening, every day.

Growing up, both of my parents allowed us to "sip" on their "adult drinks." Mom would have parties for her friends at our townhome while we were in junior high and high school, and we would take sips of her gin and tonic. We looked at this as a high privilege and much fun. I thought that the gin was so refreshing. This became my drink of choice later in life.

I clearly remember that around the age of twelve, my father brought us to a party at one of his friend's houses in New Orleans. We were sitting in the grass on the lawn, and I thought it would be cute and funny to try to get away with taking a huge swallow of his beer that he had set beside me. I knew that we were not allowed to drink adult drinks, and I was attempting to get some attention. When he was not looking, I finished what was in the can. When he picked up the can, he made it a point to say, "What happened to my beer?" But instead of giving me any consequences, he just went and got another. Since I got away with the first one, I thought it would be funny to just finish that one as well. That was my first true buzz from alcohol. And I loved it. I will never forget how good it made me feel. I was suddenly somebody! And I didn't care what Marissa might do the next time she bullied me. And that was it. I was hooked. That was the beginning of a long love affair with alcohol.

My sister and I started sneaking Daddy's cigarettes at a very early age. We also smoked with our cousin, Georgeanna. We would even pick up butts off the ground while living in the apartments and smoke the remaining bit. In junior high school, I started sneaking hard alcohol into the local skating rink on Thursday nights with my friend Andi. Then, at high school dances on Saturday nights during football season, it was a regular practice to sneak in a bottle and hide it in our locker. My friends and I got caught at both places, but that did not stop us. I got into marijuana, black mollies, and other pills as a freshman in high school. I was fourteen (remember, I was a year younger than the rest of my class). A couple of times, I took them at school. I felt like a nobody, so I used drugs and alcohol to be accepted by my peers. Plus, I loved the way they made me feel. They were an escape from . . . well, me. And the disappointment that I thought I was.

As I had to achieve something to feel "good enough," I buried myself in my schoolwork and made good grades. I remember my mom's friend, who was a teacher, once told me that it was the students who made good grades who were more likely to abuse drugs and alcohol. At the time, I thought that was very strange, and said, "Well, that won't be me!" Yet that is exactly how I ended up.

Of course, making good grades in school labeled me as a "goodie goodie," and I was bullied in high school by my peers. I was also betrayed by most of my close friends in high school. I just didn't fit into any of the cliques. Not even the misfits. I had no one to eat lunch with, and changed cliques often. The one best friend that I had in high school, Dawn—who is still my best friend thirty-five years later—ate lunch at a different time than me. She also skipped a lot of school, yet she still made good grades. She was smart that way.

One of my good friends, Chrissie, even peeled away from me in the high school parking lot with a carful of our friends on the one day that seniors were allowed to go out to lunch. We had been planning it for months. I had to go back into that lunch room in tears. I did not eat lunch that day.

I was a late bloomer, and did not develop breasts until my sophomore year of *college*. The adults told me it was because I smoked cigarettes. The teasing in high school by my male peers because I had no breasts was truly devastating, and I can remember it vividly to this day.

I remember crying after one bullying incident from a guy in my class about my small breasts. As I walked into the gym locker room to change for P.E., two female coaches saw my face and asked me what was wrong. I told them the truth.

I will never forget the kindness they showed to me that day. They let me stay after the P.E. class had started, sat down with me on the locker room bench and told me how much boobs were a pain in the ass. "Believe us, you do not want boobs! You are lucky that you don't have them yet!" They told me that boobs were heavy, and they jiggled around a lot. And bras were extremely uncomfortable, and another pain in the ass. They made me laugh.

But I could not help but think that this was the main reason that I had only had one date in all of high school. Because of all these factors, I was very vulnerable. And I was hooked on alcohol by the age of fourteen. That was the beginning of a long road of substance abuse.

Since I detested beer, I would bring a bottle of wine to high school parties and not share it with anyone. In college and graduate school, I tried the gamut of drugs available: marijuana, cocaine, acid, mushrooms, and ecstasy. By the end of graduate school, I was using these many times every semester—though usually for special occasions, such as a party or concert event. Somehow, my drug and alcohol use did not affect my grades. I would not say that I abused these drugs, but they were definitely a big part of my life.

I was so much more vulnerable than most teens. Daddy was absent from my daily life. I missed the level of intimacy that most kids got to develop with their fathers. I never got tucked into bed or had children's books read to me. I was not allowed the privilege of hugging Daddy daily, or having him teach me the life lessons so important during the formative years. How would my life have been different if he had stayed home? Or if he had at least stayed in Texas? One thing is for sure, Fred would have never been allowed to move into our home.

And then, there was the confusion of Daddy's homosexuality. I must have been around ten when my perception about his dating life changed, and that he was gay. I never thought it was his fault. But he never talked about it. Ever. Why did he keep such an important part of his life from even a conversation with me? And why did he leave Texas? Without me even knowing it, he became untrustworthy. He would visit us, or we would visit him, but then we always had to leave him again, knowing we would not see him again for a very long time. Every year from age five to age seventeen when I left for college.

And then there was the constant bullying by my only sister for twelve years. Looking back now, I can see how, as a younger sister, I was probably pretty clingy. And she was the older child, so she did hold some sense of responsibility to me. Perhaps she shut me out of her room when our friends were over because I was always tagging along. I violated all her privacy.

But all these things were happening to me. I had no choice but to take it all in. And my mind was like an absorbent sponge. I was lonely. My mom was at work, I was rejected by my father, my sister bullied me because she wanted me to stay away from her, I was bullied at school because I had no breasts, and I thought my friends didn't want me around. It was simple: I just wasn't good enough. All of this made me susceptible to the first man who I fell in love with. The problem was, Fred was an adult looking to groom a young girl. I never had a chance.

Chapter Three

THE FRED DIARIES

Enter Fred—1982

Marissa and I still argued every day. In fact, somehow it had gotten even worse. She bullied me a lot. She would shut the door to her room when our friends came over, excluding me from play. She did not start all the fights, but she started most of them. I just wanted peace. And I yearned for her to love me the way that I loved her.

It was January of 1982. I had just turned fifteen. I was in the final semester of my sophomore year of high school. Our neighbor, Bill, was on the same row as us, facing the street. He had become a family friend, and would help our family out by taking us to gymnastics and other after-school activities.

Bill had gotten a new roommate. His name was Fred. He was twenty-nine years old. He was a small, cute man who looked much younger than he was. My sister and I would hang out with him almost every day after school while Mom was still at work. We would watch old *Star Trek* episodes, and sometimes we would play cards. He would get us high every day with marijuana and sometimes hashish. I remember being so high that I could not speak the thoughts that were forming in my mind. I would think, *I want to say this. Okay, say it now. Hurry before someone else changes the conversation! Am I saying it? Open your mouth and speak!* But I could not. The synapses just would not connect. I found that sometimes getting high was fun, but most of the time, it just made me paranoid. I thought everyone was looking at me and judging me. Of course, now I know this was because I judged myself. THC is not for those who cannot love themselves. But I didn't want Marissa to have Fred all to herself.

Fred started spending more and more time with my family. We had great fun together. We would go together to movies and out to eat. And we spent a lot of time at our complex's small swimming pool. At the time, I never thought it was odd that a man almost twice our age would want to hang out with fifteen- and sixteen-year-old girls. He was the first man besides my father that was an integral part of my life. Mom had dated, but had never remarried. Fred filled that hole in my heart that Daddy had left, just ten years prior. He was the first man outside of my family who made me feel good about myself. Fred made me feel wanted. Over the next few months, he wrote me poems, and even wrote a song about me. He told me that I was beautiful.

I was keen on him and fought for his attention and approval. Eventually, I fought for his affection. My sister and I both did. And this became a problem. It was yet another reason for us to fight, and it was the biggest one yet. Marissa's bullying became worse. Jealousy tore at our already fragile bond, and ripped us apart even more. It wasn't long before we both fell in love with him. Or maybe it was infatuation. At that age, who knows the difference? I recently looked up *infatuation:* an image you portray of someone else so that they become, in your eyes, who you want them to be. You are blinded completely to the person that they really are. Infatuation or not, I considered Fred my first love.

A few months after Fred moved in with him, Bill lost his townhome. Fred told us he had nowhere to go. He had quickly become part of the family. He was already driving us to events after school and playing the role of a father. So Mom, having such a kind heart, offered him our couch. I will never understand how my mom thought it would be safe for a twenty-nine-year-old man to move into the same townhome with two young teenage girls, but she did. She did not protect us. We were already both in love with him. Following is the diary from fifteen-year-old me, shortly after Fred moved in with our little family:

THE FRED DIARIES

Tuesday, June 8, 1982

Dear Diary,

Sunday May 30th till Sunday June 6th were spent at the beach. We rented a beach house and had a BLAST! My cousin Josephine (Josie) was there with her fiancé, Russell for three days, and Fred was there the whole week except for one afternoon. I got high three times. We figured out how to ride the waves on a float. It was so fun! Sometimes you could ride for fifty feet! At night, we would walk on the beach and play with the crabs. What fun. I will never forget it. When a lot of people were there and there were no beds left, me, Fred and Marissa would sleep on the porch facing the ocean. It was so fun. What a great feeling it is to walk on the beach stoned. Especially with Fred!! I love him so, not like anyone I loved before or will ever again. I have walked on the beach stoned with Fred two times before and hope many more. Della.

Monday, June 14, 1982

Fred, I am not going to give you this letter! I'm just writing it to make me feel better. So every time you make *me mad I am going to write you about it so I won't face the embarrassment of my stupid vulnerabilities and soft feelings. Which is one reason I hate you. I cannot get mad at you, and on the rare occasions that I do, I either hold it in or tell you and start crying. That is another reason for this diary. It's just an alternative to talking to you when you hurt me. Okay, number one, when I get mad at you I don't tell you like all normal friends, as I have mentioned. I either hold it and cry later or tell you and cry in front of you. Number two, if something has happened and you hurt me and we did talk and I cried, if something similar happens, you have to stir up feelings and say something, you bastard! Now, getting specific, number three (it has to be the worst, three is my favorite number!!) all through my junior high and high school years, I have always made grades above a C, except once in seventh grade. Along with the good grades, I am classified by my peers (not friends but mostly guys) as a goodie goodie. And as all my peers know, goodie goodies are always prude, so naturally I have been considered by some guys and some let me know what they think, which hurts, as prude. It hurts especially because I really know that I'm not. I just want to save myself for the perfect guy. I honestly believe that if I really loved someone and he really loved and cared for me and we had had feelings about marriage, I would have sex with him no matter what age!! My feelings might be different in an actual situation, but anyway, I'm considered prude.*

Changing the subject a little bit, I was thinking about in the future I might just show you this, but thinking about what I am going to say next changed my mind, I know I'm not!! Besides the prudity, another thing bothered me, I was always paranoid about—gosh this is hard to admit, even on paper written to myself—my tiny tits. Some of my guy peers have mentioned their lack of size, which hurts more than anything! This is partly where you come in. On June 11, 1982, you told me, or Marissa told me, that when you first saw us, you thought about having sex with Marissa. After a while you said, "well with both of ya'll." That is when it started hurting because it sounded so much like a cover-up lie not to get my feelings hurt because it never was me that you thought of having sex with because of my tiny tits. But what really made it worse was the fact that I had thought about having sex with you, before and after meeting and knowing you. I even thought about a relationship or even marriage, but it really was a dream. I knew that would never happen. In fact, if it does, I will let you read this note!! But now, after knowing you five months, I don't think about it anymore. Probably because I'm not in love with you anymore, well I am, but not like that. Just more like . . . more than a REALLY GREAT friend. When I am really in love with a guy I dream about he and I having sex and that is what happened. I think we have a very special relationship because we really talk when we talk about feelings. Well, that's enough for now, I said what I had to say. Love you, Della. P.S. I have never said that to you in person but I really do.

Tuesday, June 15, 1982

Dear Diary,

Well I had to write this down, about a year ago, in the summer of 1981 I was hit by a car. He was going pretty slow, just starting off from a stop light. I was of course walking in the wrong lane. I was really on the side of the road on the grass with no curb, but he was coming from behind me. I was walking with my ex-best friend Andi (a girl, a whole different story). Her brother and sister were on the other side of the street and according to the driver, he was swerving not to hit them when he hit me. I'm told I was unconscious for about thirty minutes. An ambulance came but I didn't go to the hospital in it. That would have been too expensive. When I woke up on the ground there was a big crowd around me. It was really strange to see all these feet. Anyway, I didn't move until this ambulance guy told me to. First, he asked me some questions: can you wiggle your toes, etc. My mother at the time was in Las Vegas with Matt (gross scum). Andi's mom took me to the hospital for x-rays. I didn't cry till then because I was getting real sore because he hit my back (and spinal cord which is probably why I was knocked unconscious) and the table was cold hard steel and the damn nurse wouldn't help me on, off, or while changing positions on the table for the x-rays. Nothing was broken but I couldn't walk for three days. The second two were spent crawling. Della

Wednesday, June 16, 1982

Well Fred, I've decided that one day in the far future (not too far) that if we are both willing and not married (or maybe) that we will have sex. But we cannot make it a habit. Boy does that sound stupid. I feel like a slut and I'm still a virgin! Oh well, I can't think of any other way to put it. I keep having these feelings that I don't understand. Every time Marissa flirts with you or I know that ya'll are together and I'm somewhere else, my heart just fills with jealousy. And when we start talking about David (Marissa's love) I get all happy. I mean my gosh, you're twenty-nine years old, almost thirty, and I'm only fifteen. What's the deal?? I wonder, I overheard Marissa tell you that she wants to have sex with you too. Maybe I want to be first. I bet that is it. Marissa and I had a discussion about that too. We both agree that we want to make love to you (not at the same time, I hope!) AND we both agree that you would be great in bed because of your love, care and understanding. What especially gets to me is when we talk about 69 (I hope I remember what that is when I read this in the future) because when we do make love, that sure is hell gonna be included!! I can't describe why I know, maybe books, movies or logic, but I know that oral sex would and does feel better than actual sex. I cannot believe the things I am writing!! But I know for a fact that if you are upset, you write your feelings down and that's just what I am doing. Della.

Thursday, June 25, 1982

Well I actually wrote a note to Fred to give to him. I'll start at the beginning. Last night after gymnastics we all got pretty loaded. We split a joint and had some Pina colada and amaretto. Anyway, the whole night Marissa was hanging all over Fred. Boy was I jealous! Then he came to me for help, he said, "What would any other 30-year-old male do? I don't want Marissa to be jealous of Della." I mean, Marissa was hanging ALL over him. It got me so mad! So today I wrote him a two-page note saying what I felt. I'll try to summarize. I told him that while he was worrying about Marissa being jealous of Della, he never even thought of Della being jealous of Marissa! I told him that I loved him but just didn't know when to show it, or how. I told him how much affection I need and how important hugs are to me. Well we had a talk and after he read it we hugged. I was so happy. I love him so much but I have never had a relationship like this one. That's partly why it is so special. He told me that he didn't like Marissa more than me and that he thought I was special and how easy things would be if only he was sixteen or I was twenty-nine. He also said that it was cuz of me that he started writing music because he couldn't keep it inside any longer. I am so happy now!! I think from tonight and on we will think differently about each other, better!! Marissa loves him too and shows it REAL WELL!! He said he loves her too. I understand that but I KNOW it's not like he loves me! Della. PS, I love you Fred!

Sunday, July 4, 1982

Well it happened again! Tuesday night me, Marissa and Fred went to go swim in Dawn's pool because she went to Michigan for a week. When we got there, we found out that a friend of Dawn's mom whose name is Tom was staying there. We went in and smoked a GOOD joint or two inside. When we went to swim, I realized I didn't want to, so I sat on the diving board and watched. There were no lights, only the moonlight, so I couldn't see them well. But they hardly swam. They just stood facing each other and laughed once in a while. I was so loaded, I really didn't think about it. Well, I did, but I didn't want to believe it. We went again Wednesday night but Mom came. Fred wanted to get a joint from Tom and asked Marissa to go in with him cuz Fred had only met him once. So me and Mom went to swim. Thirty minutes passed and Mom told me to go get them. I knew they had both smoked, and so did Mom. She said, "what do you think they are doing?" I told her I didn't know. Anyway, I got pissed because I didn't get any, so I tried to ignore him for the rest of the night.

Thursday morning Fred offered to take me to work. I said ok and that he would be doing Mom a favor. I wanted to go on his motorcycle but Mom said no. We started talking about

Marissa on the way and he said that she was getting real brave. He said that one time he, Marissa and Mom went out to eat and he was sitting next to Marissa wearing loose cut offs and she stuck her hand up his pant leg and he got a hard-on. I was shocked! Why is he telling me this? So I asked him if she went down his pants the night in the pool when Mom wasn't there and he answered, "yes, she grabbed Herbert" (the name Fred gave his dick). I was totally shocked and managed to keep a smile until we got there. He said it like it would not affect me at all! I was miserable all day until lunch when I told my friend at work the whole story since we met Fred. I was really hurt. She told me that I should talk to him and I knew it. I said that a solution would be for him to move out, but he doesn't have the money to rent an apartment. Everyone at work knew I was upset, but I just said I had a problem at home. Well, guess who picked me up!! I tried to ignore him. He asked if I was okay and I nodded and he called me a liar. I couldn't help but smile. He figured out what was wrong and said, "Della I'm real sorry I told you that this morning. Real sorry." I tried to fight back the tears and said, "me too." He put his hand on my leg and I moved it. I could tell he was hurt too. When we got home we watched Mash on Ma's bed. I laid on the opposite end from him. When Marissa left, he rolled over to me and said, "do you think you could write your feelings down on paper?" I shrugged. He looked at me and turned away. I couldn't hold the tears back. I cried silently until he left then I ran into the bathroom and started silently bawling. I blew my nose and when I walked out he was sitting on the bed. I walked straight to my room, shut the door and wrote him a note. It was only one front page but I got the message across. It said the next time Marissa decides to put her hands down your pants, make sure I am not around. It also told about how miserable I was at work and everything.

I walked into the kitchen where he was and said, "can we talk?" He said, "yes, let's take a walk, Marissa we'll be back in a little bit." She was so mad! Smile. When we got outside I said, "I don't want people around here to see me cry, can we drive somewhere?" He said, "I have my keys, let's go to the junior high school parking lot." We did and when we got there I gave him the note. He read it and said, "I'm so sorry Della, I regretted telling you on the way back from dropping you off." My eyes began to fill with tears. We sat there for a minute until he started massaging my head with one hand. He turned my head toward him and looked into my teary eyes and pulled me close to him, kissed my cheek three times and hugged me. I started crying and I think he did too. We hugged for the longest time until he finally let go. We looked into each other's eyes again and he put his hand on my face. I held it with both hands and slowly pulled it away. He looked at me again and started coming for my lips. I regret it now but I turned my head and he kissed right beside them and we hugged again. After a minute, he said, "I'm going to have a talk with Marissa, Della." I nodded. Then I said, "Well, there goes my buzz." We had smoked a joint when he picked me up. We sat until our eyes dried and went back. I will never forget those few minutes as long as I live! On the way back to the house he said, "I still want to hold your hand and sneak a hug off of you once in a while." I replied, "it better be more often than that!" He said, "that doesn't mean I won't have sexual feelings toward you, though." I was so happy!! My theory was wrong. He still wants to have sex with me, even with my tiny tits. He said, "But that will come later." I said, "It's amazing how much we think alike cuz I was thinking that too." He said, "about what?" I said, "what, do you want me to say it?" He said, "yes" and I said "no!" Love Della. P.S. He told me I have a cute butt.

Wednesday, July 7, 1982

Well, I am finally getting over swimmer's ear! It is so damn painful! I couldn't even hardly sleep! I never thought an ear ache could hurt so bad! It is caused by a fungus. Pretty soon I'm going to turn into a large mass of fungi. I also have fungus of the chi chi [yeast infection]. What a bummer!!! Well I can't believe it! I told myself that if Fred tried to kiss me on the lips that I wasn't going to stop him. He tried (or hinted) about it last night. I was going to bed and was trying to step over his legs between the couch and coffee table and I lost my balance and sat on his lap. He looked at me and started tilting his head and moving closer. I turned my head and regretted it the first minute after I did it. Well tonight it happened!! We were watching TV on Mom's bed and when she left we held hands as usual but this time he rolled over and kissed me on the lips. I kissed him back and we parted. I looked into his eyes and just stared. Mom came into the room and he rolled back over. The next time Mom left he looked at me and said, "what's happening, Della?" I said "nothing" and smiled. I think he thinks I'm mad at him. Well he's dead wrong!! I just can't look at him or I'll get excited again. That sure does sound funny!! But it's true. We're both counting the days until we have sex! Just kidding, but we both know it's coming! I guess whenever I turn nineteen or when I get on the pill. I can't believe the stuff I am writing. I'm really not a slut!! I'm not a nasty person verbally! Does this mean that Fred is really special? I hope so! I know that whenever we finally do it, it's really going to be special and beautiful! I can't wait! Luv ya Fred, Della.

Dear Della,

I didn't know whether you were mad or hurt when you left yesterday. I never meant to do either. I was playing the game just like my brother taught my sister and I to play. The way he plays is that you must say rummy card before the other players. I can't remember us talking about the different rules we both learned so I understand why you were upset.

Della. I'm sorry it ever happened. I enjoy playing rummy ok, but what I enjoy most is the time I am able to spend with you while we are playing. Without you knowing, you, your mom and Marissa have helped me survive the pains of my separation by befriending me when I was so lonely. I know that this has nothing to do with yesterday, but I feel so awkward trying to verbalize my feeling because I get so emotional I can't think clearly. I've also been afraid that if I express how I feel that I might embarrass you to the point of being uncomfortable around me.

You are a most special person and I love you. I wouldn't do anything to hurt you or make you angry intentionally. This has been hard to write (that's what she said last night) but I have to stop now that you're here on the couch; I am getting embarrassed. With love, Fred.

One thing I neglected to tell you, I have wanted to thank you for giving me the confidence to write again. I had not completed a song in seven years until I started hanging out with you really it was more an inspiration than confidence I got from you. Hell, I don't know how to tell you how I feel. If it's okay with you when I know, I'll try again.

Saturday, July 10, 1982

Well, it happened! Last night was so beautiful! We went to see two scary movies at the theater, *Alien* and *Visiting Hours*. They were gross! Anyway, the whole time we held hands. Every time a scary part came on I'd squeeze his hand and he squeezed it back. We came home at midnight and went and sat in the back porch and swung in the hanging chairs. Marissa had cramps and went to bed and Mom finally went in her room. Fred hugged me and said, "Wanna play cards till your ma goes to sleep?" and kinda looked at me funny and smiled. I said okay. After two hands, he scooted over to me and started hugging me. I got so scared. I knew I wasn't ready for sex! I finally broke away and said, "Fred, I love you, but I'm not ready yet." He said, "Oh Della, I'm not going to make love to you. We've got several years before that. You're going to have boyfriends too." I said, "I know" and hugged him a long time. We parted and stared into each other's eyes for a year! Just Joking. He moved closer and closer. I knew it was coming. Our lips finally met and immediately our tongues were in each other's mouth. We kissed for a long time and finally parted. Fred said, "Oh Della, that was nice." I smiled and he kissed me again and laid me down on the floor. He started to rub my back and stomach. I had my bathing suit top on. So I wasn't that paranoid!

I can't write anymore. I hope I remember what happened. I just want to say that neither of our pants were even unsnapped. I did lay on top of him though. I could feel it getting hard but I don't think he came in his pants. I think he got close but then held it. We stayed up till 3:00 a.m. He told me my tits were pretty. I'm crying now, even though I didn't when he said it. I've been putting them down for so long, I'm not used to anyone saying anything good about them. I wish I had more to give him. Marissa has so much, it's not fair!! She wears her new bathing suit every day just to remind him how big they are. It works! They all hang out when she lies on her side and she does it a lot! Della.

Wednesday, July 14, 1982

This has been a surprise to everyone, but I'm leaving for New Orleans tomorrow to go see Daddy. The reservation is for 4:00 p.m. Marissa and I are going separately this year. I don't know exactly why. I guess mostly because we will get special attention. I'm going tomorrow and a week later Marissa is coming up and a week later I'm leaving to come home and a week later Marissa is leaving. Got it? I feel very differently about leaving this year. I think it is a mixture of reasons. #1—I think because of Fred and a certain night, I am much more mature about seeing Dad, I still love him very much and I can't wait to see him but I'm not all hyped up about it as usual. #2 is because of the very short notice (shock) (because of my job—the break in between the swimming sessions). #3 is because of . . . well I don't exactly know how to put it. I feel weird about leaving someone I love (Fred) and seeing someone else I love (Dad) but in a totally different way. It's really weird!! But it hurts at the same time and I don't know why. #4 Even though I will get my time when I come back, I will just always be jealous when Marissa has Fred all by herself, bitch (she wondered how many times I put that in here and this is number one). Well I guess that about covers it. Will write in N.O. but I am going to start a spiral since this is the very last sheet in this notebook. Bye. D. Luv ya Fred!

[I told Fred that he could read this diary while I was gone. so he knew exactly how I felt. I regretted it while in New Orleans.]

Thursday, July 29, 1982

I am spending two weeks with dad. First entry in this diary.

When I first got here, I missed Fred so much! I thought about him almost every minute. It was worst at night when I was laying alone. The day before Marissa got here, I wrote him a letter with Mom's. His was in a separate envelope inside Mom's, so she wouldn't think about reading it and Marissa couldn't. I told him how much I loved and missed him. I told him how miserable I was without him and that all that mattered was that I loved him.

I regretted it the next day, when Marissa came. She cried the first night but told me it wasn't my business when I asked why. I asked, hopefully, if it was about David, although I knew it was about Fred. Then she started complaining that Dad never showed affection to us and that she wanted to go home. In the next few days she was almost always depressed. I almost called Mom to tell her not to give the letter to Fred when he came back from out of town. I never had a chance. The next night when Marissa was crying we started talking. I asked why she was upset and she said because of Dad. Bull!! Then I asked why she cried the first night she got here. (I knew it was about Fred, but I thought that she just missed him and that I was stronger than her, and that's why I didn't cry.)

She said, "can't you figure it out, you're smart."

"I'm not smart enough to read your mind."

"I know you know why."

"I know who, it's Fred, but tell me why."

"You can figure it out."

"No, I can't, please just tell me!" She didn't say anything.

"Okay, I'll try to guess and you tell me if I'm right. But I know it's stupid, and I know I'm going to feel like a fool after I say it."

"Okay."

"You miss Fred because you want to have sex with him." She made this awful face like "no way." "See, I told you, I told you I would be wrong."

I was so relieved, for a second until she said, "We already did." My heart ripped right in half!! No, this couldn't be right!!

"Ya'll did it?"

"Don't say it like that!"

"Ya'll had sex?"

"Yes, we made love." It was so hard to keep my tears from flowing. I was so hurt!! Worse than I've ever been before, <u>ever</u>.

"When?"

"I can't remember the first time. July 9th."

"How many times have ya'll done it?"

"I don't know, about ten, I can't believe I'm telling you this. Do you hate me?"

After pause, "No, I don't hate you."

"Good, we were so scared you would tell Mom."

"I wouldn't have told Mom!! I won't tell anybody, you have my word, I swear it. I can't believe you're not a virgin anymore."

We talked about it a little more. Then I told her about me and Fred's night. Dumb! I don't think I will ever be as hurt as I was that night. When she went to sleep, I cried the whole night. I probably got four hours of sleep total. I hid my depression in front of Marissa, though. I didn't want her to know how hurt I was.

I asked, "Do you think Fred will care if I know?"

"No, but let me tell him first, okay?"

I didn't answer. That was how I would get my revenge. I just smiled. He was going to get it so bad!! From then on, Marissa was always complaining about how much she missed him and wanted to go home. She keeps asking if she could come home with me but I say no.

Tonight, she went swimming and I didn't want to go. From the door, all soaking wet she says to Dad, "Dad can I call Dawn, my best friend? It's her birthday."

Dad says, "Yes."

A little later I went out there and she was crying. She said, "Della, can I talk to Fred alone, please?"

Damn it, there went my damn revenge!! I was so mad I went to our bed and lied down. Marissa came in after a while and said,

"You're mad at me, aren't you?"

"No, I'm not mad at you"

"Yes, you are, you sure look like you are."

"I'm not!"

"You're mad at Fred, aren't you?"

I didn't say anything, she knew I was. I asked if she told him.

Marissa said, "Don't be mad! We didn't mean for it to happen! We just fell in love. He told me to tell you something."

"What?"

"He said that he loves you."

For the first time, I cried in front of her.

I asked, "Was he mad that you told me?"

"He said that he wished I hadn't. Don't be mad, I don't understand why you're mad."

"I'm not mad, I'm just hurt. It's going to take a while for it to go away. Just leave me alone for a while."

I cried and cried and cried and planned what I would say to him at our conversation: "How long were you going to keep it a secret? I'm not going to write this time. It hurt so bad because you had me believing it was me. You lied to me. You said you weren't going to let her touch you anymore! Well she didn't have to, you did it all for her. Why did you do those things to me when you were going to bed with her? Can I have my letter please? The only thing that's true in that letter now is that <u>I will always love you</u>. Were you just not going to say anything for a year then say, "Oh sorry, I'm leaving you and me and Marissa are going to live in Austin and get our band and you're not included, so bye." You told me all those songs were about me! You said the same thing to Marissa, didn't you? You were just going to get your thrills off of me and then go to bed with Marissa! As much as I have been looking forward to it, I will never go to bed with you, Fred, NEVER. Now I know that every time ya'll are alone what ya'll will be doing. EVERY TIME!! I will never forget this, Fred! As long as I live!!!"

I wish he would move out!! I don't know how I'm going to live with them anymore. I will think about it every day. It would be hard not to when they're always there! D.

Friday, July 30, 1982

I know now that the only way for me to get over this is for Fred to move out. As long as he lives in the same house, I will never forget and will think about it constantly. I think I will ask him to move out. Maybe he will have by the time I go home. I doubt it seriously!

Marissa says stuff to me about her and Fred that he always did to me too. She said they always looked into each other's eyes and we always do that too. We USED TO!! She said she hopes only Fred will pick her up from the airport because she doesn't know how she can keep her hands off of him when she sees him and I thought the <u>exact</u> same thing!!

If Fred doesn't move out, I WILL!! I'll tell him that too! Damn, how am I going to face him? DAMN!!

Marissa and I hugged last night. D.

Monday, August 2, 1982

Well tomorrow I am going home. I dread it so much. I wish so much that I didn't know!! It will never be the same, EVER AGAIN! Marissa told me not to do anything with him because she said that Fred was hers. DAMN. I can't believe this is happening. I'm so afraid that now that I know, Marissa is going to feel free to do anything she wants in front of me, and worse, I can't do <u>anything</u> to him when she's around. NOTHING! I probably won't even be able to sit next to him without her saying something to me. I will miss everything so much! Holding and caressing his hand, looking into his eyes, but mostly hugging him and kissing him. Why did I have to find out? DAMN IT! She told me that he told her that he would never do anything sexual with me. I don't know what to think, cuz that's not what he told me!! DAMN a million times! I want him to move out! No matter what I think later. I know now that that is the only solution. How could he do this? Why couldn't he have just left me the hell alone and not lead me to believe that I was the only one he was in love with? IT HURTS SO BAD!! DAMN DAMN DAMN. I wish I didn't know!! D.

Monday, August 9, 1982

All the way to the airport I kept wishing for time to stop! It was worse getting on the plane but mainly getting off! I dreaded seeing him so much! I knew that that day would be the last time I hugged him, when I got off the plane. I walked real slow and wondered how I would even hug Mom with all the stuff I had in my hands. When I got off the plane, I was so relieved to see that neither one of them was there. (I knew he was coming cuz when Mom called she asked if I wanted to talk to him cuz he was right there. I couldn't say no.) I followed the crowd until I finally saw them. I hugged Mom then Fred. He pulled me close. I tried to ignore him the rest of the time but without being suspicious towards Mom. I sat in the back of the car after some arguing with Ma cuz she thought I would want to sit up front. (My first real clue to Fred that I didn't want to be near him.) When we got home, Mom told me the slides of us came in that Ed, our gym coach, took of us. I went to the kitchen to look at them. He was there, he said, "Will you stay up and talk to me?" I nodded. When I was through, he was sitting on the couch. I fixed myself a glass of water and went to Mom's bedroom. Second clue. We talked about my trip and he finally came in there. We talked a long time, I think two hours. Mom finally went to bed and we started playing cards. I didn't change, still in jeans. (I forgot to say, he's trying to grow a mustache. Looks weird.) We played a couple of hands and the stereo was on. Then *Here Comes the Feeling* came on by Asia. I was mad. It always reminded me of him. Playing cards was torture! I finally got to 500 and he didn't deal again.

He said, "I'm really sorry you got hurt."

THE BASTARD!! That was the absolute last thing I wanted to hear! I know he wasn't sorry that he did it, and that was what I wanted him to be sorry of! I didn't say anything. Then he said,

"I don't want to end my relationship with you. You were so far away I couldn't tell you."

I WAS SO SURPRISED! Marissa had me believing totally different! Exactly opposite!!

I said, "But Marissa said you were hers!"

"I'm not anybody's, I belong to me."

We talked about Marissa putting me through torture and we finally hugged. I was so happy!!

"BUT," I told him, "I cannot have a relationship with you

knowing that you and Marissa are going to bed." He looked at me and hugged me.

I said, "Do you understand?"

"I understand. But I don't have to like it."

I wish I would have told him then that as soon as Marissa got back I wouldn't do anything with him. The next few days were glorious. Every chance we could we kissed and hugged. I tried hash for the first time.

Things quickly went downhill. I spent the night with Dawn Saturday night. She showed me a letter that Marissa wrote to her that told about how she was in love with Fred. Then she showed me another letter from Marissa. The Damn Bitch told Dawn about me making out with Fred, but she never mentioned that <u>they</u> did it. I was so mad!! Well if she broke her promise, I would. I told her they did it. She wasn't surprised. Brenda, her mother, knew about everything and she was really concerned. She wanted him out of our house before Marissa got back. We talked and talked about what we should do. Brenda called her sister and father for advice. Her sister said don't tell my mom, but her father said yes. As much as I hated Mom finding out, I knew it was the right thing to do. Fred was in Dallas with his mother and wouldn't be back till Sunday night. Sunday morning, Brenda called Mom and said she needed to talk to her. So Brenda went to my house and told Mom that Marissa and Fred were in love and showed her the first letter. She didn't say that they did it but said that she didn't know how far they did go. She also told her that he was in love with me too and had made advances to me. I was so nervous waiting at Dawn's. She finally came back and told me Mom was picking me up. She told me that she had told my mom about me too. I dreaded talking to her.

Mom finally came to get me, and as soon as I got in the car she started asking me questions. I told her everything except that they did "it" and I only told her that Fred had kissed me. When we got home the crying started. She said that we weren't going on a planned Labor Day vacation.

She said, "I can't trust anyone anymore, except my mother. I can't even trust my own two daughters. And all the time I thought they were innocent, but they lied behind my back. I can't believe under my own roof this happened. How could I be so blind? Fred lied and said that Marissa only had a crush, and he wished it would end."

I was so upset. Then she said, "I wish I would have known before I spent a hundred dollars on you at the expensive hotel! But no, take advantage of old mother!"

I said, "that's not true!"

She said, "Uh huh, sure!"

That is when I started crying. She went to her room and called her boss and friend. He soothed her mind. When she got off the phone I called Dawn. We tried to figure out some way for her to come over, but I didn't even want to ask Mom. I told Mom that she had another letter and asked if she could come over and that I needed her and she wanted to be with me for support. Surprisingly, Mom agreed. Mom wanted Fred out that night, so we had to pack up everything of his. When Dawn came over, Mom read the note, which I forgot was partly about me. We waited the whole day in suspense for Fred to come home. We finally started watching *A Star is Born* and at the very end, the door unlocked. Dawn said, "Della, you gotta be strong." I started bawling!

Mom went in there and said, "I want my key."

He said, "stay calm, just stay calm."

"Well, I'm not calm!"

I cried and cried and cried and cried. I couldn't go in there. I finally did and he looked so mad. I've never seen him so mad before, since I met him. I wanted to touch him, but he was so mad. When he looked at me his expression didn't change. He was so mad. His hair was in a very short ponytail. I hated it. That's the last time I will see him for a very long time and I didn't want to remember him that way. He told Mom that his notebooks were in Marissa's room. When they came back there and looked they weren't there.

I said, "I put them in your trunk." I never cried so hard or long as I did that night. If Dawn did not spend the night, I think I would have died. I wrote him a note that said, "Fred, no matter what happens, I will always love you. I didn't tell. I swear. It was Brenda. Love, Della.

I put the note in his notebook. I hope he has read it by now. There is no way he could have taken his motorcycle too, so he left it. I hope and pray he comes back for it and I see him again. I wrote him another note and put it on his bike. It says that I know Brenda did the right thing, and someday I would find Fred.

Mom went with Uncle Charlie to the airport to pick Marissa up. I went over Dawn's cuz Mom didn't want me there if Fred came back for his bike. When they got home, Mom called and said that Marissa was bawling and that she wanted to die. Mom didn't want to leave her so she couldn't come pick me up. I was glad. Brenda was gone so she couldn't take me home.

Mom finally picked me up with Marissa and nothing was said about Fred. Tonight, Marissa played rummy with me in my room and like a fool I left Fred's letter out to dry cuz my roof leaked and got it wet.

She found it and said, "Well, I guess I can read this now."

"No!" I tried to grab it from her and succeeded but not before she ripped it in half. I WAS SO MAD!! I didn't even want her to know I had it. I love you Fred. I read my diary and found out the day that me and Fred made out for the first time was July 9th, THE SAME GODDAMNED DAY YOU SLEPT WITH MY SISTER!!

Saturday, September 11, 1982

Well, he's been gone almost a month but somehow, he is still causing pain. At first, I still loved him and missed him but now I HATE HIM! A few days after he left I found out Marissa found out about my note on his bike. Dawn had told her. So she tore it up after she read it and replaced it with one of hers.

One day a friend of his came over with Marissa's pictures that accidentally got in Fred's stuff. After a while he and Mom went outside to talk and we were right by the door listening. He said that Fred really wanted to talk to Marissa!! I was so mad. A few days later he called Dawn and told her to tell Marissa not to kill herself and that he wasn't getting back together with his wife. When Dawn said, "what about Della?" he said, "Well I barely did anything with her." DAMN. He told me that he called what we did "making love" and now it's "barely anything."

That is when I started hating him. Then Marissa started calling him on Wednesday nights when I had gymnastics, and one Wednesday she went over there. DAMN. Now they are planning to get married when she gets out of school. NOW I REALLY HATE HIS FUCKING GUTS. All that time he had me believing it was ME he was in love with and now he's going to marry my fucking sister. I HATE MARISSA NOW, TOO. For the first time in my life, I hate her. I REALLY DO!

Mom knows everything and is getting hurt really bad. Last night she caught Marissa in a lie about where she had been and slapped Marissa across her face for the first time. Marissa ran out of the house and sped away in her truck. She is treating me like total shit and I can't fight back or she threatens me that she won't take me anywhere anymore. As it is I have to take the bus to and from school!! She won't even give me a ride to school! Mom said, "How did I raise such a BITCH?" If me and Marissa ever say anything to each other, we are arguing and calling each other names. Mom had a long talk with Marissa about him. Marissa wants to move out and Mom is going to let her, but not until his divorce is final. She can't see him till then and Mom is demanding that she know where Marissa is every minute.

As if that is not enough pain, I am having friend problems at school. This is my junior year of high school. Since my best friend, Andi, ran away, I haven't had a best friend. Tammy is a girl I've known since the 6th grade and that is who I eat lunch with but it seems like she doesn't want me around anymore. Before Andi left, me, Andi, Tammy and a girl named Theresa (little red head) hung around together. Andi left in the summer and the next year I ate with Winnie, who lives in our townhomes and is one grade younger than me. That was my mistake. Tammy was in my English class and so half of the school year I ate with her. It was too late because she got a best friend named Mitzie. She is sweet. All through the summer, Tammy never called me once and every time I called her (five times) she was never home. This year I eat with Tammy, Mitzie, and two others, Chrissie and Angele (pronounced Azhell). It is now almost a month since school started and I have gotten only one note, it was a short one from Mitzie and I have written Tammy and Mitzie twice and Chrissie & Angele once.

I have been getting to be better and better friends with Dawn since the F crisis (it is too painful to write out his full name) and thank God, she writes me. She started out as Marissa's best friend, they are in the same class, but Dawn cannot stand the way that Marissa is treating me. And Marissa treats her bad sometimes too, especially lately. Dawn and I get along really well, and we never fight. We "get" each other. She is like a nice sister to me. And she has helped me through some pretty rough patches.

Well, there's the trauma of my life right now. I hope things will get better. F is even messing me up in school. This really sucks. Della.

Tuesday, September 28, 1982

Well things haven't gotten much better, if not worse. Marissa has been secretly seeing F every day. She goes over there after school and before work at 5:00 p.m. I wasn't supposed to know, but I found out when one day Marissa said she was one place and Dawn said she was somewhere else. I knew immediately. Marissa has been treating Dawn like shit lately and Dawn couldn't take it anymore. Dawn once said that she's only friends with Marissa so she can get rides to school.

One day Marissa and I went over Dawn's house, and Brenda slipped and said that Dawn didn't want to go to the movies because she felt uncomfortable around F and Marissa together. When Marissa went to work, she called Dawn and asked if I heard what Brenda had said and asked what I had said. Then Marissa started bitching her out and Dawn blew up and said that she didn't want to be her friend anymore. Marissa called Mom bawling. The next day, for some reason, Dawn called Mom and told her that F had given us pot. Bitch. Mom blew up once again, and told us that she hated us! But after a while, she apologized.

Then Mom called Dad and told him EVERYTHING. Mom asked him to come down because she couldn't make decisions about it anymore by herself. So he did and one night he had a long talk with Marissa and the next day he talked with Mom, Marissa and F. I left cuz I really never want to see his fucking face again. Mom told me that she made a big deal about how hurt I was. F said that it hurts him too, and that if I wanted to take out all my anger on him, he would listen. THE FUCKING BASTARD!! I wouldn't give him the pleasure!! Although I had thought about yelling at him and everything. I don't know. I really need some advice. Should I call him and yell my head off at him or just hold the grudge for the rest of my life? I DON'T KNOW!! I really need a friend right now. A CLOSE FRIEND! A BEST FRIEND. SHIT! I'm in such a bind right now. What am I going to do? Della. P.S. Dawn and Marissa are friends again. Frown.

One time Daddy and I were in my living room alone. I tried to tell him how I was not doing well. How I was hurting. I showed him lyrics to a song called *Do You Remember When* from the J. Geils Band album, *Freeze Frame*, which described a little how I was feeling about F. He read them, but didn't really have a response. I felt like I was being ignored, forgotten, that Marissa was getting all the attention. The song expressed my feelings that every time someone mentioned him, that my heart felt the pain. And that time was moving very slowly for me.

Saturday, April 9, 1983

Wow, it has been a while, hasn't it? A whole lot has happened. Daddy hates F. Then we all went to a psychiatrist several times and spent lots of money trying to break them two up. He was a jerk. He told me that I should definitely see a psychiatrist by myself before I try to have a relationship with any guy. I didn't really think about it. Anyway, Mom said she could move in with him as soon as he got his divorce, which was right after Christmas. Since then, I have been trying and trying to forget him.

After a while he started wanting to go to choir concerts and stuff cuz he is tired of missing things Marissa is involved in. He said he even wanted to go to Oklahoma (the school musical I was in, which Marissa had nothing to do with). So finally, Marissa told me he was coming to our choir concert at the coliseum with a lot of elementary, junior and high schools performing. It would have been the first time to see him in eight months. Then my boss said that if I didn't work that night (I forgot to tell him about it till that Tuesday and the concert was Thursday) that I would be more or less fired. (I work at Bob and Linda's Sandwich Shop. Started March 5.) So I didn't see him then. The next concert was the Mozart Mass at another high school in our district. Of course, he wanted to go. Because I didn't want to see him for the first time on stage, we decided for me to go to the beach with them. I cancelled out. On the day of the concert, we had to practice from after school (the day I went to the beach in oceanography class) till 6:00 p.m. and the concert was at 7:30 p.m. so we were in a big rush to get ready. So Marissa said it would be faster if me and Portia (friend and fellow choir member) got our clothes and dressed at her and f's apartment. So we did.

I work with a girl named Lisa and we have become pretty good friends. She is twenty-four and has a five-year-old son. Anyway, I told her the WHOLE story from the time me and Fred met to present date and asked her how I should act towards him. She said, "It sounds to me like he is a real jerk, and I would make him pay for what he did to you. So what you do is act like nothing ever happened and just be a smiling bitch!" I did. When I saw him for the first time in eight months, all I said was "hi" and he said "hullo," kinda in a sad-mad voice. It was really good that I didn't have time to be depressed and I sang great in the concert.

So this brings us to today. Chrissie couldn't take me home so I asked Marissa to take me. She said yes and asked if I would go to the bank with her. On the way home, she forgot me and started going towards her apartment. She was about to turn around, then suggested that I stay at her apartment till she has to go to work at 5:00 p.m. I reluctantly said okay. Of course, Fred is there. I did exactly the same thing as before but this time it was a lot harder cuz I stayed a lot longer. I never really realized how hard it was being a bitch until today. Especially to someone you love. Yes, I realized also that I still love him. And watching him (with his now full-grown mustache) made me want a hug from him SO BAD. He is so much cuter with his mustache and layered haircut. It is exactly the length I always loved it. I can't believe that in trying to hurt him, I am doing a great job on myself! I would love to say, "let's forget the whole thing, I forgive you" but the woman and hurtness inside me won't let me. It has got to stay like this for a long time. I just hope he doesn't think that I am completely over it and that is why I act so gay over there. As soon as I took the first step into my house, I was crying.

Guess what! I had my first real date on Friday, April 1st. His name is Ron, he is a senior, he is maybe an inch taller than me and has fuzzy red hair.

Sunday, June 5, 1983

I hate Ron now, and besides, I don't want him in here because this is Fred's notebook. I am seeing a lot more of Fred now. It is still very hard on me every time I see him. It has almost been a year now since everything blew up! Lisa is now my best friend. Dawn and I are in a fight. She can't stand me having Lisa as a friend, but she sees JoAnne anytime she wants. She can be a real bitch sometimes.

Anyway, I thought about the fact that when I am a "smiling bitch" to Fred, like Lisa said, I was afraid that he would think that I am okay now. I talked to Dad and he said that F will know how I feel by reading my face. It makes sense, he probably knows. It was funny, yesterday Mom, Marissa and Fred came to Bob and Linda's to eat. Thank goodness Lisa made sure to make his fucking sandwich. Anyway, after I rang them up, I went into the back room and stayed there the WHOLE time. I'm sure F got the message cuz Mom came back there and asked why was I back there. Duh! I told her that Lisa was slicing and we were talking. She probably knew the real reason and was probably mad, but I am NOT going to be nice to the BASTARD!! Every now and then I still want to hug him very much. It's funny. Sometimes I think "wow, I have a boyfriend" just like last summer (Fred), then I realize he is Marissa's now, and I feel sad. I swear, how fucking long is it going to take? Will we ever be on friendly terms? Now and then I want to just talk to him. Lisa is now saying, "it's up to you, if you want to." I don't know. I don't know. FUCK! This is really driving me CRAZY! I want to call him up and say, "meet me at the junior high and let's talk, I'm tired of the STUPID games." Sometimes I even still want to make love to him. I can't deny it, I really do. Lisa says, "don't you dare let it go any further than just friends. Marissa will hate you for life." It's true, but damn it, she did it to me! I know it's not worth the risk, but I'M GOING CRAZY! I want my virginity GONE! I'm an old lady compared to most virgins! I keep thinking about going to a male whore house to lose it. But then I think, no, let it be someone special. I wish he would hurry up! I've decided I'm not going to be sixteen because that is when Marissa lost it.

So I've decided on seventeen, for Mom.

I still cry every time I read my old diary and F's letter to me. Not a whole lot, but it's there. His hair is too long now. It hugs his neck. I WANT A HUG FROM HIM. But I won't. NEVER!!! Really.

Oh yeah. I forgot. Mom is going to rent a beach house again and guess who's coming. GOD, WHAT AM I GOING TO DO? Memories from the last time are killing me. I'm crying again. How am I going to act? What am I going to do?!?! I wish they would just move. How about Mars! If Russell comes [my cousin's fiancé] it is really going to be bad because he loves F. What if everyone (except Mom) wants to take a walk on the beach at night and get stoned and chase crabs? I can't not go but it is going to KILL me. SHIT!!! Will I ever stop loving him?

I really can't carry on a relationship with a guy anymore because of F. Ron was a really sweet guy, but now I hate him. I started liking this guy named Randy. He gave me a hickey. But now I don't know. I was liking Larry again, but now we're just friends. It's because I change the feelings I have for F. I need a psychiatrist. BASTARD. Is it true? Can I have a relationship with a guy anymore? Has he ruined my life? The only guy I feel real close to right now is Victor, and that's only because I know we will never be more than great friends. He came over yesterday to swim. It was fun. Della. P.S. It is getting better. I THINK! How do I know?

Sunday, June 12, 1983

Wow! Today was the best day I've had all summer! Lisa, Ethan (Lisa's five-year-old son), and Lisa's little brother, Bruce (who is 22) and I all went to the beach. It was a blast! The waves were great! Bruce has a Subaru Brat and it had two seats in the truck part to sit in. We all had turns sitting in back, even Bruce. It's really fun going down the freeway backwards, in a chair, outside of the car. I got sunburned on my face and chest. We took the highway which was the way to Bruce's and Lisa's big sister, Selma's house. Or should I say farm? We stopped there on the way back. I got to hold a little baby chicken for the first time. They're so cute! They had baby geese too. Bruce said he promised he would take me horseback riding this summer. I can't wait. He's kinda cute, but he has a front tooth missing. Somehow that kinda turns me off. He's a great person though. (I'm hungry!)

For two weeks, we had plans to go to "The Hop," me, Lisa, and Mom, so we did. It was also a blast. Off the subject, Mom went to a male strip club for her 40th birthday. She told me all about it and it sounded great. She took ten people including my cousin Josie. She said you put a dollar in their G string and they dance in front of you then give you a kiss. Anyway, they had male strippers at The Hop, which we didn't know about till last Thursday. They were great! The best dancer was a black guy. The best looking was a guy named Flash (Lisa's nick name). But . . . the best kisser was named Night Rider. Yes, I did it! The first time I asked, when they were in their G, Mom said, "No, you're too young." But at the end they all came out in clothes and danced around. I finally got my way and got to kiss one. I put the money down his pants. We kissed for about a minute. Really! Mom started yelling for us to stop! Really! He was so good! He smiled real big when we were through.

I've made a decision. I want an older guy for a boyfriend. Not forty or anything! Just around twenty to twenty-four. They kiss so good, and believe me, I've had both. Fred and Night Rider have been older and kissed great! Whereas Greg (gag!) and Ron (gag!) kiss AWFUL!! They really do! There is one exception. When we were playing truth or dare on the back porch when I was about thirteen, I kissed a guy named Lester (he was sixteen) and he was okay. Anyway, one time I went over Greg's house and I swear, he kisses like he's dead! All he does is just sit there. He's GROSS!! YUK.

I like the Night Rider! Della. P.S. I wish I knew his real name!!

Monday, June 13, 1983

Well, I don't have much to say, since I just wrote yesterday. Except that I finally started my period! I wish I hadn't. I always wanted to have sex and not worry about getting pregnant. Without having to worry about the pill or rubbers. Too late now! I wonder if last night had anything to do with it. Probably not. Della. P.S. I'm starting the novel *The Thornbirds* tonight. 692 pages!

Friday, June 17, 1983

I finally took my driver's test! I PASSED!! My cop was a cutie! He was real nice too. When I said that it was my first time he asked if I was nervous. I said a little. While we were driving, he asked if my super kinky curly hair was perm or natural. The first thing I did was parallel park. I got in the space all right, but I hit the back flag. Thank goodness, he didn't fail me for it. I was lucky I got him. My score was a 76 percent. (I'm listening to Rick Springfield right now.) He said I needed to smooth out my approach to and turning a corner. Typical! I can't wait till I get a car! Mom works with the wife of a used car salesman. He is going to give me wholesale price. That means around a grand (hopefully). I want some kind of small Toyota.

Tuesday, June 21, 1983

Last night, Mom, Marissa, F and I went to a new restaurant. I didn't really have a choice cuz when I was over visiting Marissa, he asked what night I had off. I guess I could've not gone, but I did. It was a real nice place and all but it really hurt being with him for five hours. He did the sound and lights in the place. It was gorgeous! I couldn't help wanting him again. The more I see him, the more I keep thinking that someday we will make love. I know that will NEVER happen, and I'm just hurting myself. Damn! When is it going to end!! He talks to me like nothing happened. But what choice does he have! I was pretty quiet most of the night, though. I'm sure he knew why. I do still love him and always will. That will NEVER change! He took a very special part of my heart and it will never come back. Marissa had her hand under the table most of the time. BITCH! In her little way, she is still saying, "Ha ha, I got him, not you!" The beach is going to be pure hell! Mom is renting a beach house for the 2nd, 3rd and 4th of July, and as usual, they are coming for all three nights. DAMN, DAMN, DAMN! Marissa is going to be ALL OVER HIM. That's not all I'm scared of. I'm scared we are going to make up, and I don't want to! I still hate him so much. DAMN! When will it end? It has been a whole year now! I think I should just stop seeing him. TOTALLY AND FOR GOOD. I think it's the ONLY way that I will get over him. If I ever do! There is also the Journey concert July 1st that I have to see him. That's FOUR FUCKIN DAYS in a row! I need Lisa. I'm going to see her in two hours but that's at work! Mom doesn't understand anymore. I got bitched at last night because I didn't thank F for spending $20 on me. I COULDN'T. I just couldn't! How can she not understand what I am going through? He hurt me too much! Della. P.S. I took my senior pictures yesterday.

Friday, July 1, 1983

Just got back from the Journey concert. FANTASTIC! TOTALLY AWESOME! I love them so much. Steve Perry is FINE! I love him. So does Texas. He said that six years ago, we made them come back out again and again for encores, and it hasn't changed since. He came back three times. WOW!! I just know he loves Texas. He should, all three nights sold out. That's a lot of $! S.P. IS FINE!!!

Well, the beach is tomorrow. I'm not that scared anymore. I talked to Lisa and she really helped me. When I said that the holiday was going to be pure hell, she said, "You're the one who makes it pure hell. You want to suffer. You want to hurt yourself." Also, "Facing him and saying to yourself 'you're an idiot' in your mind is the only way you are going to get over him." She is right. Lisa is starting to be my best friend. She knows and has experienced "men" and she is passing it all to me. I don't know what I would do without her! Dawn is still my best friend too, but I can't talk to her about F. Well, I can, but she doesn't help much.

Marissa and Fred are staying in a different beach house, thank God. Mom rented two small ones this time. I only wish my cousin Josie and her boyfriend Russell were going to be there. That hurts me. They are vacationing elsewhere.

One more subject. (I gotta get to bed. Rise in five hours!) I finally quit Bob and Linda's. I put my request in for the Journey concert two months in advance, and they scheduled me to work. That started it. Lloyd had a talk with me (I listen) and I decided to stay. Then, they said that my vacation was choir tour. Bullshit! So I told Lloyd I was going to give my two week notice and quit, and he said, "Hit the door." I said "Fine, bye." The Bastard! This was last Tuesday. I got my last check today. $94.41. Della. P.S. No car yet.

September 5, 1983—letter to Fred

Fred, I am writing this on Labor Day, September 5. It has been a while since I have written you, hasn't it? In fact, it has been fourteen months. That's a long time! I'm not even sure that I am going to get the courage up to give this to you. It would take me a lot of courage. Or risk the chance of Marissa getting a hold of this.

Anyway, do you realize that we (or I) made a major breakthrough today? We actually had a long conversation with no one else around. I don't know if I like it or not because I still have mixed feelings about me being nice to you and all. I broke my "silence vow" today. I guess that is good, but like I said, I have mixed feelings about the situation. I am so scared, Fred. I am frightened to death that we will touch a soft spot in a conversation, and I will start crying. You know I am giving up a lot of pride in telling you all of this! All that I have worked for for a year in trying to pretend you didn't hurt me. It's no use pretending anymore. You hurt me so bad that it took me a year and two months to accept it. I don't think I will ever get completely over it. Never! I don't think I could ever see or talk to you without it hurting. You not only hurt me mentally, you physically hurt my heart. You took a part of me that will never heal.

I might as well say it! I am so scared of you because I am scared that we will hug. I mean scared to the point of panic. My heart has rebelled you for so long. I am trying to protect myself from gettting hurt again, which may happen. What if I get too close and have to break away <u>again</u>! That is just getting hurt all over again. Fred, I want to talk to you about it. I <u>really</u> do. But I am afraid of you. We can't get close again, yet if we talk about it, I couldn't help but be close to you again.

Fred, somehow, I will always love you. <u>Always</u>. That will never change. You were the first to steal my heart. My first love, and my own sister got you. So it is impossible to forget you. You will always be around. The main reason why I could never see or talk to you without it hurting is because I know you are Marissa's love. I don't think you realize how much I still hurt.

Well, since I have totally spilled my feelings, you must do the same. I must know how you feel about everything. You owe me that much, Fred.

Will things still be the same? Or do we have to go back to the "awkward stage" because of this meeting? I hope not. I have found out that lately I don't hate being around you as much. In fact, I enjoy it. Is that good or bad?

Della. P.S. I will admit that with each passing day, the hurt goes away a little more. P.S.S. OK you have exactly five seconds to tell me which movie this quote came from: "I wish we had made love." (Arthur)

Saturday, September 17, 1983

Wow!! It has been a while, hasn't it diary? Three months to be exact. A whole whole lot has happened in three months. It is gonna be hard but I gotta write in chronological order.

The beach house was pretty bad at times. The first night I walked to F and Marissa's beach house (thirteen houses down) and we got stoned. Pretty soon we were talking like nothing ever happened. I always forget to be mean to him when I am stoned. Then, when I come down from the high, I'm mad that I was nice to him. The next two days weren't good. I had memories of the last year's beach house and it got me sad. They left early on the last day and I watched them leave through the window. I finished *The Thornbirds* on July 5.

I think the dates that I went to New Orleans were from July 14—August 7. I worked for Dad for money for three weeks. He bought a house on Canal Blvd., and is staying in a tiny apartment. I slept on his tiny couch. I was supposed to help him move, but I had to leave to start school. My senior year of high school! Didn't think about F much. I think I cried once.

School started August 17, a Wednesday. Hurricane Alicia came on the 18th. Went to Jamaica with Mom August 19-22. Blast. The people there <u>are real</u> friendly. One Jamaican pinched my ass while I was in the water at the beach. We brought back lots of neat stuff. We went dancing every night. The first night we went to a beach party. Me and Mom both got drunk off of the rum punch. If you pay an initial price, you get a bamboo cup that you can fill as many times as you want. I met a guy there named Malcom. He was around 25 and adorable. I asked <u>him</u> to dance first and we kept it up. The next two nights were at discos. First the Fantasy (Casa Montego Motel) then the Cave (Fine place!). I saw Malcom again at the beach and got a picture of him. I lucked out because of Alicia and didn't miss any school.

Now, for one of the biggies! On August 29, 1983 (a Monday), I got my first car!! It is a maroon liftback Toyota Corolla with white stripes. It has two speakers in the back, one on each side, gear shift between the bucket seats (automatic) and no power steering, but who cares, I love it! Still trying to think of a name, though. September 7, started work at a drug store. Mr. Dumbass is still there, and as big a jerky tight wad as when Marissa worked there.

The BIG biggie. September 5, Labor Day, Marissa and F came over for swim and barbeque. Coach Ed (our gymnastics coach) came too, been a year since seen last. Anyway, Ed had to leave after BBQ and Marissa and Mom swam. So just me and F had a long talk on the back porch. We went around the edges of the hurt, but never really touched it. One time when neither of us was talking for a while, I said, "Nobody is saying anything. We're just sitting here. I guess that is normal for us." That night I wrote him a long hairy letter because I made a breakthrough that day. Just talking to him stirred up my feelings and brought them to the surface. One time Marissa came to the back porch and said, "What are ya'll doin?" F said, "Just talkin. I haven't talked to your sister in a year, maybe more." I said, "A year and two months. I know my dates." On Saturday night, September 10, I went over to F and Marissa's to watch a movie on cable. Actually, we had planned to go to the theatre with my aunt and cousin. But F got pissed at Marissa cuz she was nagging at him, so he took her truck and left her at our house. Marissa started crying, so I took her back to her apartment in my car, and they wanted me to stay. Anyway, I didn't leave until around 12:30 a.m. so F walked me to my car. On the way to the car I told him that I had written him a letter but I wasn't sure if I could get the courage up to giving it to him. He said that he would really like to read it. I said that I didn't have it with me anyway, so I left. The next Monday he called me at work. He said that if I had something to say to him that he would really like to hear it. The first thing that popped into my head, I said, "oh, well, uh, uh, it would have to be a day that Marissa works and I don't. That would be Wednesday. Give me a call at home. Also, I don't want Marissa even knowing about us meeting." He said, "if you mean destroy the evidence, I will." So it was set. We were FINALLY going to make up. I started bawling at work and couldn't stop. I mean BAWLING! I was so scared. I mean actually scared to the point of panic.

    Wednesday September 15. I knew it was him when he called. I could feel it. Dawn had called earlier, and I knew that wasn't him calling. He was on his way. We hung up. Then I heard the back-gate open. I was confused. Did he want to hide the truck? No. It was Mom. DAMN!! The only thing to do was tell her. DAMN!! I told her that me and F decided to settle things and that he was on his way over. He came. I was shaking. We went back to his apartment in his truck. We went in. He said to go into their room. I sat on the bed. So did he. Summary of conversation:

I said, "First of all, why do you care what I feel anymore?"

"Because I still love you, Della"

"Damn it, don't say that!" I threw him the letter. He read it.

He said, "I love you, Della. I always have. But I couldn't do anything about it because I couldn't talk to you. I have always loved you more than Marissa."

"Then why the fuck did you choose her?!"

"I didn't choose her, she chose me. After I got kicked out, she called my roommate every day for three weeks until I was home. Then she wanted to move in. I swear to you, I bought her that ring for the sole purpose of to make her shut up. When I was living at your house, she used to set her alarm clock for 4:00 a.m. every night and come fool around with me." I started to cry.

"I *really* wish you didn't tell me that."

"I'm sorry."

"Don't say that either!"

"I'm sorry. I have to say it now for all the times I couldn't say it and wanted to." I was still crying. The tension was getting stronger and stronger.

I finally said, "I can't take this anymore" and I threw my arms around him. He was ready and did the same. I cried on his shoulder for a long time. He bent his head down to kiss me but I pushed him away and said, "No!"

He said, "Come on, Della, just let me hold you." He put his arms around me again and we stayed that way. I had never been so happy as I was in those few minutes. We talked more about how Marissa would do ANYTHING to get what she wanted. ANYTHING. She is really a vicious bitch, and even Fred said so. We looked at the clock and it was 6:47 p.m. Marissa would be coming home soon. I didn't want to leave him. I really didn't! He drove me to my house with his hand on mine the whole time, except to change gears, just like we used to. We hugged a last time. He later told me that on the way to my house and back to his, he was shaking too. When I got home I had to go pick up my check from the drug store. The whole way there I cried with joy!

So this brings me to tonight. It is now 1:07 a.m. and I started writing at 11:00 p.m. Mom and I just got back from a barbeque at Fred's apartment. Fred managed to get in a wink at me with no one else watching. I love him so much.

Well, I knew I would forget something from the rewriting. The most important thing.

Fred said, "What do you want me to do, Della?"

After a long pause, "I can't tell you that." After an even longer pause, I said, "Do you really, really, love, love Marissa?"

Fred said, "Marissa is sooner or later going to get sick of me. I really don't think we will get married. Della, don't ever tell anyone this. Okay?" I nodded. Fred said, "I love Marissa, but I give you my promise, Della, I will never love Marissa enough to marry her. I will never marry Marissa."

I was so happy! He asked again, "What do you want me to do?"

I replied, "when I grow up, I want you to be unattached."

Fred asked, "When will you grow up, Della? I will try to be unattached when you are in college."

Way before, he asked me what I wanted to do with my

life. I said I was going to college to study oceanography. He also said that he was going to set up Marissa's hair salon first.

Fred, I love you!!

He also said that he has never felt the way that he did when we made out on the living room floor nude from the waist up. I now have hope again that one day we will make love.

Saturday, October 1, 1983

I find it very frustrating and heart-aching every time I go over Marissa and F's apartment. Last Thursday Fred was supposed to fix the sink in Mom's bathroom. I went over there after school and I took Fred back to my home at 5:00 p.m. when Marissa went to work. It was glorious. We kissed like we never have before! It was the greatest feeling in the world, and we were standing the whole time. I told him that when Marissa called here crying when they got into a fight, I realized that I was taking the most important thing in Marissa's life. I was crushed. Although I love Fred more than ever, and he loves me, I still love Marissa and so does he. Even though it was selfish on my part, I asked him to promise me that if he had the slightest hope that he and Marissa would work out, that he would try to make it work. What I was really saying was that I don't want it on my conscience that I took him away from her. He promised me. Then came up the problem of "Well if Marissa and Fred do work out, how will we ever make love?" I started bawling when this thought entered my mind and I told him it. I also said, "There is no way I can do anything with you when you and Marissa are living together." All I have done with him is make out. I wouldn't even let him see my boobs (or whatever there is of them!) He told me that he loves them. Weird!

One time when I went over there with Marissa gone, we started making out on their bed (gross) and he was on top of me and I could really feel it getting hard. I kinda got scared. Even though I was sure nothing would happen! Will I ever be ready? Fred also said that he wants to make love to me more now than before "the crisis." I love him so much. I know that I will never marry (or maybe even live with) Fred, but I would love to be his lover. He keeps telling me that he can't wait. God knows I can't! Love you Fred, Della.

Saturday, October 8, 1983

Saturday night. I just got back from ZZ Top. Fantastic concert! It changed my whole feeling about them. For some reason, I hadn't really liked ZZ Top. I liked their songs a lot, but I thought of them almost like I think about ACDC (YUK). But boy was I wrong about them. They are terrific! They have beards almost down to their belts. As Nolan would say, "kick ass." (I wanted to go to homecoming with him, but he has a girlfriend anyway.)

Again, the heart-ache of Fred came up. Marissa is always hanging all over him. Sometimes I wonder if she is still trying to make me jealous. I really hope I don't get an ulcer. Sometimes I want to hug him so bad, and I can't. When no one is looking, we blow kisses at each other. I am scared to look in his eyes, afraid that Marissa will suspect something. I can't wait for the days when we don't have to hide. Boy I sound like a sinner. I feel guilty. I guess it's because we have done this before (make out without Marissa knowing).

I keep getting off the subject. Back to the concert: I tried hiding from Mom that we were smoking pot at the concert. It worked. Mom never even had a hint. But when I got home, she totally blew my mind. She said, "I'm not trying to lecture or anything, because the concert was fine. It's just like drinking, but I hope you don't make a habit out of pot. A guy at work says that pot has five cancerous substances in it that cigarettes don't have." I was too stunned to say anything.

Well, I had told Fred that I wouldn't let him see my teats when he was living with Marissa. It didn't last very long. Last Tuesday was chorale night, so I didn't have to work. I went over to his apartment without a bra on purpose. He says that they're bigger. Big deal. (It is a big deal, but I don't want to admit it.) Tonight, when Mom was dressing, we were on the back-porch smoking. Marissa said, "Della, look what Fred did with my keychain that Dad gave me. Fred show her your thing," (it was hooked to his belt loop). He didn't hear the first part and questioned her. Then he said, "I thought you meant 'show her my thing,' I was thinking 'sure, I'll show her my thing anytime.'" I blushed. I'm surprised Marissa started laughing at the comment. I loved it.

I don't like to think about this next subject. I love Marissa more now than I ever have before. She feels the same about me. She wrote me a note and told me so. The thing is, now I love Fred more than ever also. I feel a little guilt, but not nearly enough as I should. As I said, that is why I feel guilty. I confess to God every Sunday for doing it, and I hope I am being forgiven. I am really in love, though. No one person has ever loved me as much as Fred does. Help! Luv you God, Della.

Sunday, October 16, 1983

Last Thursday I went over Fred's and confessed to him that I wanted to take a shower with him. He said he'd love to.

Last night was a very, very important night and it will be

cherished in my heart for the rest of my life. Saturday night I went with Marissa and Fred to his home town where he grew up. We spent the night with Fred's brother, Buck, and his family: wife Melissa and two boys John and Todd. I love this family a lot. Melissa reminds me a lot of me. She is a very sweet woman. I am hoping that our friendship will grow and be strong, as I want to visit there a lot.

We got there at around 9:00 p.m. and after introductions were made, us four kids went to play pool. When the game was over, (me and Todd lost) we started watching the late movie. It was "The Battle of Midway." (I am going to skip night time and come back to it at the end. Best for last.)

The next day was very fun. I got to sleep late and we had breakfast. Buck, Fred and their other brother went to the oil fields. Us four kids went bike riding around the little town and saw everything. Most important, Fred's elementary school with the slide fire escape that I've heard so much about. This town has one bank and two churches. The countryside is so beautiful and peaceful. I must spend part of my life living in one! We got tired of waiting for the guys, so we all had a lovely lunch. We laughed a whole lot. We watched two movies after that. One Chinese Godzilla movie and one called "Werewolf meets Frankenstein." After the guys got home, Marissa cut both boy's hair. Buck's two boys are like the generation immediately preceding it. The oldest, John, who is eleven, is fat and resembles his father, Buck, also the eldest. Todd is eight and reminds me so much like the picture in my mind of Fred as a kid. He is very skinny, has a small frame, has stringy blonde hair and loves to climb trees. Amazing.

Now, back to the night of October 15, 1983. Actually, it was early Sunday morning. The late movie was supposed to end at 2:00 a.m. I wanted to go to bed, but I had a glimmer of hope that Marissa would go to bed early and maybe Fred and I could get in a good-night kiss. I was right. Marissa fell asleep on the floor and Fred took her to bed. I made myself keep my eyes open until the end of the movie. At 2:00 a.m. I rose and announced that I would see them (Buck and Fred) in the morning when they got back from the oil fields. As I hoped, Fred came in my room. He said, "Can you stay awake for me to come back in a little while?" I said, "Hell, yes."

Ten minutes later I was reading in bed when he opened the door. He shut it behind him, turned the light out and came to my bed. Marissa was in another room. We hugged for it seemed like five minutes. Then our lips found each other. It was great, lying next to him in the dark kissing him. Then he got under the covers. As we were kissing, he started massaging my thighs. I was wearing my old Journey t-shirt. To my surprise, he slowly worked my underwear to my ankles and took them off. I wasn't very scared at all. He was just rubbing the surface. Then, he got up and took his jeans off. I was a little worried, but I trusted him. He laid back down and started kissing me again. I told him I was scared. Then he moved to the end of the bed and did what I had dreamed of him doing. It was fantastic. His experienced tongue felt exciting and stimulating. Although I really wanted to, something stopped me from coming. Most probably fright, that Marissa would walk in. When he felt that he had done enough, he gave it a final kiss and laid on top of me. To my surprise, he didn't have his underwear on. I could feel his hardness on my stomach.

He said, "Can I turn the light on?"

I said, "No, let's take one step at a time."

As we kissed, I could feel him getting harder. He took my hand and led it to his penis. I didn't resist. For the first time in my life, I came in contact with a male organ. I could feel it's stickiness.

I said, "What do I do?"

He said, "Just move your hand around him." I did. With my hand, I explored the area and tried to visualize it in my mind. I was surprised that hair grew half way up it. When I told him, he laughed. Then he repositioned his cock to head straight in me. Although he wasn't in, I could feel it growing and moving in.

I said, "Fred, please don't."

He said, "Okay" and kissed me again, but he didn't move it. I felt it grow even more. It started to hurt.

This time I stopped kissing him and adamantly said, "Please don't, Fred, I'm not ready."

He said, "Ok, Della, I'm sorry" and moved it.

I said, "Don't apologize. It's my fault."

He started moving it in and out of my pubic hair. (I know that sounds gross, but what else can I call it?)

When this didn't thrill him enough, he said, "Will you do 69 with me?"

When I didn't answer, he turned around and straddled his legs across my neck and went to work on me. I put his penis in my mouth. It really didn't taste like anything. It grew and grew. Pretty soon, it was taking up my whole mouth and I could barely breathe. He heard my gasps and got off of me. He turned on his side and asked if I would do more. I did. I could breathe a lot better now. He started to finger me. Feels great. It seemed like it took him a year to come. I will remember what he said to me as long as I live. He had to tell me twice, and for some reason it struck me to be very funny. He said, "Della, not quite so much teeth." I made an attempt to laugh but it wasn't easy. To be playful, I gently bit down. Fifteen minutes later he finally came. I remember reading sex scenes in books that it came in little spurts. They were right. He spurted six times. I can't remember how I knew that it tasted gross, but I was right. After he pulled it out, I kept it in my mouth cuz I was going to spit it out. I wiped my mouth on my shirt sleeve and gave up and swallowed it. I will always remember the little white stain it made. It is hardly noticeable, but I will always know what it is. I gave out a "YUK." To my surprise, he leaned forward to kiss me.

I said, "You mean, you really wanna kiss me now?"

He didn't say anything and backed away. I could scarcely see it in the dark, but I think he was hurt. I quickly said, "Well, I don't care. If you want to, come here."

He did. We went into the bathroom and I rinsed my mouth out. We kissed again, and said our "I love you's" and "goodnights" and went to bed in our separate rooms. I found it hard to sleep. Naturally, I could not stop thinking about what had just happened. It was my first intimate experience with a penis!

Early the next morning he came into my room and got something. He was walking out when I said, "Hey."

He turned around, surprised that he woke me and said, "what?"

I replied, "I said, hey."

He came to my bed, pop-kissed me and left the room. I am in love!!

The next day, the first chance I got to be alone with him, we were in the kitchen near the bar and I said, "Boy do I feel weird!"

F, "I know, so do I"

D, "You do?"

F, "Yeah."

D, "I feel like a totally different person! My heart goes mad every time I see you."

F, "You are a different person. You have done something that you never did before." He was right. Last night he told me again that he couldn't wait to have sex with me. I'm not scared anymore.

Chapter Four

OFF TO COLLEGE

BLAME AND SHAME

I honestly don't remember how many times Fred and I had sex after he weaseled his way back into my heart while he was living with my sister. I must have blocked it out. I am guessing less than ten. I had not had a conversation with him for fourteen months after Marissa moved in with him. I hated him so much for causing me so much pain. But I came to realize that we had to talk, or my only sister would not be in my life. I had no idea that I was still in love with him. Until he told me that he did not want our relationship to end. And he convinced me to have sex with him.

Thankfully, I moved away to college in the fall of 1984. I have reference in my diary that we did have sex once when I came home for winter break my freshman year. Marissa would become pregnant with their first child that December, and so the date had been set for their spring wedding. I do remember crying to him after we had sex, telling him that I wished the baby was mine. That was so painful for me. He said nothing. He must have known that the situation was tearing me apart. It makes me very sad and ashamed that I consented to sex with Fred after such news. It did not occur to me that he was lying to me the whole time, and continuing to do so. How is that possible, that I could not think of that? Perhaps the evil Casey was in control, and she was mad. Casey, you see, is the inner child that I created to contain all of the shame that I could not face.

That winter break in my freshman year of college was the last time that Fred and I had sex. The physical and emotional nightmare had lasted from January of 1982 to January of 1985. Unbeknownst to me, however, the psychological damage of my immense shame and secrecy would be a far worse injury, lasting decades. Casey had locked herself in her dungeon that she built, and threw away the key.

Fred had taken advantage of my vulnerabilities, and my love and trust for him. He had manipulated my sweet and defenseless heart. Because my junior and senior years of high school were filled with the never-ending roller coaster of love and pain for Fred, I never dated in high school. He had stolen those years from me. He was with my sister publicly, and our intimate relationship was kept a secret from everyone. So it was hammered home in my mind that I was second best. I held so much shame and guilt for what I had done to my sister that it skewed my reality. I was having an affair with my sister's fiancé. If it ever became known, I would be scorned publicly. And I knew that if Marissa ever found out, I would lose her as a sister forever. She would never forgive me. In my subconscious, it was just so wrong, and the guilt I felt was immense, but I justified it. After all, she had stolen him from me first, right? And she had bullied me for so long. Fred had told me that he loved me more. That they would never get married. Perhaps the shame I felt for my betrayal of my sister had a greater impact on me than the pain I felt for losing my first love. And Casey would never let me forgive myself, although her stealth was keen.

For reasons I still do not fully understand, my mind could put no blame on Marissa or Fred for the events that transpired over that time period. So I put all of the blame on me. I blamed myself for continuing our sexual relationship after we started speaking again. And especially for having sex with Fred. I had no way of knowing that the shame that I carried deep inside of me would shape my entire life and the decisions that I made about men. I buried my guilt and shame for my unspeakable secrets deep down inside for three decades. The sexual and psychological abuse, and subsequent self-blame that I endured, froze the development of my ego, soul and body. The development of trust in myself was shattered completely, and I didn't even know it. I had loved and trusted Fred with all my being. And everything in my life that I trusted had fallen apart in the formative years of my adolescence. My inner child, Casey, that remained deep within me from the age of fifteen, would always seek attention, understanding, love and respect from men. To the point of searching for unavailable or disrespectful men to repeat the love/pain pattern, or scaring every good potential mate away.

I have since learned that self-blame is one of the most toxic forms of emotional abuse. It magnified my imagined feelings of not being good enough. I was always second best . . . Almost Della. Casey was locked away in her dungeon of silence and shame. So I numbed her pain and confusion with alcohol and drugs. I truly thought that if I just ignored the pain long enough, that it would go away. At some point in college, I began to drink heavily. And it never ended.

I bottled my confusion of synchronized hatred and love for Fred as he became my brother-in-law, and hence part of our family. I really cannot remember when or how I blocked the pain and suffering that he had caused me over those horrible three years. I only knew that I had no choice but to accept my life with him in my family. So I did. It never sunk in that my former lover was now my brother. I repressed this feeling for years. But we were amicable, and I enjoyed being with my sister and her family.

Thankfully, my sexual desire for my first lover abated completely. I became godmother to my beautiful nephew, Joey. And three years later I became an aunt again when they had a daughter, Alexa. I didn't know it then, but those children were the only children I would know closely. I adored them as if they were my own.

In the end, Fred was right. My sister did grow tired of him, and they divorced after only seven years of marriage. I found out later that he did not treat her with respect during their marriage. He had many violent outbursts. He once smashed his guitar to bits right in front of her face during one of many fights, and he regularly called her horrible names such as *bitch* and *cunt*. He later told me that he was even high on acid on their wedding day. Was my sister ever scared of him?

I was so full of shame for cheating on my sister, and for then justifying it, that I never told anyone what I had done. Not even Dawn, my best friend. All I knew was that I had to protect Marissa, Fred and their two children from the truth forever. My awful truth. Fred had asked me to burn my diaries. I felt that it was my duty to keep our secret to protect him and my sister's family. I felt that sex with Fred was my choice, so I never considered myself or my sister victims of sexual abuse and rape. Casey would never allow that. Shame was her food, and she was always hungry.

Hiding My Pain with Substance Abuse and Men

During my freshman year of college in the fall of 1984, I doubled my efforts in my drinking career. I made friends easily, and we partied a lot. But I had permission to drink heavily: all college students drink alcohol! And most binge-drink on the weekends, right? It is an accepted behavior. I thought it was normal to vomit from drinking too much. Almost every weekend. I thought I was being smart by getting the alcohol out of my body to prevent the intensity of my hangovers! In graduate school, I dabbled in cocaine, acid, and mushrooms. I had a lot of fun.

The three years of intimacy with Fred eroded the pillar of my belief that love leads to sex and replaced it with a belief that sex leads to love. That was a travesty of my mind. Plus, I had zero personal boundaries. I didn't even know they existed. My "picker" of men to have relationships with was broken. I did not heed the advice from the card-playing psychiatrist and seek therapy. I perpetuated a pattern of self-punishment by choosing bad men. For thirty years, I proceeded to go through one failed relationship and heartbreak after another. My pattern of choosing relationships was dysfunctional, and it impacted every aspect of my life. I did not realize it, but I sought unavailable men and men who were emotional abusers. I developed serious relationships with controlling men, a married man, a womanizer, a cheater, a few liars, a thief and con-artist, and one with bipolar mental illness. My criterion for a potential date was that they wanted me. That was it. And then there were those who didn't want me as a girlfriend, but they wouldn't let me go either. I repeatedly crawled back to their beds to have sex with them after they treated me with no respect. And the good ones, I just fell out of love with. Or love was never there to begin with, but I stayed anyway, hoping my feelings for them would change. My belief was that I had to be *in* a relationship, at any cost, to be "happy." Kind of backward, because it caused me so much misery. Not surprisingly, I would never have a relationship that lasted over two years, including my later marriage. I was broken.

The first few guys that I dated in college each dumped me, and it always ended in a bowl of tears. But that is kind of the point. I didn't see them as dates. I saw them as boyfriends right away. I could not separate the physical acts of intimacy from the emotional impacts they would have on me. I was constantly seeking acceptance, love, and approval from men. I thought that sex implied a relationship. I expected too much, and that scared them away. Perhaps my pattern was created when Casey took form at the age of fifteen, during the time when Marissa and Fred first moved in together and I stopped speaking to him. I was in such jealousy and pain. And I wanted Fred to hurt like I did. I remember the time my friend Lisa from the sandwich shop told me, "You want to suffer. You want to hurt yourself." It was a pattern that would replay itself for many years to come.

Molestation as a Sophomore

As a sophomore in college, at the age of eighteen, I was molested by my employer for an entire semester. He was an older man that I gardened for at his home. He had put a flyer on the school bulletin board for a gardener. He had several large flower beds, a vegetable bed, and a greenhouse full of tropicals. Plants were his hobby. Pretty quickly, he asked if I would like a drink after work, and headed for the garden shed. This became a habit. He would get me drunk on rum and coke, then molest me in the garden shed, while his wife was in the house. He said he would give me a full day's pay extra. I knew it was wrong, but I justified it by telling myself that it was for the extra cash. Sex became a currency, and I used it with many men in college. Too many.

During this time in college, I had my first "real" boyfriend. Ray and I were in the same major and we had a few classes together. We soon became good friends. I was not all that attracted to him, but he was a cadet in uniform. And he sure was attracted to me. This fit my criterion. I thought it would be enough. I believed I could make it work. We dated for a few months before I had sex with him. I knew that I was not in love with him. I hung on to him for over a year, way too long, and so unfair to him. But I was on a natural high while hanging out with his fellow cadets and their girlfriends. I felt like a part of something important, a community, and I needed so much to belong to anything. Cadets in their junior year could take their girlfriends onto the football field during pep rallies, which we called yell practice. It was a joy I had never before experienced. Then, when he got his senior boots at the end of his junior year, I was a girlfriend of high status. Senior cadets were distinguished from the other classes by knee-high leather boots. But we were doomed from the start, and I broke his heart. He tried so hard to make me love him. We were so young. That story and others are told here as I continue with my diary:

The Early College Diaries

Spring 1985

Wow! It has really been a long time since I have written. A year and nine months to be exact. I really don't know why I am writing. Had the urge, I guess. But it is not like the urge I had before to write. I probably would have gone crazy without spilling my guts to someone! Why not me?

I just reread the Fred diary. I shouldn't have. It stirred up some feelings that are supposed to be dead. Most of them are, but I have always and will always love Fred in a special way. I'm sure that love is returned from Fred. I wish I knew just how much he still loves me. He once told me that he used to cry for me. That melted my heart.

Well, I guess I should get in to all the "happenings." To put it very bluntly: Fred put a bun in Marissa's oven and they got married. The glorious wedding was held April 14 (I think) and the beautiful bouncing baby boy is due the first week in August. As probably guessed, Marissa's tummy is huge. Just think, I'm going to be an ant. Me. (I know the damn word has a "u" in it.) By the way, no one knows for sure what the critter is (gender!) but I know it's gonna be a boy. Gut feeling.

Shit man, what about me? I have been through a full year at Texas A & M University and am now officially considered a "pisshead." That's cadet talk for a sophomore. I am now back home taking a history class in summer school at the local community college. Great teacher. I have the stupidest, lowest paying job I ever had selling cutlery on commission. I now hate sales. I am being the most opposite person that I want to be, an asshole. I am being forced to be an asshole to get paid. That's the good ole US of A for ya.

The main reason that I wanted to write tonight was to tell about the guys (men, no, boys) that I have gone through in just nine months. More than my whole seventeen years before that! What happened?

Anyway, first comes Evan. He was a counselor at fish camp. This is a camp for incoming freshman that takes place just before school starts. It is a fun week-long camp that teaches about the history of the school and the long-standing school traditions. And there are a lot of them. TOTAL BLAST! Anyway, Evan had gorgeous baby blue eyes. I was so in love. (Yeah, right.) He was very tall and skinny and not too foxy. He had blonde hair and had a slight slump, probably from kissing too many girls shorter than him. Ha ha! Anyway, he had kind of a baby face and had a slight gayish accent. We had a great time making out under the bleachers in the moonlight on the last night of fish camp while the dance was going on. We also had a great time on the first Thursday night at the local boot scootin joint here, slow dancing, if ya know what I mean. After that, he dropped me. He just never called unless it was to return my call. Someone told me that he has his girls call him. Screw that! I hate calling guys. He <u>really</u> broke my heart. I used to wait outside my psyche class just to watch him and his senior boots walk by every Tuesday and Thursday. I think I was in love with his seniority and boots.

Next came Jacob. I met Jacob at a cadet party at the Q-Huts I guess around October of 1984. This is gonna sound crazy, but I am going to recopy something that I wrote in December while visiting Daddy in New Orleans. This is how I felt about Jacob then:

I remember when I first saw you at the Q-Huts. You were wearing a white shirt, were short and had light green eyes. We caught each other's eyes. I thought you weren't that cute, but I wanted to dance. Besides, I was drunk, so I asked you to dance. You said, "you read my mind" and we danced and were together the rest of the night. I still didn't like you. I couldn't believe it when you told me that you were a senior and a cadet.

We went to yell practice together and I loved kissing you when the lights went out. You gave me senior privileges as a freshman! I could stand on the wood [bleachers] during the yells and I could even "whoop." I loved it.

You called me the next night and asked me out. I really didn't want to go. I had just broken a date with Chip, my neighbor, to study. But you convinced me to go to a movie. We went to Hauffbrau's and had a drink first. I ordered a white Russian and I think you had a seven and seven. We talked about you going into the army after college. We both agreed that we wanted to visit other countries like Italy, Japan, Germany and Africa. You said that that was the reason for joining the army, to travel. We ordered another drink and it was happy hour so we got two more each. We walked over to the theater in the same square. We were early, so you held me in your arms and we talked some more. You said my jeans fit me good. I told you that they were hand-me-downs from my sister. I was feeling good from the drinks. We saw *Thief of Hearts* and we held hands the whole time. In fact, my hand was very close to you. I didn't care. We both liked the movie. You suggested that we go to Research Park for a while. I didn't mind. I was driving and I had no reason to be home. We sloshed through the mud. You said that I had to see the ducks. When we got there, I could barely see them, but we heard them. We kissed. (I remember touching the back of your hair, but there was almost nothing there, yet more than the underclassmen. I loved the feeling of cadet heads.) You kept telling me "kinda nice, woman." It drove me wild. I loved it when you said that. Jacob, Jacob, Jacob! I drove you back to your dorm and we kissed some more. You said you would call me.

You did. I have been to your dorm three times since then. You made me so excited when we kissed on your dorm bed. One time you kissed my stomach. You asked if it felt good and I nodded. You asked me if I wanted to make love to you and I replied, "someday." I meant it Jacob, I really did.

Well, kinda detailed, huh? I was so in love with him. I always wrote his whole name all over my notes. I saw it on his dog tags that I found in his dorm. Anyway, I didn't know it then, but he would never call me again. I kept wishing and hoping, but he never did. After we went to the Rice game (we scored a lot of points, too, so we kissed a lot. The Aggies kiss their dates when the football team scores) he gave me back my ticket book so all ties were broken. It took me a couple of months to realize what he was after and didn't get quick enough. He was just a big-headed senior who would go through a lot to get some, but not too much. I think, after my heart mended, I realized that I was infatuated with the uniform and the boots, just like I was with Evan. It was different with Jacob, though. I was attracted to him. Besides, he was short like me. Oh well, all over now. I saw him once on campus by the arches. I don't know if he saw me, but if he did, he kept right on walking.

Once my friend Charla and I snuck into his dorm and taped a note on his door that said, "Jacob, I want your body. If you know who I am, give me a call." Don't know why I did it. Maybe I still had a tiny flicker of hope, or maybe I just wanted to get him back, or maybe we were drunk and felt like doing something crazy. Anyway, I found out later by a guy in his dorm that he had switched dorm rooms. That meant that everyone on his floor probably knew about the note before he did. I hope if he had a girlfriend, that she found out about it too! Oh well.

Next came Carson. Actually, he came before I knew that I had heard the last from Jacob. I had NEVER dated two guys at the same time and got worried about making a decision between the two of them. I asked Big Brother Bill (a senior in the band that I worked with at the horse center) what to do about telling them about each other. He said don't, unless they ask. I didn't have to worry, though. Both of them stopped calling at the same time. My luck. Carson is now the director of intramurals in Off Campus Aggies (OCA). He is a jerk and has a head bigger than my new house and doesn't deserve to be in here, but I dated him. I was an Apartment Council President in OCA at the time. (I am now Leader of Spirit and Traditions. Whoa, an exec!)

Anyway, I met Carson personally the time I went to cut for bonfire. I had seen him at meetings before. Yes, I cut some trees for bonfire with OCA. Blast! We drove down to the cutting sight with Michelle and another creep who turned out to be my cutting partner. After lunch, we managed to pair up and cut down our tree. We even put our initials on the tree with our axes. He was just a bit taller than me, has blonde hair (well, reddish, sort of) and a blonde mustache. After cut, everyone went home and showered and met back over at Carson's condo for a soggy spaghetti dinner (he overcooked the noodles). There were six of us in all. After dinner and cake, we walked across the street to an OCA Bonfire Party for everyone who had ever cut. We kinda stuck together and kissed for the first time. I had even turned down a Michael Jackson concert ticket that night with Mom and Marissa.

After the party, we went back over to his place, etc., etc. He kisses pretty good, but what I liked most was when he stuck his tongue in my ear. A first for me, I thought it felt great! Not much more to say, cuz after a couple more times at his place (no, we didn't) he didn't call anymore. In fact, he would barely even talk to me at OCA meetings, much less dance with me Thursday nights at The Hall. About a month later he finally started dancing with me again. I'm glad because he taught me a lot about country dancing and doing the jitterbug. He would even do a lift with me. So much fun. I never found out why he quit calling, and I really don't care. My guess is that a bad and untrue rumor about us spread to OCA and got back to him. He really does think too highly of himself, though. He is immature at twenty-two and always has to have his way. Typical!

Adam was the next. Babe and a half! He is definitely my favorite, and I am still in love with him. He is a senior now, I think. Anyway, he is a little taller than me, has brown, kinda wavy hair kept short and a brown mustache. He has got one terrific body and a not too hairy chest. (My heart is pounding!) He is originally from Waco and has a slight Texas accent. I met him one night at Teasers with the OCA gang. He is Melissa's really good friend. Anyway, when we were first introduced I about fell over. He would wander around the club with his friend and come back to talk with us. I was getting discouraged because, unlike The Texas Hall of Fame, the guys just didn't ask unknown girls to dance. I told this to Sharon, she nodded, Adam asked her what I said, she told him, and he asked me to dance (pound pound goes my heart). We danced about four songs in a row. One of them was *Relax* by Frankie Goes to Hollywood, my fav. Then he came back and we danced the last song. It was that night at Teasers that Melissa told everyone that she was getting a group together to go to Port Aransas for spring break. I was all enthusiastic and told her that I was a definite. During the last slow song (heaven) he asked me if I was going to Port A and I told him probably. I prayed that he would go!

A week later OCA had a party at the Q-Huts. On my shift to check ID's at the door he came in. I about died! When my shift was over, we talked, drank and danced the rest of the night. He told me that I was in his agronomy class. How could I not know that? I remember that he didn't want to ruin the soles of his boots by dancing on the concrete. *Let's Go Crazy* by Prince came on and we were both tipsy, so we danced. During the song, he kept telling me that the song was titled, "Let's Get Crazy" and I kept telling him that I had the album and that it was "Go." He kept insisting and finally said that if he was right, I would have to cook him dinner. I asked him what we were having. He asked me the same. At the end of the song we walked over to the DJ booth and looked at the album. He was going to fix me dinner.

A few nights later he called Melissa to see what night the dinner date was supposed to be and she said tonight, so he called me and apologized for forgetting. I understood. He had had two beers for my every one. We set the night and he came to pick me up and take me back over to his place. I bought a $4.25 bottle of Lancers wine and he fixed broiled chicken, corn on the cobb and another veggie. When he brought me home, he didn't even lean over, so I just got out of the car. He has a Subaru Brat truck. I really didn't know if he would call me again, but he did. He asked me to his softball game that night at 10:30 p.m. Hell, I didn't care. His team lost, but I yelled every time he batted. I sat with a bunch of his teammates' girlfriends. Fun! (Yes, this is sarcasm.) When the game was over he did something that eased the tension, he tapped my foot with his foot. Same story when he drove me home. I was getting kinda worried. Was there something wrong with me or was he just a real gentleman?

He called one night and asked me out to a movie on the same night that I told my good friend, Charla, we would go to the Q-Huts for a class party. So we went to the movie (*Falcon and the Snowman*) and then went to the Q-Huts. By the time we got to the Huts, Charla had already been there and left and it looked boring, so we danced a couple of songs and went back to his place to watch TV. He put his head on my lap. How sweet! Then, get this, he kissed me on my cheek! What was I gonna do with this guy? I had to hint my head off to get a real kiss when he brought me home.

Melissa gave me the news one day. I was happy the rest of the day. Adam had paid his dues for him and a friend to go to Port A for spring break! Happy Heaven was me! I had told Adam the night that he cooked dinner for me that I would cook dinner for him one night, so I asked him over for Friday night. We had fajitas and au gratin potatoes. He brought lemonade (whoa, potent stuff). For dessert, I bought two huge slices of New York cheesecake. Expensive, but delicious. He enjoyed it. I think so, he ate enough.

    Spring break started on Saturday, March 9. Carson drove me, Tommy drove Sharon, Michelle and Nancy, Gary and Kyle and two others followed each other. We all had CBs in our cars except for M and N. So we talked and bullshitted the whole way there and tried to keep M and N in someone's sight. When we got there, we saw Adam and his friend Jeff at the beach house. We had to wait for Kent and his sister to pay for the keys to get in. Later, Melissa, Mark, Julie and her three friends came. We had three rooms for twenty people. In my room, it was Adam, me, Jeff, Michelle, Nancy, Sharon, Kent, Kristi and Carson for two nights. The rest were in the other two rooms. After we unpacked, we went to the beach for the rest of the day. That night the sleeping arrangements went like this: Michelle, Adam and me in one bed and Kristi, Jeff, Sharon and Carson in the other bed. Kent was on the floor. They never put that many in a bed again, but it was funny.

    The next morning after breakfast we went back to the beach. Adam and Jeff brought most of their own food. At nights, we usually went to the beach where EVERYONE either walked or drove up and down the beach, or sat in their cars and watched. I got a ride in a sweet '65 Corvette! One night we drove to Corpus and went to a dancing club. We had a blast. One day we bought ten pounds of shrimp, peeled them and ate 'em. I drank beer like it was coke. I had never drunk so much beer in seven days as I did on spring break. Wednesday, it rained most of the day, but we were all sunburned too bad to go to the beach anyway. We saw a lot of Aggies, mostly in the Corps of Cadets, and talked with them a lot. You can always tell them, cuz of their buzz haircuts. The guys played a lot of hacky sac.

Every night me and Adam were on the same bed. Sometimes with Michelle and sometimes with me in between him and Jeff. That was fun. I loved waking up next to him. But he snores. The last night it was just us two in the bed. He had not touched me the whole time until that night. The rain had caused a leak in the ceiling right above the bed the night before, so we both had to get on only half of the bed. Tough break, huh? It was wonderful being under one blanket with him. I was in high heaven. And all we did was kiss! He asked me to rub his shoulders and while I was, I started kissing his back.

I don't know what I did that night, or that week, but he never called me again. We barely even talked in class anymore. We used to walk to the Academic Building together, but he started taking the bus with this bitch who was also in the class. They sat next to each other behind and over from me. I didn't know what she was to him, but I remember he brought some flowers to class for Valentine's Day, and they weren't for me! I asked him to the OCA banquet and he reluctantly agreed. We sat with our friends.

Saturday, July 27, 1985

This summer I got a job in sales selling cutlery. Long story, but in our four-day training class I met a guy named Nolan. I sat next to him on the first day (only because I was half an hour late and it was the only chair left and it was in the front) and I noticed him because he was part of a demo in class. He winked at me in class. The next day he took me to

McDonalds on our lunch break cuz I didn't have my car. He insisted on paying for my lunch, which I thought was very nice considering we had only just met. That night he took me to get my car from the shop and we went out. The next day after training we got high and went to Luther's Barbecue, and then to play pool. We went out with his friends that night. We went out after the third day of training also. I knew at this point that I liked him a lot. He is about half a foot taller than me, is skinny but not a rail, has dirty blonde hair, and has moon eyes like me when he smiles. Daddy always loved my moon eyes. He drives a silver and blue Dodge Charger with tinted windows that he did himself.

Our last day of training was three days later and we went out again. We played Putt Putt till midnight. I think we get along so well because we both like a lot of the same things. He asked me if I wanted to go to Robert Plant the next Saturday, and I said yes and he got my phone number. He didn't call all of the next week. On Friday, I convinced myself to call work for his phone number and call him myself. I called Saturday morning and he told me that he was just about to call me. I said, "yeah, right." He couldn't get the eighth-row seats like he planned, so we went to a scalper and got really good seats in lower prom. We went dutch, meaning we each paid for our own ticket. He started calling me after that and we started taking turns driving out to each other's house. Forgot to mention, he lives an hour from me. Real nice neighborhood. He told me that his dad is a private investigator and guards the president when he is in town. Wow! He has many guns in the house and both Nolan and his ten-year-old sister know how to shoot them. Just thought I would throw that in.

On July 4th weekend, Dawn had a big swimming party and I invited him. Marissa and Fred came too (and baby too in Marissa). I was scared that it would be awkward, but the pot took care of that. [There I was again, using drugs to numb the pain.] *I guess it is a common language if you smoke it. Marissa and F didn't show up till 4:00 p.m., but it was okay. We had a great time. We swam, smoked, ate, swam, and watched rented movies on the VCR. At 1:30 a.m. he came back over to my house and didn't leave until 3:30 a.m. We had a great time in my TV room, but we both kept our pants on. It was then that I kinda knew that we would someday make love. It felt so good to have someone love me who was closer to my age. He is nineteen and Fred is thirty-two. We have been having problems lately cuz I just can't love two guys at the same time, but that is a different story.*

On July 23rd, it was my turn to drive, so he invited me over to his house. I got there at 3:00 p.m. We played pool for two hours, went swimming, ate at his house, went to the boat docks and played cards with his friends, then went to a wild party. We played quarters. When we went back to his house we started making out on his couch. He started undoing the buttons to my jumpsuit. I knew that if I was going to stop him, I would have to do it then. I didn't. I wanted him. I had known Nolan for almost two months and I figured that if he only wanted sex from me, he would have dropped me by now. He had tried once before in early dating, but I told him no and asked him, "what kind of girl do you think I am?" He said, "you are just a nice girl who likes to party." He later apologized when he took me back to my car.

Anyway, back to subject. He got my jumpsuit off half way and I wouldn't let him go any farther until he took his clothes off. While he did, I finished taking off my jumpsuit. It was then that I saw his hard penis. I was shocked! He is so huge! Not only longer, but wider than Fred's. I couldn't believe it.

I let it slip, "Oh Shit!"

He replied, "What can I say?"

I replied, "Nothing at all."

He tried going in, but I wasn't excited, and with his size, he killed me. I was almost in tears. Also, it had been almost eight months for me. He wanted to go outside and make love on the hammock. What a cool dude. I was game. It got a lot better, but he still killed me. We kissed a while and I couldn't wait to grab it to feel the size of it. I swear, I couldn't touch my middle finger to my thumb wrapped around it. And I am tiny down there anyway. What a match! It got better when I got a little wet (gross) but I still hurt when he went all the way inside me. It was so neat making love under the stars, though. That was a first for me! After he came, he took it out and we rested. We were both sweating all over our bodies. After we cooled off, he wanted to go back in, but I was too raw and sore. I tried to give him a hand job (like Billy Squire says, "Stroke") but I wasn't too good at it. He hinted for me to suck on him. At first, I refused, but then I thought, why the hell not? I did Fred. There was absolutely no way I could get that whole thing in my mouth, but I tried. I still had both hands wrapped around it too. Huge! After he came, he did me for a real short time. What he did felt good and soothing, but he stopped. We kissed some more and he wanted to put it back in. I reluctantly agreed. He couldn't get very far, and when I tried to put it in, it just wouldn't go. I was too sore. I said, "You just don't get enough, do you?" He shook his head and smiled. We finally stopped and he walked me to my car. I asked if he was going to grow anymore and said that if he did, we were gonna have problems. We kissed again and I went home at 2:00 a.m.

The next day I couldn't wait to tell Dawn and Marissa that I was no longer a virgin, ha ha ha! Dawn screamed at me for doing it "when I barely know him" and Marissa was mad that I told Dawn first. But they both accepted it. Two nights ago,

I spent the night with Dawn and we stayed up till 2:00 a.m. talking about sex. I was so glad! I had been wanting to tell her that I wasn't a virgin since Fred, but that was out of the question. She wanted almost every detail and I gave them to her. I'm glad, cuz she gave me some good advice. She said to try some lubricant beforehand and it won't hurt nearly as bad. She also said to let him go down on me first, "to get it wet," but I already knew that. My ultimate fantasy is to come during sex at the same time my partner does, and I can't come twice in the same night. At least, I don't think I can. When Fred used to keep sucking after I came, it just got numb. I don't like a lot of stimulation after I come once. Don't know if that is normal or not, but it is the same with Dawn.

   I was afraid that Nolan wouldn't call me again, but he did. I don't know what I would have if he didn't. I have been hurt so many times already! Why don't boys call after the first time they have sex with a girl? Maybe they cannot handle the intimacy? I have been frustrated the last two days cuz every time he called, I wasn't home and visa versa. But I finally talked to him this afternoon. I think he wants to stick with me. At least until school starts, anyway. I like him so much!!! I don't think I really love him cuz I don't know love when I'm in it. When I think I'm in it, I'm really not. But Nolan is everything I ever wanted in a boyfriend . . . especially now! He is not too sweet, which I hate. For instance, I open my own doors. He is cute and has a great personality. Sex could be a lot better, but that takes time. I think I need to teach him what Fred taught me. There is definitely a big difference in experience and skill, but that is expected. Fred has had thirteen years more experience. I don't think I can teach him, though. He needs an older, more experienced person to teach him like Fred taught me. But I'm glad I expected it. I told Nolan before he entered me to be gentle. He said, "don't worry" but then proceeded to ram it in to me. I don't think that that is right. Guys should care about the girl that they are making love to! Fred always told me to tell him if he hurt me. A lot of the times I did, but a lot of the times I didn't. I will try to get the courage up to tell Nolan to go down on me first and to go slower when he puts it in. Who am I to tell him, though? I am younger than he is. But maybe he really doesn't know how to make a girl get pleasure. We will see. Next weekend Dawn and her boyfriend have invited Nolan and I to a condo on the seawall in Galveston. Maybe then.

Added note, Mom and Lukie are tying the knot. Hooray! They need each other. Lukie is a sweet man, and they have been together for ten happy years.

Friday, August 9, 1985 — A Child is Born

The greatest miracle in my life happened today. Marissa and Fred had a beautiful bouncing baby boy! God bless . . . I'm an aunt! I think I am still in shock. Wake up, Della. There is a new baby in the world and he means more to me than anything in the world at this moment. God, how I love that child. He is part of something I love dearly . . . Fred. But more than that and more importantly . . . he is my nephew. My sister had a baby! It seems so weird that Marissa and mommy are one in the same person. I love her more than I ever have. What made everything incredible was that I watched it happen. I will never forget that experience as long as I live.

His name is Joseph. Fred thought of it, but Marissa loves it. He wanted there to be another Joseph after his deceased brother and grandpa. Marissa says she will call him Joey, so that will probably be his nickname. Anyway, he was born at

7:28 p.m., weighs seven pounds twelve ounces and is nineteen inches long. He has a thin layer of brown hair and dark blue eyes. Thank goodness he has a bottom lip, unlike Fred. He has Marissa's nose, eyes and ears, I think.

The birth was . . . fascinating is not good enough. Marissa's water started leaking at 7:00 a.m. She called Fred at 7:30 a.m. and they were in the hospital by 10:00 a.m. Mom and I came at 2:00 p.m. and stayed. She started having somewhat regular contractions at 2:30 p.m., just after we went for a walk. At 4:00 p.m. the contractions started getting really painful and she stayed with her "hee hee" breaths until 5:50 p.m. when Fred convinced her to have an epidural, which took away 99 percent of the pain. They put something between two vertebrae in her lower back and left it there throughout the birth.

After that she dilated six inches and by about 7:00 p.m. they started preparing for the drop out. The doctor came in at the last fifteen minutes to help it out. He used two spoon forceps to pull, then he cut her. I cringed, but I watched. We slowly saw the head, then shoulders, then the rest came out. He cried immediately, yet now extra loud. Dawn called two seconds later and heard him cry. (There was a phone in her room.) Mom and I started crying, but Fred held his back. We took pictures with my camera, but the other doctor had a Polaroid and took two. One of the baby and one of all of us in our caps and gowns. My cousins, aunt and two of Marissa's coworkers were waiting in the "stork club," so I took the picture of the baby and yelled that it was a boy. Everyone was excited, my cousin Georgeanna especially . . . now her boy has a playmate. They are the first two in this generation.

The rest of the family and friends couldn't see Marissa until the doctor finished sewing her up. Then, they came back and saw the baby and visited. After their visit, they all left except for my aunt. Marissa breastfed him then. That was neat. He's a good sucker! Then Dawn and her boyfriend came by and brought flowers. Sweet. They left with my aunt and we brought Marissa up to her hospital room. She had been dying for a hamburger all day so Fred and I left to get her one. We stopped by the house first to call a friend, smoke a joint, and tell our next door neighbor. Marissa savored every bite of that burger. She hadn't eaten all day and had been through a lot! Mom and I went to look at the baby through the window. He is beautiful! I just know he is going to be a good baby. While other babies were bawling their heads off, Joey just laid there and looked around. I think a reason is because Fred sang to him in Marissa's tummy for six months. Whenever Fred sings, he stops crying. I want to go to sleep now. Tired. Aunt Della. P.S. I told you it was going to be a boy!

Thursday, September 5, 1985

It is now 12:30 a.m., I'm drunk and I want nothing more than to lie down on this bed, drown in my sorrows and go to sleep. But I feel this is important to write down. I just got back from The Texas Hall of Fame and I'm crying my eyes out. And I hate myself for it! Last Monday, first day of school, I met a cadet named Greg at the Howdy Dance at The Hall. Damn it, I told myself that I wasn't going to let myself feel enough for him that I could get hurt. But it didn't work. Monday night he asked if I was going to be there tonight and I said yes. (By the way, he is another fucking senior. Why do I always get them?) Naturally, I thought he was at least a tiny bit interested. I figured that he would at least ask me to dance on Thursday (tonight). I saw him at the bar last night and thought things went pretty well. Even though I was with my friends and he was with his, we talked a while and I really enjoyed being with him. Tonight at The Hall, he never even asked me to dance. I asked him once and we danced two and a half songs. The last song was *You Never Even Call Me by My Name* and we sang and kicked at the front with the band. I loved it. But he never came up to me to talk or dance. I promised myself that I would only ask him once. And I did.

SO, WHAT. Big deal. The same thing that happened with Evan and Jacob is happening and I CAN'T STOP IT! I met him less than a week ago and I'm already crying over him. His friends were so close to us that I had no choice but to keep an eye on him, and he knew where I was! Adam too. Why does this happen to me? I get a fever every time! I feel that I am too immature to take rejection. I hope and hope and then I get crushed. EVERY TIME! Lord help me. How much more can I take? I'm gonna get an ulcer.

My First Real Boyfriend, Ray

Wednesday, November 27, 1985

Wow. It's been a while. It feels good to write again. Joey is now almost four months and has changed a lot. He lost most of his brown hair and it is now almost tan. He is not a "non-crier" like I thought would be. He screams a lot, when I'm there to hear him. He wears a leg brace now attaching his legs to a bar and his legs are strong. He stands very well with help when the brace is on.

About Greg, I keep trying to tell myself that I am completely over him, but I don't think I am. I still ask him to dance at The Hall, and I still hurt when he chooses someone else over me. I can't seem to write too well tonight cuz I just took a few hits. Oh yeah, I wanted to write about Ray. Have I ever mentioned him? He is a cadet in my MWF Ag class and Tuesday lab. We met in that class and he asked me to his squadron party. They had a big screen TV and we watched the Alabama game, then danced at half time and after it was over till 12:00 a.m. I had a great time with him. I was also surrounded by many cadets. I know, I know, they are just guys, but they are guys in the Corps of Cadets. Some are total jerks (speaking from several experiences), but the majority are nice, polite guys. Ray is one of them.

He asked me to the first home game against Arkansas. Then the second, third, fourth and fifth home games and one away game, TCU in Dallas, which was an awesome blast. I like to be with him, but not when I am with the OCA Hogs. I don't like to mix the two. Too much controversy. I love to be with his outfit and their girlfriends. It's an easy way to make friends. It also makes me feel like a part of them. I love going to yell practice with him on the field, juniors guard the band and they get to invite their girlfriends. And going to the football games with him is fun because we are always all together. He asked me to the University of Texas game. Oh yeah, for the switch-off game (girls get to ask the guys to this one) I told him that I was asking someone else. I think he got hurt. Oh well, I told him from the beginning that I dated other guys. He said okay, but he always asks me how I feel about him. I think he wants more of a relationship than I do. This has nothing to do with sex. I told you, he is a gentleman. He is. Totally extreme opposite from Jacob. Ray has never tried anything, and we have known each other almost three months. He wants to hold hands all the time. I do, but I shouldn't. How can I date other guys if I hold hands with Ray constantly? The third week I knew him he sent me a dozen roses. What a sweetie! I kinda felt bad too, though.

College is not a place for a steady boyfriend. Bedtime. Bonfire was tonight and it is 3:30 a.m.

Saturday, January 4, 1986 — Cotton Bowl

Wow, I can't believe it is already 1986! It seems like I just started college, but I have been in a year and a half. Lots has happened. The Texas game was awesome! We won 42-10, which meant we went to the Cotton Bowl. Whoop! Well, that was January 1st, and Ray and I just got home from Dallas two days ago where we spent four wonderful days together and watched Auburn get the hell beat out of them by our awesome Texas Aggies. What a game! Quoting the Dallas Times Herald, "Auburn had Bo, but the Aggies had more." Bo Jackson even won the Heisman!

Ray met my cousin, Josie and I at my apartment in College Station and we drove to Dallas from there on December 30th. Josie decided to ride with me at the last minute to meet her boyfriend at the Dallas airport on the 1st. (By the way, I am on an airplane to New Orleans and this flight is very bumpy!) Ray and I were supposed to stay with his cousin, but she came down with a virus. So we stayed at a hotel. This got me worried for obvious reasons. Josie decided to treat us to Ninfa's for dinner. Ray then took me to Billy Bob's Texas, what a fun place! They had all kinds of games, a shooting gallery (that was fun!), plus a dance floor with a band. It is a lot like Gilley's. It wasn't really crowded and contained a lot of Auburn fans, but we had fun. Five of us Aggies yelled our "Beat the Hell."

On Tuesday, December 31st, 1985, New Year's Eve, Dallas, Ray's whole squadron all met at Luther's, ate, stopped by the liquor store, and went to the Fairmont where most of the outfit would spend the night. I wanted to stay there as well, but we already had a paid motel room. Half of the outfit went to the Sheraton Aggie Party where we played drinking games till 11:00 p.m. We then went to the Aggie yell practice held a few blocks away. It was a blast. I got wasted, but I remember everything. At midnight I kissed Don, a cute guy in Ray's squadron. Heaven! I guess I should tell the story about Don, and me and Ray's problems. I am attracted to Don (he is Italian like me) and Ray is in love with me and he knows my feelings for Don. Wheels spinning? I kissed Ray first, of course, then his whole outfit. It was a brand new year, after all, and that is the custom. We proceeded to sing all of our songs. Then I saw all the OCA Hogs and gave them all big hugs. After the crowd dispersed, we went back to the Fairmont and partied till almost 4:00 a.m. Ray and I went back to our hotel. We made love for the first time. It was wonderful. And it didn't even hurt. Even with the rubber. Shock!

I have a feeling that even though I wanted him, it was a mistake. Number one, I blew any chance that I could have had with Don; and number two, Ray is now more in love with me than he ever has been. He told me during that his dream had come true. I have never experienced anyone so in love with me before. Maybe not even Fred. He does anything that pleases me. I feel guilty that he spends so much money on me! He got me a James Avery ring for Christmas. He told me that he would have sent me roses if he had known my address. I paid for nothing the whole darn trip of four days. We got no sleep, for we had to rise for the Cotton Bowl parade. Beautiful! The Aggie Band and cavalry marched. We whooped! We also froze our butts off! Don was there too. Then was the awesome game! We sat with his parents, his roommate's parents, and Jim from his outfit. We all ate at Red Lobster, then went and saw the movie *Spies Like Us* (bad!). We left for College

Station in the morning. When it was time to say goodbye, Ray told me for the first time and with great difficulty that he loved me. What am I going to do??? I love him too, but I am not in love with him. I am breaking his heart, but he wants a relationship and I just don't want that right now. Not in college. Hell, we may end up being married someday, but I don't even want to think about that for three years. I need my freedom right now. I want to have fun. Letter Time . . .

Dear Ray,

You are driving me crazy! Not bugging me, just driving me crazy. What do you want from me? In our talks, the word "relationship" always pops out of your mouth. We have been to every home football game but one, and two away games. We go out every weekend. We see each other almost every day in class. And we study in the library together. I am with no one person more than I am with you. If that is not a relationship, I don't know what is. And now we have even made love. And you ask me if you have a chance? A chance for what? What do you want from me? It hurts me to know that I am hurting you, but what more could I possibly give you besides a commitment? And you know the answer to that one! I can't. Not right now in my life. My freedom and independence mean too much to me right now. Later that will change, but I don't care about later. Ray, I cannot give you any more than I have already. If you want more, then we have to stop dating all together.

Back to me: I couldn't handle that! I was too scared to give this letter to him. Sometimes I scare myself shitless wondering how I would feel if he all of a sudden stopped loving me. How long would I hurt? I am not prepared to go through that again.

Thursday, January 30, 1986—Love Comes

It has been ten days since we have been back in school. I know now that I truly do love Ray. It seems like I love him more every day. I seem to be fading fast from my "independent, free, dating other guys" mantra that I was so in love with. Ray and I don't spend much more time together than we did last semester, but it has much more meaning now. We write little notes on each other's notebook in class and we talk differently on the phone. Sometimes he spends the night and we sleep with only our underwear on, yet not always making love. That means a lot to me. I love to wake up with him on a Saturday morning and just hold him in bed. On our "big talk" day, we wrote each other long letters describing our feelings to each other. His mainly said that he loved me and wanted me to love him and to "be careful, you've got my heart and it shatters easy and hurts like hell when it does." He also said that he understood my "freedomness" and wouldn't give me any crap about dating other guys, not that he wouldn't be jealous. I wrote mine after I read his and told him that I do need to be free, but that I wouldn't date another guy on a "more than just friends" basis. How can I? I am making love to Ray! I also told him to back off the "I love you's" cuz even though I loved him, I couldn't say it to him. Well, I did today. He had given me a "thinking of you" card in class so I whispered in his ear that I loved him, just to get him back. It was funny to see him melt. It is so funny to sit next to him in class and think about hugging him, or kissing him, or other, and not be able to do anything except tell him on his notebook, "kiss kiss." In a way, it is so hilarious! I guess cuz of the mixing of feelings with class atmosphere.

I can't help but wonder how or why my feelings for him are changing. Last semester, sometimes I wouldn't even get near him on lab field trips. And I didn't like it when he came to The Hall with me (or worse, just show up!). I went to The Hall tonight with Debra, my new roomie, and all we did for almost the whole night is talk about each other's boyfriends and sex. I danced, but a lot less. Besides, Carson had a hurt arm. I danced mainly with Kent and Chip. Debra is really open and will talk about anything. I like her a lot and have a feeling we will get along great. Especially since we both have boyfriends. Notice I keep calling Ray my boyfriend. I would never tell him that, but what else can I call him? Man, I am changing my attitude about him almost in a 180° turn. Was I just scared shitless about a relationship last semester, or did I really not love him? Making love to him definitely started that turn! Why? What is going on inside of me? I haven't thought about Fred sexually since the summer, so he couldn't be the reason. I can actually see myself someday marrying this guy and owning a business with him. Debra says that's normal and you do that with all guys you date. But is it? I am still so baffled by Ray's love for me. It seems to grow, as mine does. Why, why, why? Why was I so different last semester? Am I changing emotionally? (Besides physically, my boobs are bigger than they ever have been, and are still growing. Not that they are as big as Marissa's.)

    Oh, I forgot to mention, I got on the pill last Sunday. Besides making me nauseous and gain weight, they make your boobs get bigger. I want to tell Ray that he is lucky he didn't meet me a year earlier, cuz there was almost nothin' there. Even Daddy and his partner, Ron said something about them. I look at them and can't believe my eyes. They took <u>so</u> damn long to grow! God, why did you have to wait till I was in college? It would have saved a lot of heart-ache if you could have pushed that button while I was still in high school!

    If my handwriting seems bad, it's cuz my brain is moving

faster than my hand. By the way, like this green pen? Isn't that supposed to mean "horny?" Maybe just "plants." D.

Monday, February 10, 1986

Sad day, Mom's boyfriend of seven years, Lukie, has moved out of Mom's house. He has a gambling problem and stole some checks from Mom.

My love for Ray is still growing! We went to New Orleans for Mardi Gras with two other friends and stayed with Daddy over the weekend. Besides Michelle's fits, it was a blast! It meant so much for Ray to be there. I loved holding his hand on Bourbon Street and standing so close to him during the parades. I do not mind calling him my boyfriend or him calling me his girlfriend. How can I? We are! I doubt I will date anyone else in college, unless I go out with a guy friend.

Daddy moved in to a beautiful blue house on Canal Boulevard several years ago. When we park in the garage and come in the back way, we can smell the Butterfly Ginger blooming before we even get out of the car. He has an entire row of this specific variety of ginger growing against the garage wall. It is a cousin to the culinary ginger root that we eat (it is actually an underground rhizome, which is a stem, not a root). In the tropics, there are hundreds of varieties of ginger. But you can't buy this one at a garden center. It has a delicate white flower that is the most aromatic flower you have ever smelled. And it propagates fast if you keep it watered. Daddy had dug some up from the neighbor's yard after he got permission many years and homes ago. He just digs it up and brings it with him when he moves. Daddy's Butterfly Ginger.

My Second Real Boyfriend, Ricky

Saturday, September 12, 1987

Wow! It has been one and a half years since last entry. It feels very strange to write, kind of childish even. Oh my God—am I becoming an adult? Me? NEVER. I am only 20. Anyway, so much has happened! It was mostly downhill for Ray and I after Mardi Gras. He began to choke me with his love and obsession. I couldn't breathe. I wanted to date other guys and not be so tied down. We broke up the next summer, June or July. He had gotten a summer job in Houston, and smothered me for my time. I did love him for a while, though. My only regret was losing a friend. He just wasn't for me. Yet, part of me wanted a boyfriend. Why did my love for Ray disappear?

The next fall I met a guy named Aaron. I didn't know till it was too late, but he was the lowest wimp I ever knew. He not only broke it off on my birthday, and broke my heart, but he spread untrue rumors about me and gave me a bad reputation in the OCA Hogs. Things turned out all right, but my Christmas was tainted. God, why did I cry so much for that asshole? If it wasn't for two people, I would probably still hurt today. The first was Gary, who was my shoulder to cry on (literally, I poured my heart out to him), and was my inside connection in the OCA Hogs to spread my truth. I was satisfied. The wimp never even came back to college.

My second real boyfriend was a guy named Ricky. He was my downstairs neighbor, and had become a good friend to hang out with. My previous excellent roommate, Debra, had decided to move in with her boyfriend, and moved out. Ricky filled a void. We started going to Duddley's Draw, my local bar where the cool folks hang out, to play pool four to five times a week. I had just gotten a new roommate the spring of 1987 who turned out to be a total bitch (and her fucking cats). I found myself spending all of my free time downstairs. We would play pool at Dud's and cook each other dinner (steaks and marshmallows on the Hibachi). I had found the best friend I could find at a time when I needed one so desperately. When I got better, I started looking at him romantically. He is from New Jersey, going to school, and in the Army (which he had just spent four years in). One day my dream was shattered when he called his "babe" on the phone in New Jersey. Oh well, I thought, at least I have a great friend. I loved him for that. We went on, playing pool and spending time with each other. He would bang on the ceiling whenever I was home to get me to come downstairs and I would pound on the floor for the same. It was great fun to get high with him and his friends, David, Jack and his roommate, Patrick. Ricky called him his "room dog." I remember Patrick's twentieth birthday party. We all drank tequila and got really wasted. We had great fun whenever we were together, no matter what we were doing. One time, I helped them blow up their battleship models with firecrackers in the bathtub. Silly boys.

I guess he felt the same way as I did. One day we were sitting on the couch and he told me that he felt very comfortable with me. Of course, it was mutual. I will never forget that magical Monday night on February 16, 1987. As usual we went to Duddley's to play pool and stayed till the bar closed and we got kicked out. We had an especially good time with friends and my pool skills were actually decent. We were walking home, like we always did, and neither of us were talking. He turned to me and said,

"You know, Della, five or six guys in there asked me if you were my girlfriend, and all I could tell them was 'I wish.'"

I was jumping for joy on the inside. Then I remembered, "but I thought you were already attached in New Jersey!"

"Where did you get that idea?"

"From your 'babe!' That is what you called her on the phone!"

He smiled the biggest smile I have ever seen, "that was my sister!" I was the happiest person in the world at that moment. Later that night, he kissed me for the first time. When he left my apartment and walked downstairs to his apartment, he let out a big "whoop."

Graduation

My relationship with Ricky was really intimate and healthy. He was the best boyfriend I have ever had. We were young and in love. In the fall of 1987, I moved in with him and his roommate, Patrick. Then, in December of 1987, he dropped a bomb and told me that he was quitting college and moving back home to New Jersey. I was, of course, devastated. We did the long-distance thing for a semester.

I took the fall semester of 1988 off from school and did an internship in my field in New Jersey while living with him, his mom, and his sister. It was a grand time. I got to meet his friends, and visit New York City for the first time. I learned how to drive a stick shift with the company truck in the snow on the New Jersey Turnpike. So comical. Those drivers behind me at the toll booth were not horn-shy as I was still learning to navigate the clutch . . . on the icy roads!

But after the internship we were back to the long-distance thing. It was awful. I do not recommend it to anyone. At the end of the spring semester in 1989, he flew from New Jersey to come to my graduation. I had achieved a Bachelor of Science! I was proud of me. Daddy even flew in. But I knew that moving to New Jersey was not in the cards for me. Without realizing it, I inadvertently introduced Ricky to my agriculture colleagues as "my good friend." Somehow in my mind, I had already broken up with him, and forgotten to tell myself. Or Ricky. Right after graduation, and after all of my family left, I ended the relationship. I asked him if he would make love to me one last time, and he looked at me like I was the devil. My view of the world was under selfish lenses. I will never forget when he walked out of my apartment and walked to the bus station. My tears were bittersweet, because I knew that I had made the right decision. He actually came back to the apartment because he had forgotten his wallet. That was awkward. My tears dried fairly quickly as I put on a Rush album, *Grace Under Pressure,* and sang as loud as I could. It was a clear moment.

About fifteen years later we reconnected. He came to

Houston to attend a business training workshop and stayed with me. He was working for a bowling alley, doing something with the ball return apparatus. He had become a raging alcoholic, and I judged him, because I could not face the fact that I might be one too. But I noted the fact that I drank a *lot* less than he did. I did not need it to wake up in the morning! I did not even drink every day. Yet.

After the intense pain of Fred, Casey seemed to look to repeat it. She expected, then demanded, too much from men. And she had a habit of becoming too attached too soon. And she knew all of this. Yet she continued to repeat the same pattern with most men she dated. Her tears from heartbreak were too frequent. Her heart was always open for the next heartbreak. As I mentioned, she had no boundaries. She had never been taught how to have a relationship. It was like she was looking for pain to be attached to love. It was all she knew.

Chapter Five

FORBIDDEN FRUIT

GRADUATE SCHOOL

In the fall of 1990, I entered graduate school to study plant research and get my master of science. I was twenty-four years old. I had worked for a research facility during the previous year, and discovered I had a love for plant research. I loved my office on the fifth floor. It was the best I have ever had. One whole wall was a window that looked out over campus. There was tropical ivy laced all over the ceiling. Since there were not enough graduate students, I got the office to myself for most of my three-year stay. I became a teaching assistant for an entry-level class laboratory, and found another love: teaching. Even better, I found out that I was really good at it. That love would change my career, years down the road.

Since most of my friends from undergrad had graduated, I got a whole new group of friends. And they had friends that played in a few bands. I found a love for live music, and got to know the musicians well. Even dated a few of them.

One gig, I will never forget. The band was invited to play

at a nudist colony about an hour away. They invited one of the girlfriends and me. We only live once, right? We were invited to stay the night, if we brought our own tents and camped on the grounds.

The day started with swimming, billiards, and foosball. I remember worrying about my boobs slamming against my body if I went off the diving board. I had to get several strong drinks in me first, but then I joined the nudies. I am not a very shy person, and was pleasantly surprised that there was no boob pain going off the diving board. It all felt quite natural. Then, I was asked to be a partner playing doubles in pool. Well, this was not a natural experience playing nude, but I got the hang of it. For one shot, I had to lean across the table. Lots of giggling ensued, and I was not penalized for moving the opponent's ball with my left boob.

That night, there was a big dance. Attire was cowboy boots and a hat. And that was all. The band joined in the party attire, so we did too. It did not seem fair that their guitars covered their private parts. I think they adjusted the straps for the occasion. As my date was in the band, I found myself being asked to dance by the locals in the colony. I refused a few times, but eventually decided to go with the flow. I said yes to a gentleman who was very well endowed in the private area. I tried to keep my eyes high. It was a two-step. The straight-a-ways were not a problem, but to my horror, every time we rounded a corner or did a spin, his "endowment" would slap against my thigh between the second and third step. This was not a comfortable feeling, and I didn't quite know how to react. That was the longest song ever. I just could not get myself to say yes to him again. But I enjoyed myself watching the band play.

Within a week of beginning graduate school, I met a fellow graduate student from Costa Rica named Leo. He was married with two children and twelve years older than me. Leo's office was on the same floor as mine but on the other side of the elevators. I really did not like him when we first met. He seemed arrogant and full of himself. But we soon became friends and were regularly visiting each other's office and helping each other out. He and I had coffee together in his office every weekday morning. He always had this yummy Costa Rican coffee shipped to him, best in the building. I soon found myself looking forward to morning coffee. He even gave me a key to his office, so that I could start the coffee before he arrived.

He was foreign, with a funny accent, and had a great sense of humor: both turn-ons for me. Soon the chemistry between us exploded. We could not stop the freight train that was overtaking us. We both tried. So many times! I had never experienced the level of passion that I felt when I was with him. And honestly, I have experienced it only a few times since. Because it was forbidden, it was heart-wrenching and exciting all at the same time. We finally gave in to our passion and began a physical love affair. It was two years of pain, lust, and tears . . . but also, I believe, true love.

He made it clear from the beginning that, although his marriage was on the rocks, he would never leave his kids. But my mind and body were so taken over by this man that I made the decision to do whatever it took to be with him. I was willing to wait for him until his youngest left home for college. Love and passion had so blinded me, I did not see that this was not normal. Insane even! I did not see that I was digging a very deep hole for my heart. I did not see that it was completely unfair to me as a human being. I had never learned that I deserved respect, or how to give it to myself. He even admitted to me before we became romantic that I was not his first affair. But adultery, to me, was no big deal. I had committed it with my sister's fiancé. I was a mistress, again. So what? Casey was in the lead, and she was determined to repeat the love/pain cycle.

It was around this time that drinking only Thursday through Sunday became any night of the week. I had my favorite drinking hole, and would always run in to friends there. I dabbled in cocaine, mushrooms, acid, and of course, marijuana. But hey, didn't all college students experiment with drugs? I remember one time some friends and I went to a park on the outskirts of town where cows had grazed to pick mushrooms. The hallucinating kind. It was quite comical when we had to explain to the campus cops that we were collecting plants for a biology class. Oh, the things we do in college . . .

The Leo Diaries

Friday, October 12, 1990

Three years and one month to the day since I last journaled. I am twenty-three years old. Why I am writing I haven't quite figured out. School starts Monday and I finished a Dean Koontz novel and wasn't sleepy, so I started reading my diary from the beginning, June 1982 to present. It is now 5:15 a.m. Three years is too much to try to catch up on, but Ricky and I were together until May of 1989. He had moved back home to New Jersey, and I refused to follow him. We did the long-distance thing for a long time, but it was too much to handle. And too hard. I did, however, have myself convinced that I was going to marry him. It was a wonderful, yet frustrating two years. I guess he was my longest relationship ever and since. I still love him, and would probably still marry him should he ever move back here. But he is working on a year anniversary with his new girl. I called him to see if he was going to be called to active duty and deployed to the Middle East. We are about to go to war, I fear

After Ricky, I went into a pretty promiscuous phase—slowly. I graduated with a Bachelor of Science on May 15, 1989. I am still in this town, now getting my Master's! Crazy, huh. I just can't seem to get enough of College Station. Plenty of heartbreaks, but no big relationships to speak of. Moved in to a party house with three friends, Jack, Jim and Kelly, after graduation. I got an internship at a plant research facility here in College Station with a dangle to go to Japan. Fell in love with plant research. I moved back into an apartment near campus when I got accepted in graduate school. I teach an undergraduate plant lab. I started my graduate research extracting RNA from maize endosperm yesterday. Neato!

Sleepy. I think I'm getting boring. No, just a transitional phase from "party organism." To what, I don't know. The bar is getting old.

Thursday, November 8, 1990

Leo came to my major professor's house last night where I was cat sitting to have a beer. We listened to Elton John's *Love Lies Bleeding in our Hands*. Sadly, I fear this will become our song. This morning in his office he told me that he left last night to save our friendship. And that he had previously had an affair in Costa Rica. Letter time . . . for my eyes only:

Dear Leo,
Why did you do this to me? Why did you tell me about her? Do you understand that you just undid what it has taken me two months to decide? I am in such turmoil that I can't even study. Don't you see? It is okay to want each other, because we have the option of never doing anything about it, and then laugh about it occasionally. I can deal with that. Making it known that we both felt the same way made it even easier. But I thought that our reasons were the same. Sure, our friendship is very important and to risk harming or even destroying that is very big. But there was a much much bigger factor in my head that made it so easy to say, "it will never happen and we just have to deal with it together." That factor is the two most important people in your life: your children! I could lean on them to help my strength to say "never." But you threw a wrench in the engine. You took away my pillar! Now, how can I be strong to say "no?" Because there is always a possibility that it would either not effect, or even strengthen our friendship. Not much of one, but a possibility.

And when you told me that THAT is the reason you left last night: to save our friendship . . . don't you see? It is not black and white anymore. The probability of us making love sometime in the next two years just went from 10 percent to 70 percent! Did you know that I could spend the rest of my life with you and be happy? Costa Rica would be awesome. I need to talk to someone, but the only answer will come from me and you and time. I love you, Leonardo! More than you will ever know. When I am studying in my office and I hear your voice down the hall, I smile because I know you will come visit me. It is truly music to my ears.

Della, you MUST be strong! Situation: we do make love. How will you feel the next day? The next week? The next two years? You see him at department functions with his wife, his kids. YOU would be the other woman! YOU would feel like scum. YOU would hurt like you have never hurt before, because she would be sleeping with him that night. A heart-wrenching pain that would last until he graduated and left. And how could you possibly be friends with someone who did that to you? YOU COULD NOT. And that is why you will be strong. You love him too much for that to happen. I think I have built another pillar. Back down to a 20 percent probability. Every time you are in the situation to consider making love to him, read this. Think what you would be destroying. Not the three people, Leo and his kids, but yourself! And maybe even grad school. NO ONE person, especially a married one, is worth that. It is YOUR life. Be the best friend Leonardo ever had. Love him, but keep it a joke. God, thank you for the ability to spill my guts to paper!

FORBIDDEN FRUIT

Monday, November 19, 1990 (Leo read this)

We can't control what we feel inside. So we must control the way we act. The physical and mental attraction that we feel for each other is extremely strong. Maybe even stronger than either of us can realize. We control it now, but how long can it last? The more we see each other, the more we weaken our strength to fight it. Especially when alcohol weakens us even more. Is it inevitable that we will break down and give in? Can we control how inevitable it is? Can we maintain a friendship when we feel so strongly attracted to each other? Can we drink beer together and maintain our sanity? Should we even attempt to trust ourselves even one more time? Or will the next time be the straw that breaks the camel's back? Is our friendship doomed because we both feel for each other? I have no answers. We are both tearing each other up. Should we stay away from each other for a while? I refuse to stop being your friend, Leo. I love you too much for that to happen. So is it now down to "stay away" or "give in?" What would happen to us if we did either? Or do we just play dumb and play it by ear? You have too many important things going on in your life for some grad student on your floor to jeopardize the time you need to spend on them. And so do I.

Sunday, November 25, 1990

Note from Leo on my office desk:
You are very ugly, so please use your mask. The Shadow.

Wednesday, November 28, 1990

It is already happening. I am hurting already, and nothing has happened. For me, Leo, and especially our friendship, tell him you CANNOT make love to him right now. Tell him you think about him all day and all night. Tell him you are already jealous of his wife. Tell him you would eventually hate him if it ever happened. You CANNOT make love to him and not fall in love with him. I believe I am already in love with him. Tell him! Make it NEVER! For us. Be strong. Don't destroy our friendship.

I did tell him that night. Then he told me the same thing last day of fall semester.

Thursday, November 29, 1990 — The Very Next Day

I love you. I want you! I get so excited—but we can't. But never say never. I will hurt worse if we do it, and think about you more. But you told me you are a fantastic lover. I bet I would surprise you also. ☺ We would be so passionate; the memory would last a lifetime. I will make love to you. Someday, I promise. I WILL MAKE LOVE TO YOU. You do not want to hear it. You said, "No! We can't think that way." I can. I must, or else I will lose my sanity. Just a twinge of hope is all I need. Just a "someday" to keep me going. I think I may be stronger than you, even though you are much older. Maybe you think about me, not more, but more intensely? You woke up mad last night after I told you "never,". I did not. You almost kissed me last night. You thanked me for being strong. I almost wish I wasn't. My heart beats so fast. Because we love each other, we can't have each other. It is NOT FAIR. But then I think I am already in love with you. How much harm would we really do? How can I think so differently from one night to the next day? My thoughts are so mixed up. Twelve hours ago, I was positive that we could not. Why? Because I would want more than sex. I would hurt every time you went home to your wife. DAMN. Why do I have to be so FUCKING emotional? Why can't I use you? It is a Catch 22. I want you, but I can't have you, because I love you.

Monday, December 3, 1990 — A Birthday Card from Leo

Della, it's your birthday . . . a special time to tell you how special you are to me! Happiness today and always! I will always treasure our talks. I will always treasure your memories. You can always count on my support. You can always count on my friendship. I wish you a very happy and fulfilling life, Leo.

Wednesday, January 16, 1991

Christmas Break I missed him terribly. I talked to Fred about it. The first time Leo and I had a chance to talk when we got back, I told him that we would regret it for the rest of our lives if we don't.

Yesterday he came over to smoke a joint before we went to the Wing Joint to drink beer. After we smoked I went to the kitchen to get water. As I was putting ice in my glass he surprised me, grabbed me and kissed me for the very first time. It lasted a long time and he was pulling me closer to him. I felt his penis and got scared. I was not ready. I pulled away and suggested that we go. Later he told me that he was about to take me upstairs if I hadn't pulled away. When we went to the Wing Joint for a beer, he told me, "Someday I will make love to you."

Our first time to make love was January 31. He came over and sat on the couch. I asked him if he was nervous. He said, "Of course!" I liked how direct he was. The second time was February 8.

Monday, February 11, 1991

Leo, I have so much flowing through my head that it is taking up the whole thing. When I force it out, I still can't concentrate on my studies. I know that you would be mad to hear this, so you never will. It is 90 percent good thoughts. I do not regret finally being one with you. I don't think I ever will. I do love you very dearly though, and I know that will haunt me for a long time when you leave. But I want to enjoy to the fullest the time we have together. We worry about one wanting more than the other. I think that this will work itself out. If we didn't respect each other's wishes, we wouldn't be as close as we are now. And that is the key—to respect the other's wishes, always.

You have a beautiful body, Leo. I am so happy we can share with each other and maintain our sanity. SO HAPPY. But can we? It pleases me so much to sneak kisses from you on the elevator and make out with you on the roof or in your research chamber. Or sneak back to my place on a Friday afternoon. I don't really look at you very differently, either, like I was so scared I would. Today we talked as friends and fellow grad students without so much as one sexual innuendo. We can play both sides of the fence, and be happy. Yet, I do worry about you. You seem to be having a harder time dealing with it than me. Last Friday was a graduate council party. It seems like you feel more awkward than me around your wife and/or kids. I am really shocked that I don't feel as awkward as I should. I remember my first letter—scared shitless about being "the other woman." I can only think of three reasons why I'm not. 1) I have been there with Fred and Marissa. 2) I know your marriage is falling apart. 3) I am an extremely open-minded person. Will I go to hell for this? Who knows? I guess I would rather live for the time that I am alive instead of what comes after. Funny, I even kinda like your wife. What a hypocrite! I hope that I can write you forever once you are gone. I love you! Della

Reading back through the first four letters, I laugh. I was so wrong about my own feelings. Defense mechanism from Fred, I'm sure. I don't hurt because of your wife. It may be just a shield now, but I don't think so. She sleeps with you, but do you make love to her? It doesn't matter. I love you too much to let that bother me. I will enjoy the time we have, and hopefully, keep in touch with you always. January 31 will always be a special date in my heart, Leo. You were so scared. I felt like you were a little puppy in my arms. Funny, I lean on you so much for control, yet not when it comes to being alone with you. I wish you hadn't got so angry when you could not get a hard on. Tired.

Wednesday, February 13, 1991 (*Leo read this*)

Leo. I know too well how important communication is, yet many times I don't open my mouth when something is wrong and I go away hurt or frustrated. This happened last night. I knew it was silly and that I was overreacting, but nevertheless, it was how I felt. So I am writing you this letter. I guess I am sensing that you are getting scared and backing away from me.

First, because you made it a point to tell me a reason why you came to my office last night (like you need one) and second, because you never made an attempt to even get close to me. I feel like you are not telling me something. I pour out my thoughts to you, Leo, you must do the same. If I feel you are not, I can become very cold without even realizing it. We have both said before that we are scared that one of us will want more than the other. Well, that will probably happen anyway, since no two people are ever that much alike. But it is so easy to work that out. First is through communication, and second and most important, is to respect each other's wishes. Leo, we already do that. Otherwise we would not be where we are now and we would not have waited so long. What we have is so special, yet limited in time. And extremely fragile. You already know that I am just one huge lump of emotion. Always talk to me, Leo. I told you once that if we ever made love that I would never expect anything from you. I lied. I expect to be held in your arms at least four times a week. That is all. We both agree that sex is not important, so there is no problem there. Don't make it one. Love, Della.

Added after he read the rest

We worked this out on the roof under a gorgeous sunset. He admitted I was right. Things are going great.

Thursday, February 14, 1991 — Valentine's Card from Leo

Since I came to college many good things have happened to me. It so happens that knowing you is one of them. On second thought, it's the best that could occur. Thanks for your sincere friendship. It's so good to know that I have someone that will always be there for me. (I hope!) God bless you always, keep it going with your studies and research (if not, I'll kill you!!) and never look back (unless he has a tight ass!!) Yours, Leo

Monday, March 4, 1991 — Note from Leo left on my Desk

Do you want to relax? Does your body feel tense? Well!! On your next "break" come see your friendly neighborhood "tension reliever" a.k.a. Me!! Free quickies. First fifteen minutes free. Free everything. Friendly service. No cover, no minimum.

Tuesday, March 5, 1991 (Leo read this)

Hey! Taking a study break, 2:00 a.m. Ugh! Remember the last day of last semester when you came to my office and told me the dreadful news? I was so devastated. And then, the next day at David's moving party, while cleaning his fridge, you came over to me and kissed me very softly and sweetly on my lips. The thought sends a big smile to my face. My heart sank to my feet and came back up with a bang. Kinda funny to think about how when I decided to be strong and say never, you were devastated, and about a month later when I was ready to give in, you turned around and decided never. Then one month later we both gave in. Well, back to studying biochemistry.

It is now 3:20 a.m. Does the song *Behind Closed Doors* ever enter your mind when you think about us? Our situation is difficult, but in many ways, it is fun and funny. I am happy with it. Are you? I think that it would be much more difficult if we were fighting it all of the time. (If we never gave in.)

Studying would be worse. It is much easier for me to know that, at least for now, I have what I want. I will purposely avoid the "attachment" issue. We have plenty of time before we have to worry about that large hill. Although, my ears are always open if you want to talk.

So, as you would say, "what else?" Alternate conversations seem to pop in your head so easy. Why? Juan wants to go have a beer Thursday after my exam. I have an appointment at 5:30 p.m., but free after that. My roommate works at 9:00 p.m. (hint hint). Although if you can't, I will always understand. Do you think Juan likes me more than a friend? I hope not. He is a very good friend now, and I would hate to feel awkward around him.

Thank you for always being there, and wanting to help me—Amigo. You know.

Saturday, March 16, 1991

Now I am getting really scared! Last week was Spring Break. I had several thoughts to ponder while riding in the car to and from Corpus Christi while missing Leo. Thursday March 7th he came over and told me that we were going too fast and that he wanted sex to be more special. We have only done it twice. Anyway, he said that we should not do it. Well, after two beers and two bong hits our clothes were off and we did. Well, we attempted. Next time completely sober. Afterwards he told me that I had a beautiful butt. I told him that I was just thinking that I loved his face, his balding head, his eyes, his little wrinkles coming off his eyes, his lips, his chest and his calves.

The next day in his office he told me that I scared the shit out of him saying all of that, because he doesn't want to fall madly in love with me and he doesn't want to mess up my life. So in thinking all of this, I decide that he is obviously going through something that needs to be worked out, so I will lay off and let him come to me for a while. I decide that maybe we should just be friends for a while, till he gets this worked out. So after missing him a lot and thinking about him, I come home March 15th and CALL HIS HOUSE (which I have done only once, ever) and ask him to go look for bikes with me today, Saturday. He says yes and we plan to meet at noon. We go turn in my CD player to be fixed and the bike shop was closed, so we went to look at Michelle's bike. He asks me if it was really bike shopping that I wanted to do and I say, "yes, what else did you have in mind?" and he refuses to answer. He asks me to say whatever is on my mind, that I am biting my lip and I deny it. I tell him to talk to me and he says he has nothing to say. I told him that I wanted a hug and he says no. Maybe a kiss on the forehead, but no hug. I didn't say anything. Back at the office he asks me to help him do something and I nod. In the car—I did not know if he was joking or not, so I think maybe I can get to hold him now.

Later he comes to my office, leaving. He touches my back and my arm, as if to say, "I'm sorry." But I turn away and tell him to leave. And he leaves. I am very hurt that he cannot hold me. He once said that he cannot hug me without it being sexual. I said that I had no problem with that and that hugs are very important to me. He asked me to show him how and I say I wish I could. Anyway, he is obviously (or he thinks) that he is helping us. Maybe this is his way of slowing down. Well, I can't STAND IT! I laugh. How can we EVER go back to being just friends? I really thought that I had the situation under control, but this one tiny incident proves that I do not. We have not seen each other in over a week, and he will not hold me. That hurts. What the hell am I going to be in for when he leaves? Worst part is I cannot talk to him about it for fear that he will stop seeing me to protect me. If he thinks that I am out of control, he will cut me off. That would be much worse! I would start hating him and being cold to him. What we feared the most would happen. But I try to see his side. "Maybe if we don't touch each other as often, we won't fall madly in love with each other." Does that make sense? Am I too blind to see it? God, I want him! All of him. He is the forbidden fruit.

I guess it does not matter if it makes sense to me. If this is what he feels he has to do, then I should listen to my own words and respect that. If it makes him feel better, then I must comply. Do not write him a letter saying anything different. Let him call the shots. Please try, Della. I know it hurts. I know you want to hold him. But for us, let him do what he feels is right. And try not to let him see your pain. Yet, I am too honest. Sooner or later I will blurt it out. But I will try hard. When I feel I am about to unload, I will think of us and repress it.

later entry

But you didn't, bitch. I cannot repress my feelings and probably will never be able to. When he did cut me off, I could not hate him, even if I wanted to.

Tuesday, April 2, 1991

I WANT YOU SO BAD FOR THE REST OF MY LIFE. I want someone like you to take care of me. To look after me. To hold me. To have my children. To grow old with me. To hold my hand as we walk through a park. To laugh with me and make me laugh. To dance with me under the moonlight. To make love to me so sweet and tender. To kiss me all over my face. To look into my eyes and know that I will be yours forever and ever. Leo, I am so scared to even say any of this to you. Scared you will feel so guilty that you would not feel comfortable around me anymore. You have told me you cannot give me anything. That you will not give up your kids. So how can you face me when I still hope you will somehow change your mind? I have told you that I accept that decision. I was lying to myself and you. Now I know the truth, but I cannot tell you. Or I will never stop hoping that you will change your mind, Leo. NEVER. Tonight you told me, "I care about you very much, and I do love you." Della.

Thursday, April 25, 1991—So Fatal Attractions!

Oh No! Another letter. I debated a long time whether or not to write this. I had decided not to, but the way I feel has affected my mood today and the way I have acted towards you. As you probably guessed, it has to do with you leaving so early last night. And, I guess it hurts most because you threw me for a loop. You surprised me. Ever since the last time we were one, we said that the next time we would spend three hours together. We planned a shower, remember? Leo, Wednesday you walked in to my office and made it a point to tell me that we were going to shower. I don't give a shit whether we take a shower or not. That is not the point. The point is that you only gave me a little over an hour. So then, naturally, I started thinking, "what did I do or say? Maybe it is my fault. Maybe because I said that I might want to go out with the girls." What was it? That is a two-way street, Leo. You said it could not be Friday because of the fight on TV. Fine, no problem. But I gave up my entire Thursday evening to be with you. I am not saying we need to change anything. I am telling you that you must be very careful with me. I have accepted the fact that I am "the other woman," but "being used" can very easily go along with that, and that I could not handle.

    I hope that this did not scare you. I don't feel that I demand anything of you, and I have been very careful not to give you that impression. If I ever do, let me know as soon as it happens. But if we say we are going to do one thing, and don't, yes, I am going to get hurt. I feel that is a completely normal reaction. Especially since you went to the library then came here to the building. Do you see how it is easy for me to feel like those things are more important than me? I know they are not, and I know that your feelings for me are genuine. But I must hear it and see it in the things you do. I really did not want to make a big deal out of this. But I feel it is more important to communicate my feelings to you whenever something is wrong, and hope you do the same with me.

    Leo, the time that we spend alone together is so incredibly precious. I put it near the top of my list. I don't take one minute of it for granted. Just be careful not to let me think . . . just, be careful. By the way, the time that we were together was extremely nice. Love Della. P.S. Meet me on the roof sometime this afternoon.

Sunday, May 5, 1991 (Never gave this to Leo)

    Dear Leo. I know that you do not want to hear what I am about to tell you. Therefore, you must trust me enough to know that I feel it is important for you to know. Spending so much time with and becoming closer to Diego, my roommate's friend from Geneva, Switzerland who is staying with us, revealed a lot about me that I was not fully aware of. You have always told me to find a boyfriend and I have always shrugged it off and thought to myself that I do not want one. Mainly because of you, but also because I just don't want one, even if I did not know you. My priority is school. Right now, I have the best of both worlds because I have both you and school without sacrificing time for either. And I am very happy with this situation. I did not want to bring Diego to the Barn Dance, but he had nowhere else to go. He wrote me a card that says he likes me. But I could not leave him at home. It was smart of you to never let us be in the same ring. I felt so bad. That night I told him that I was in love with someone else. I had no choice. I cannot describe what I was going through because of what I was putting all three of us through. Those two days made me realize how deeply in love I am with you, and it scares me. Because the pain I foresee in the future will be many times stronger.

Leo, don't you dare even think for one second that we must stop seeing each other. I would have to leave this town if you did. I felt that I had to share this with you and I am truly sorry if I hurt you. But I have had my share of pain as well.

You hold all of the cards in your hand, Leo. And I will play them any way you deal them. But either way, time will make everything work out in the end. Love Della.

Thursday, May 23, 1991

Leo, this may be a cliché, but I have never been more sure of anything in my life. So if you are planning to dump me, you better wait until you leave, or else you will have one humongous fight on your hands. It will be easier for you to fight me from Costa Rica.

Later that day

Leo read the above note. Last night Juan, Rob, Leo and I drank beer on the roof and had a good time. After they left, we went to his office to hold each other and somehow started talking about the future.

Like he has said a million times, "I can't give you anything."

Well, I had had just enough beers and had been holding it in so long that I told him, "you are talking within the next five to ten years. What about after?"

He said, "I thought about living with you, but I can't. Besides, you want children and I don't want to give you any, although they would be cute. I believe in population control, and I have already had my two."

I was SO hurt that I had to hold him to hide my face. I couldn't talk much after that. We left and he insisted to follow me home. He was worried because I had been drinking. I tried to tell him that I would be okay. I just wanted to get away from him so I could cry. But he insisted and I knew he would not give in. I rode my bike very fast. He left me at the corner store and the tears came immediately. I rode home and threw a fit, like the one when he told me that we could not sleep together, before Christmas break. I even overturned the coffee table and sent the large ash tray flying. I WILL NOT DIE WITHOUT HAVING CHILDREN! How could I even sleep with him after that? I went to the bar, played spades (a card game with partners) and got drunk. Sheri and Liza showed up, so I talked with Sheri about it. She said not to worry, that he was just saying that because of his own kids. This morning I lied in bed a long time and thought about it. And finally realized why he said it. In his own way, he was trying to protect me, to get me to not want him. He cannot say that he will never have children again, no one can. My hurt then turned to anger.

Who is he to know what is wrong for me? While we drank coffee in his office (like we do every morning) I was very quiet thinking about what I should say to him. How far should I go? I was tired of being treated like a damn butterfly. He needed to know my true feelings once and for all, even though that meant jeopardizing the time we have left here in grad school. What if he changes his feelings and it backfires? I had to take that chance. He told me that I was being very quiet. I told him that he upset me very much last night and that we needed to talk. We took a walk to the research farm. Again, he told me that he could not give me anything. He could not stay in the states. That was all it took.

I blurted, "When we first started seeing each other I accepted that we only had the time that we were here. But then I fell even deeper in love with you. I knew what I wanted. What I want is you, and if I have to follow you to the ends of the Earth and wait until your youngest is in college, then that is what I will do. You will not be married to your wife forever. It doesn't matter if we live in Alaska or Costa Rica."

He laughed, "I am very flattered."

"I am not expecting you to make any decisions right now, and I might even change my mind. I just wanted you to know how I feel. I was mad at you because you think you know what is best for me. Well you don't. You can't say that you will never have more children. Were you trying to get me to hate you?"

"No, and you are right." He replied.

"Are you more scared now than you were before?"

"You bet." Then he said, "You would not like Costa Rica. It is very noisy."

"It doesn't matter, and that is not going to work."

He never gave me any hints as to how he felt about any of it. I am really scared that I blew everything. But I could not delay it any longer. It was inevitable. Whatever happens will be for the best—I hope.

Also, we decided a few days ago, no more finger fucks. They are getting old, and we want it all. I hope we will make love again. Oh, God, what if he says no. I love you forever, Leo. FOREVER.

Tuesday, May 28, 1991

Dear Leo,

I am really glad that I had the chance to be away from you these last few days, because it has made me realize what a selfish bitch I have been to you. I put you in a very uncomfortable—no, painful position then told you that you can't get out of it until you leave. I was only thinking about myself. It was very unfair, and I am so sorry. I can now see my reasoning for doing it. I was worried about the time that we have left together here in graduate school. I didn't want things to change as they were—even if you knew that you had to let me go. But things did change because of what I said. I put more of a burden on your shoulders than was there before. Even though it came from the very bottom of my heart, I am regretful for what you must be going through right now. I guess it took being with my family and friends this weekend to realize that I am a very lucky girl. I am young and pretty with a good body and a family that will always be there for me. So you must know that if and when you let me go, I will go on with my life just fine. And I will find someone who makes me as happy as I am when I am with you. It is inevitable, Leo. I am telling you all of this because I love you and I am very concerned about you. I want you to worry about you and your family. But more than that, I don't want you to worry about me. Please.

I have said what I had to say. If you want to talk about anything, let me know. Della.

Leo's Reply That Day

Della,

This is not the Dear John letter, but maybe I'll be able to tell you what I feel and think "your way." Yes, I was feeling a big burden last Friday. Yes, I was feeling the pressure, and yes, I am (and was) very selfish. Even more than you. Why? Because I have two worlds and did not want to lose them. It is very selfish of me to have a family and then have you.

The problem started when I thought I wanted to be "with you." I felt very bad because, one, I felt I wanted to be with you just because of the physical stuff and two, who the fuck do I think I am to "take possession of you" and play with our feelings?

I'd rather have you as a friend (a very dear friend) than to have you as a lover. I'd rather feel like being able to see you happy than see you being miserable.

I don't want to jeopardize our standing and our lives. I have mine and yours is just starting. Yes, it will hurt once you find someone that will make you happy. (You know I never had any doubts you'll find someone—if you don't already have.)

But then it is so nice to be with you. If in case you didn't realize it, I need to thank you for a lot of things. You make me feel good (and attractive) about myself. Yes, I think you are a lucky girl, as I am an even luckier guy. There is only one problem, and here it goes! Whoever told you that you are a pretty girl must be fucking freaking blind! Yes, that is a joke.

Yes, it will hurt not being close to you (it may already hurt, because I may look that way, but I'm not stupid) and not being one with you again, but it feels better to know that you are happy, or will be.

Anyway, I'm not going anywhere for the next year or so, so if you ever need a friend, hey, you know the way to my door (and my heart). Thanks again for all your love, I will always be in debt with you.

Your friend always, Leo

P.S. By the way, what are you doing today from 5:30 to 9:00 p.m.?

Friday, June 7, 1991

I have nothing important to talk about, but just wanted to write and think about you. I am surprised and shocked by how totally in love with you I am. Last night was so good. And it didn't matter if we didn't come, because it felt so nice just to hold you, kiss you, caress you and shower with you, with my skin totally next to yours. But of course, we both came. I am scared, Leo. I love you too much. I want to grow old with you. I want to have my children with you. Last night you did not use a condom for a while. You told me that neither of us had the money to take care of the problem if it should happen. Leo, I could never kill something that we made. I could not. It would be different if it were Brian's or Devin's. I would not think twice about getting an abortion. But if there was a chance it was yours, (and I would probably know for sure, because I can't make love to anyone else right now) if I got pregnant with our child, I would raise it by myself if I had to. And I have always said that nothing would come in the way of my education. NOTHING. Well, I was wrong. I know for sure that I could not kill something that came from so much love. I would have to finish my Masters in nine months and go home and live with my mother.

And Leo would hate me. God, he would hate me. Seeing me walk down the hall carrying his child would break his heart because he would not leave his daughter. She has a much stronger hold on him than I do. Nine years stronger. I am sure that we would both have bleeding ulcers. But better that than to kill our child. No, I would have to leave graduate school. I love him too much to put him through that misery. I could not let him leave his daughter. I want to hate that little girl. But I can't. I am just very jealous of her. Last night when he was drying me off with the towel, and he told me to dry my own private parts, I knew that he had done that with her a thousand times. And then he even said, "remember, I have a little girl, we used to shower all the time." I knew.

But I can never tell him any of this. I just can't get pregnant. I just can't. That was the first time he ever went inside me without a condom. And the last. Although it felt so good. The whole two and a half hours were ecstasy. I was so damn happy and in love that I wanted to cry. I kept wanting to look deep into his eyes and see what he was feeling. To communicate without speech. It has been a whole month to the day that we had made love. And then we went through the truth scene at the research farm. He now believes that I want him forever. So now he is either, one, hoping I will fall in love with someone else; two, planning on letting me go no matter what when he goes back to Costa Rica—for whatever reasons, i.e., for me and/or his daughter, or three, taking me with him back to Costa Rica. I wonder if he knows at this point which one it will be. Probably not. He has told me that if I don't ever find someone that I love as much as him, that he could not live with an indoor pet. That was one of the happiest moments of my life. But he can't know what will happen in a year. Neither of us can. So we live day by day and enjoy each other now. And try to keep "future thoughts" at the back of our minds. But that is almost impossible. At least for me. At least once a minute last night I thought "this is why I want him". And almost none of it had to do with sex. He was very different last night than he has ever been. Foreplay was longer and heavier. He was biting and licking me all over. It was only the second time he had ever gone down on me. (The first was in the back seat of my car!) I know now that he doesn't like to. And it shows. But he absolutely loves to play with me with his fingers. So much, that I get a little raw just from his hands. But he lasted longer than he ever has before. And it didn't take as much for him to get hard. Every single time we have made love it has been better than the last. Not counting the finger fucks, I have six written down. I don't think that I would forget to write one down, but I don't have anything from February 8 to April 17. I don't remember not being one with him for over two months! But then, we finger fucked quite often back then.

Thursday, July 11, 1991 (he read this)

Leo,
 I can't blame you for what you are doing (or not doing). I would probably be as scared as you are if I were in your shoes. But you need to know the events and feelings I went through leading to that day. In New Orleans, I was able to look back on that day and mostly understand why I felt the way I felt. I saw myself from the outside, and didn't really like what I saw. I made a vow to myself to try to better myself. I realized that I can be a pretty selfish person on some things—one of those being you. You said it yourself a while ago, that I was possessive. But I never would have said anything that day if it wasn't that one damned day of the month on my period when I can't control anything I feel or say. You have seen me before that way, plenty of times. My hormones are so active and my mind is uncontrollable. I hate it! When I woke up that

morning and realized that it was that day, I told myself not to say anything. But it did not work. I am not trying to excuse myself or say that those feelings were not real. They were just magnified a thousand times. If you can believe me, I am (or was) happy with the way things are (or were). When I am alone with you, that is all that matters. And I would rather be alone with you in my apartment once a year than be with you at a movie or restaurant with a bunch of other people around. This month I was eight days late starting my period, but that day was the day that I was supposed to start, but didn't. Part of it also was that I was jealous of your anniversary and never talked with you about it. I just let it bottle up inside of me. But please try to see my side. I am scared because you are a married man, and there are times when I am going to be jealous. No other woman in my shoes wouldn't be. Let me know when you are ready to talk to me, but please don't put it off too much longer. This pretending that nothing is wrong is driving me bananas.

His reply (same day)

Della, I'm not putting off talking to you, I don't need to be ready to talk to you, so don't go bananas. If I'm acting as if nothing has happened, that is not my intention. L.

Thursday, July 18, 1991

Dear Diary,

Leo, give me the strength to be your friend for the next year plus. I have never in my life wanted someone so bad to be my husband. And possibly never will again. I will go on to get my PhD—for you Leo—to pacify my time waiting for your youngest daughter to leave home. Yet I am a realist as well as a hopeless romantic. I will not pass up the opportunity of marriage to someone else if I find someone who makes me as happy as you do. But my standards will be set so high and my love for you so strong, that this chance is not very likely.

Also, will you still want me in five to six years? So many things could happen. You could fall in love with someone else, as well as I could. Why is it so hard for me to accept that the chance of us spending the rest of our lives together is so fucking freaking tiny?

Thursday, August 1, 1991

God, so much has happened. It may be over for good. Although I won't know until he comes back from vacation. He has been gone ten days and has four more till I see him again. God, this is worse than Christmas break! But then, everything is different since then, except for the fact that I still (and will always) want to spend my life with him. But I now know that that cannot ever happen.

I reread this entire diary and got so mad at myself. I am surprised that he put up with me as long as he did. I lied to myself and him, over and over. How many times did I tell him that "I do not expect anything from you" and then I go and tell him that "I want you no matter how long it takes?" And then I tell him that I need more. And I compare him to an asshole who lies to his mistress (look who is talking). God, he must hate me. I made him physically ill the day he had to give an oral session at the meetings.

Sometime after our June 6 wonder-night with the shower, I came to him and told him that I either need to get closer to him or get farther away. I told him that I couldn't look down the hall towards his office anymore. GOD—WHY—I HATE YOU

FOR DOING THAT TO HIM!! YOU RUINED EVERYTHING, DELLA.

We talked it over that night on the roof, but didn't really solve anything. I told him that I could not stop seeing him, that I could not go back to being just friends. Things have never been the same since, and never will be. I told him—SHIT—that we never go out, to a movie or dinner. He said that if he doesn't even have time to do those things with his kids, that he will not take the time to do them with me. GOD, DELLA, YOU ARE SO SELFISH. WHY?

Soon after that I went to New Orleans for a week and thought a lot about what I had done and hated myself. I wrote him a letter to try to make things better, but it didn't (dated July 11). His reply was full of anger and guilt. We had a week before we went to the conference at Ohio State. God, I had been looking forward to that for so long. To be with him out of state by myself. Well, that week was awful. He would not talk to me and I would not initiate it.

He finally did on July 21st at Ohio State. I could not concentrate on the speakers on day one. After the speakers were over for the day, we found an empty classroom and sat down at two of the desks in the back. He began the conversation. He told me, again, all the things he has told me from the very beginning, and a lot more. "I can't give you anything. I am in love with my kids, and not you, my wife or former mistress is going to separate us. I've got to go back to Costa Rica for five years."

And more, "I would be an outcast from all my friends because they were my wife's friends first. A divorce over there is very different from here. They really look down on it." And, "I will not have my kids only every other weekend."

I began to silently cry. He continued, "Aside from a few white lies, I have NEVER LIED TO YOU!" He slammed his hand on the desk for emphasis on the word "never." I jumped because I was so startled at this unusual anger from him. I let the tears flow. He continued, "I was so angry when you said I reminded you of that asshole in the movie. I have never lied to you about us. I will not use the word 'love,' because it is overused these days, but you are growing inside me. But I love my kids more. Your heart is screaming inside, Della. I can hear it."

And so it was. He talked for half an hour in the classroom where he would give his talk the next day. He kept telling me to say something, but I could not say anything except, "I'm sorry." I realized that he was and is going through just as much pain as I. Maybe more because he's got guilt on top of all that hurt. And seeing me hurt that much made him want to stop being intimate with me for good. "Making love involves a relationship and I can't give you one. And I can't make love to you anymore if it means you will hurt this way. And it is only going to get worse the longer we do. Can you be friends with me, Della?"

The tears were flowing heavily by this point and I honestly could not answer him. "I don't know. I don't know." I replied. Thinking I would want him every time I see him and know that I could never touch him again broke me. My heart has never hurt as bad since that infamous day in New Orleans when Marissa told me about her and Fred. I was on the bottom of the world. I have never loved anyone so much in my life, and I can't have him. Never have I been so sure that I would drop anything I was doing to be with him—forever. We finally left the classroom and walked around campus. He tried so hard to cheer me up. Swinging me around. Chasing rabbits. I finally asked him to hold me, and he did not hesitate (even though in the classroom he said he could not). We held each other very tight for a very long time. Someone even walked by us, but it did not matter. When we finally let go, we walked to a bench and sat down. He asked me to promise that we would still be friends. I was still hurting so bad. I said I promise but I knew that I could not promise. God, I love him too much. We walked again to find a place to smoke a joint. As we were walking under a tree near a building he stopped and hugged me again. He pulled me away and looked into my eyes. I had to look down or I knew that we would kiss. When I finally looked up again, he kissed me. Very softly at first but growing and growing. I did not hold back. He grabbed my butt and started squeezing. I was getting very excited and could not hold back a soft moan. We kissed for a very long time. When we finally parted we moved out of sight and sat down and lit the joint. We smoked in silence.

When it was gone, he said, "If we don't go, I am going to do things to you right here in the grass."

I replied, "I don't mind."

"This is not my idea of a good place."

"Then let's go back to your dorm room."

"Let's go." He replied. Oh my God, my heart jumped wildly and landed in my throat. I was so incredibly happy at that moment. At least I was going to get one more chance to be with him. We got a coke on the way in. When we got to his room he poured the coke into two glasses. Then he turned around and faced me and looked deep into my eyes. The light was out, but there was light coming in from the window which was wide open. He kissed me. I began to caress his chest and nipples and shoulders. He did the same to me. He began to take off his shirt and me mine. I looked toward the window and he said not to worry, that no one could see anything. We quickly undressed ourselves. When we were both naked we embraced and kissed each other very hard and passionately. I almost knocked off his glasses, so he took them off and put them on the desk. He felt me and discovered, to both of our surprise, that she was already very wet and ready. This made him moan and he asked for the condom. I gave it to him and he put it on quickly. He asked if I wanted to lay down, or could he take me standing up. I said, "surprise me." He felt for me with his fingers, bent his knees and rammed himself inside of me. The pain was very quick and exhilarating. He slowly pumped in and out, and oh I was so juicy. Thinking of this got me even more excited and I said, "I am so wet." He pumped a little faster, but I was ready to take over. God, I was getting close. I grabbed his ass and pulled him toward me roughly. I began to move faster and faster and squeezed his cheeks tighter and tighter until I exploded in orgasm—my entire body quivering for what seemed like five minutes. My body had never quivered so intensely before. I had never had an orgasm quite like it. There was so much emotion and love. I held him tightly for nearly a full minute, jerking a little every few seconds.

He then laid me down on the bottom bunk and slowly reentered me. I was sopping wet and ready again. He pumped a little faster and the bed started to make noise like old springs in a cheap motel bed. He gently moved my leg under his and rolled me over onto my side and entered me from the rear. He then rolled me slightly back over and put my foot on a rail from the top bunk. This was very comfortable and did not make any noise. He'd done that before, I guess. We both rose to a climax again, and again. By this time, we were both sweating drops, as there was no AC in the dorms, only my little fan in the window. He then began to caress my legs and suck and nibble on my nipples. I began to lick the sweat off of his forehead and he laughed very quietly. He kissed me softly on my lips. Then I got on top and started pumping again. He asked, "talk dirty to me." All I could think of to say was, "you feel so good inside me. It feels so good. I love you inside me." I was never good at that. He asked, "Do you want me to lick your clit?" I licked my fore lip and he said, "yes, oh yes" and he climaxed again. I was following soon after.

Afterward he said, "I came so many times that I don't have any cum left."

I said, "I lost count of mine a long time ago."

We held each other's sweaty body. I did not know how long we had made love, but my guess would be close to two hours. In less than three minutes Leo was snoring. I took a sheet and climbed onto the top bunk. It took me a very long time to get to sleep, on account of his snoring. But I didn't mind. It was the best night of my entire life.

Wednesday, August 12, 1991

Dear Diary,

Leo. Damn it! I made a promise to myself not to initiate any conversation about this, but I am a very unhappy person right now. I used to wake up with a smile. The thrill of buying a new bicycle was taken away from me. I feel like I am on the edge of tears most of every day. But your pre-lims come first, so I have been biting my lip up to now. But it is becoming harder and harder to even be around you. And our first promise to each other was to always be friends. Even before we ever made love. Remember? Well, my end is in grave danger, Leo. We have to talk. But I will wait until after your pre-lims mid-September.

Wednesday, September 11, 1991 (from Leo)

Della, I'm off, I am meeting with my major advisor tomorrow. I may (maybe not) be back tonight. He is leaving the test in my box tonight so I want it answered by the morning. I took a quarter from your upper right drawer. See you later, L. P.S. I hope you solve those biochemistry problems in a jiffy!

Thursday, September 26, 1991

We finally got to talk about us. The first time since Ohio State two months ago. Leo told me that we could not see each other anymore. He said:

"If I was living alone, I am pretty sure that we would be living together right now. I shouldn't tell you this, because your head would swell, but you are the best lover I have ever had. I will never forget your face that night at Ohio State. I have never seen a woman come like that before. You are a good lay. Some days you look so cute in your tight jeans, and I want to hold you and kiss you. And I see you looking at me too.

"I know in my heart that this is the right thing to do, so I can't be sorry. I can't see you hurt like that anymore. It got to the point where I did not want to be at home and I did not want to be here with you. I can't live two lives. I will not risk losing you as a friend, and it would get to the point where you will be angry with me for not choosing you."

Thursday, October 17, 1991

I can't believe I actually get to write this, but I want to get caught up first. The next day we met at a local dive for a beer. He had already had a couple of pitchers with David at the bar before he got there, so he was pretty buzzed already. But I didn't like his face. He seemed upset. I asked him why and he said that I would find out some day. He finally said that the past three months had been really hard for him—and he knew it was hard for me too. He said that if he started seeing me again, that he would have to leave his kids (I guess for me) and that thought made him want to throw up. Then he told me that he wanted to tell me something that did not imply anything, but he wanted to tell me before someone else did. He said that his wife and kids were going to Costa Rica for Christmas to see the family, but he was going to stay here alone. At first I thought he was telling me to stay away to avoid temptation. But the more he talked, the more I thought that he wanted me to spend it with him. I am not going to speculate so soon, because I still don't know what he has planned, but I really hope we can spend some quality time together. Who knows?

October 19th was his 37th birthday. I wrote him a poem—included after this entry—and gave him a certificate for a lunch and beer on me. Specifically, alone with me. The next day Mom called—Paw Paw was not going to make it through the weekend. I immediately went home. He passed away on Friday and the funeral was Monday. Leo was the only person I called. Twice—no, three times. I had to break my rule and call him at home to see if he was going to the lab, so he could get my teaching materials and quiz for Monday's lab to my substitute. The materials were in the notebook under Leo's birthday card. He could not keep the poem for obvious reasons. It was also in the drawer with this diary. He had to get them and no one else. Anyway, he cheered me up as much as he could and tried to prepare me for the mass and funeral. He was a true friend when I desperately needed one. But surprise, huh. Well, the whole five days I was home, I thought about him constantly. How I wanted him there with me to lean on and love. Pretty scary, huh? I am going to be in a world of hurt for a long time when he leaves. For a very long time.

Especially right around my Master's defense, and especially since I still have hope for us. A part of me truly believes that we will spend our lives together. It doesn't seem to matter that we are not sleeping together—well, almost.

Anyway, since I came back on Tuesday, I have wanted him so bad. Monday night when I came up to school he was here. He gave me a sideways hug and repeatedly told me that he was glad I was back. Well, all day Tuesday and Wednesday he was in my thoughts—sexually. I considered finding someone else, ha ha.

Wednesday night, last night, was Armando's birthday party. Armando invited me, but I did not want to sit at a table with a bunch of people I did not know (except for Juan) speaking a language I did not understand. But I had gone to Foley's to look at shoes and it was on my way home. I thought, I will just have a couple of beers and go home. To my surprise, Leo was there. He had been there about an hour. He told me soon after I arrived that he was going to have one more beer, then split. Ha ha. We both stayed until 12:30 a.m., leaving with a pretty good buzz. He said, "Let's go smoke." I said, "Where?" He said, "At the building."

He got there about five minutes before me and I found him waiting at the car. He said he didn't know if I was going to show up. Ouch, that hurt. He said that he was freezing, so I said let's go to my place. We did. He sat on the couch next to me. As I was pulling the joint out of my purse, he stole a quick kiss and said, "that is all you get." I called him a tease and he said that he should not even be there. We smoked a few hits and he got up to go. I let him go, but he turned around and hugged me. Then he kissed me quick again. We pulled away and he looked at me saying nothing. Then he teased me some more, "what I am about to do is called sexual harassment." He grabbed my butt and pulled me close to him. I felt his hard-on and moaned. Well, that was all she wrote. Our hands were all over each other and we kissed very deeply and passionately. It had been three months since we had touched. I was surprised when he undid his pants, then my pants. It was just like we used to do on the roof, but pretty rough. He said he did not want to finger fuck me, but he was. He asked me to suck on him, which I was glad to do. But he stopped me and said that it wasn't fair to me. I said it didn't matter, but he insisted. We kissed again and he said, "Della, you are so special." I was in such ecstasy. My hands were roaming all over him. I sucked his nipples. I whispered, "I love you so much" but was unsure if he heard me. By this time my pants were pretty far down, and he was getting closer to me. He whispered, "I don't want to get you pregnant, do you have a condom?" I nodded and led him upstairs. My roommate could be coming home anytime. We did it. It was very quick, but passionate. He walked to the bathroom to wash, but he did not shut the door. I could not help myself but watch those buns taper down into those gorgeous and massive thighs, and then into those beautiful calves. I hope I never forget that picture. He turned and saw me watching and teased, "this is private, you know." I smiled.

We got dressed and went downstairs. I hugged him tight. He said, "you know how I feel, and I know how you feel." I nodded. That was all that needed to be said. He left. We did not say one word about it today, but it was on our minds.

Monday, October 14, 1991 (Leo's birthday card)

Dear Leo,
What do you do for someone's birthday who is very special in your life, but who won't take anything from you? I thought and thought, and came up with this certificate that you can

keep and use whenever you wish. However, you may not "not" use it. I would be very hurt and offended if you did not graciously accept this gift. Just for the record, it is redeemable with me and me alone. I am selfish with the time that I spend with you. After that is the other half of your birthday present. I wrote you a poem. It doesn't rhyme, so don't expect it to. As you may have guessed, it is something that you cannot very well keep. But if it brings a light to your eye and a smile to your face, then it is worth it.

Please don't throw it away. Give it back to me with this letter.

Hope your birthday and your life is happy and fulfilling!

(I will not say it, because I know you don't like me to.

But if I did, it would be in this spot right here)

P.S. Thirty-seven! Golly, that's almost forty!

SUNSETS ON THE ROOF

You have meant so much in my life
You bring me up when I am down
If that doesn't work, you swing me round and round
You point me in the right direction
Whenever I go astray
You build my confidence in me
When I feel I am not worth this MS degree
You make me feel so special
Like the person I truly am
You have been such a true friend
But you have been so much more
I can't even begin to say
Although you do have your faults:
You are one of the most stubborn assholes I have ever met
You don't believe in your self-worth

You can't take a compliment
You insist that the coffee is all yours
And after all we have been through,
I STILL owe you twenty dollars
You say that I got the losing end
But you are so wrong
I have had the privilege to know, love, and be loved
By one of the most special human beings in the world
And that means more to me than you can imagine
In knowing you only thirteen-and-a-half months I have gained a lifetime of memories
Your sweet smile, the way your eyes crinkle up like mine
Your sweet, soft lips that kiss so fine
And, oh, that beautiful, beautiful chest!
(Forgive me, I lost it there for a second)
Let's not forget those shapely calves
And, for the record, I like your balding head!
Those countless sunsets on the roof
All those hugs
Those few times surrounded by potato plants
Those stolen kisses on the elevator
A few other hot spots around the building
And those 7 beautiful nights we shared as one
Along with the countless memories of friend hood
These "Sunsets on the Roof" I will never forget
And we'll hopefully add one more to it
For the memory of all memories
But if not, it is nice to know that we already have one
July Twenty one Nineteen and ninety-one

His reply (same day)

Dearest Della,

Very few people indeed are able to say that they have been blessed because so many beautiful people have shared with them. I am one of those few, so I know how it feels to know people like you.

Keep it going, never stop. Because one day, hopefully soon, your heart full of joy, and your chin high, you'll get your degree and fly.

I will always be your friend. Leo.

Friday, November 8, 1991

Leo. I'm really sorry about your car. I know you don't have much time to read this, but there are some things you need to be aware of. This has been an extremely emotional week for me—the worst ever. If it had not been for my closest friends, I think I would have gone insane. Many people have commented that I look tired and have even offered to listen to whatever my problem is. I did not realize that I was that transparent—except to you. I know you can read me like a book. But I can't talk to them. And it scares me that they see something is wrong with me, because they might figure out that my heart hurts for you. I don't really know why this week has been worse than all of the rest, besides the fact that my emotions get magnified when it is my time of the month. But it must be more than that. I have cried almost every day, and it has affected my teaching and my studies.

Part of it is you trying to avoid me. But I think most of it is that I am finally realizing that when you leave with your little family, I will never see you again. It is so damn frustrating to me that not only can I not have the one thing that I want most in this world, but I can't even fight for it. I can be a very stubborn person, like you, but in this case I have to just lie still and let this happen. And I know that this is the way that it has to be for you, but that does not make *it easier to let you go. So I think, what is the best way to get over you? Of course, the answer is to get away from you. BUT WE DON'T HAVE THAT OPTION.*

I need to hate you, Leo, but I can't for many reasons. First, I have tried, and it is mentally IMPOSSIBLE for me to hate you. Not only because I love you, but also because of the wonderful person that you are. Second, and most important, because people will see that I am avoiding you and they will figure out that something is wrong between us. And it would not take a genius to figure out what is going on. Third, I could not go through that. For me to hate and avoid you would be too devastating for me. I could not handle coming to school and seeing you. And fourth, we have to work together for the next year. As a fellow graduate student, I need your help to do it.

Stop thinking that it would be best for you to avoid me. You really need to see that it is making things worse. We need to try to lean on each other instead, and be there as friends. I need you, more than ever, to try to be that friend that I knew a year ago. And, yes, it will be hard for both of us until you go, but we have to believe that it will get easier. And it will. And if you catch me looking at you, don't tell me that you don't like it and to stop. Let me go through it and heal in my own way. It is only natural. Let's set a day next week to sit down and talk about this, ok?

Thursday, November 21, 1991

God, help me. I can't tell if the problem is as bad as I am making it. I don't want to hurt for the next year, but what choice do I have? I want him so bad. I would do anything for him. Today, I thought that I might even die for him. Men used to die for women back in the chivalrous days to prove their undying love for them. I love him that much. And I am trapped because I cannot have him and I am not being allowed to get over him.

So I hurt. And feel sorry for myself. And wish. And hope. Maybe someday, he will leave them for me. But he must not love me as much as I love him. The bastard even told me that he loves his former mistress more than me.

Sunday, December 1, 1991

Dear Leo,

I have been thinking a whole lot lately, as I am sure you have. I have realized that you are probably going through the same grief that I have been. Ours is a very testing situation, and we both have our faults. But after several bong hits and a good friend to talk to, it came to me. Like the light at the end of the tunnel. Leo, we have to agree that we will never be one again. Only then can our friendship endure, and we can spend this last year as something we can look back and smile on. Our friendship is one that may not come too readily in a lifetime. And that is why I fell in love with you. I guess it backfired, didn't it. Well, for all of the pain, I can't regret it. What do you say we make a fresh start? I'm almost ready.

Monday, December 9, 1991

Leo did nothing for my birthday. Not even a card.

Saturday, December 14, 1991

My stomach turned to knots when he danced with his wife at the department Christmas party.

Saturday, December 21, 1991

His wife and kids were in Costa Rica. I asked him if I could spend the night after dinner. He said no. He could not see me go through the pain I went through before. He said he loved me too much.

Monday, February 10, 1992

Well, it got to the point where I could not even be around Leo at all after his wife and kids came back around January 6. I talked to my old friend, Max about it, and leaned on him. So much that we spent the night together. I started to fall for Max, and the very next day and subsequent weeks, I was able to be friends with Leo. When school started, I learned that Leo would be my teaching assistant for a graduate level class. I asked him if it would hurt the healing. The tables had turned 180°. Now he is hurting a lot and not me. He told me twice that he was having a very hard time. My feelings are mixed. Of course, I feel bad for him, but at the same time, now it is his turn to get a taste of what I went through. Yet, I know I am getting over him. Finally.

Thursday, February 13, 1992

He took me to the roof today. The words he said made me feel so good that my eyes filled with tears:

"I dream about you almost every night. If I never sleep with another woman, I would be fortunate because I have already known you. I look up to you and I respect you. The reason I did not get you a birthday or Christmas card is because you were hurting so much at that time and I was trying to back away. I see you getting your life back together, and it is so good to see you happy all of the time, instead of crying. But I get selfish and jealous that I don't have you anymore. I still want to jump your bones. Everyday. And I want to hold you and kiss you. Can I pinch your butt once in a while?"

I told him that he blew our once in a lifetime chance December 21st to wake up together. But I could not be angry, because he did it for me!

He continued, "I do still love you very much. I will never admit saying this, but you have a beautiful face."

Sunday, February 16, 1992

For Valentine's Day, I walked into my office and saw a little rose plant, a bottle of Johannesburg Riesling, and a card on my desk. I cried, and loved him. I was smiling so wide. He popped his head into my office at that moment and said that if I was not careful, I could eat my ears. I wrote him a Valentine that said there will be one more time, and that he could not say no this time. He had to leave before we could meet on the roof. Yesterday we made beer in the lab. When we took it to storage, he asked if he could hold me. We kissed for a long time. God, it felt so good. Later, we smoked a joint on the roof and talked and laughed. It was just like old times.

God, please don't let me hurt again like I did! Please let me have the strength to know and believe that I can NEVER have him. He will NEVER leave his kids. Don't let me hope. Let me love him and be one with him without pain. PLEASE DELLA! It has to be possible. He will not be in my life for very much longer.

Remembering Leo, and then Jim Happened

That was the last entry of the Leo diaries. Not since Fred had I endured so much emotional pain over a two-year period. And less than ten years later. I tried so hard to convince him to choose me. It didn't seem possible that he just didn't want me enough. I convinced myself that I would wait until his daughter was in college. I just had to have him. There was no fighting it. That is crazy! I made myself crazy.

How could I have been so stupid and blind? So selfish for that "love feeling" that I set myself up again and again for such intense pain? How could I have absolutely zero respect that I jumped into this relationship with a married man – doomed for certain failure before it even began? How did the attraction – strong as a tidal wave – overtake me completely? How could I allow it? The escape route was so clear! All I had to do was head in the other direction. Put one foot that way, shift the weight, pick up the other foot and pass the first. But instead I ran toward the title wave and became consumed. I drowned. And when I came up for air, I dove right back in. Again and again.

When Leo finally cut me off sexually, we attempted to salvage a friendship for the time that he had left in graduate school. Several months later, he passed his prelims, became a PhD, and went home to Costa Rica. I did not go to the airport to see him off. My therapist says that I wanted him so bad, not despite the impossibility of having him, but *because* it was impossible. She said that the combination of Daddy leaving us, seeing him only a few times every year and the sexual abuse from Fred created a pattern of choosing and pursuing unavailable men to repeat my pain. It was the love/pain cycle again. It was all I knew. The pain kept Casey alive.

What finally turned off the Leo faucet of pain was the love of another man. I met and fell head over heels in love with Jim a few months before Leo left. He was sexy, funny, all smiles and my age! I was twenty-six years old. I found him on my couch one day when I came home and my roommate was having a party. Oh, he was so cute. For the first few weeks, we were inseparable. I was on the rebound with my foreign, married lover, but I just knew that this one was THE ONE. We ate almost every meal together. He spent the night at my apartment every night, or I his. We had so much fun together. And the sex was the best! I never had to use a lubricant with Jim, which was extremely unusual. I wanted him all the time. I was elated. We planned a trip together to New Orleans. And I was ready to move to Ohio, where his job was, to be with him.

But it was too good to be true. After only seven and a half weeks, he dropped the bomb. His ex-girlfriend from Paris had contacted him and wanted to give their relationship another try. I could understand her foreign allure, but I knew it would not last between them. I kept saying that he could not possibly feel the same way I did, or he never would have let me go. "He would know," I kept repeating to myself. I was beyond devastated. How could I be right back in the same boat I was in just a few months ago? The breakup was long and drawn out. He moved home to Ohio and we wrote to each other and talked on the phone. I was convinced that when she dumped him, I would be waiting in the wings. It did not occur to me that this showed absolutely no respect for myself. Because I had never developed self-respect. Casey was in control again.

Jim's relationship with his ex hinged on her completing school in Paris within the next several months. Meanwhile, I asked Jim if I could come visit him in Ohio. He hesitated, but agreed. That should have been a sign right there. But I did not know how to look for signs. I only saw us together in the end. We talked about the chance of my moving there and finding a job. The clarity finally came when he told me that I would have to get my own apartment and we would have to start over. That was just not possible for me. So I finally ended all communication, and it was over for good. I heard through a mutual friend that Paris-girl had broken his heart a few months later. But by then, it was too late. He had dumped me and then stepped on my broken self. I guess adult Della finally took over for Casey. A few months later I finished my studies, defended my thesis, and passed my prelims. At least I was successful in school, and I had a Master of Science to prove it.

Chapter Six

OFF TO EUROPE, BACK TO MYSELF

The Europe Diaries

Saturday, October 23, 1993 – Madrid, Spain

Well, after I became a Master of Science, I could not seem to get one positive response to any of over sixty resumes that I sent out, so I decided to take my car down payment and take off for Europe. By myself. With no return ticket. Have an adventure. I am so psyched! My plan is to save money by staying in youth hostels and traveling by train on a Eurail Pass, which lets you travel ten train trips anywhere in Europe with no time limits. Because Air Hitch makes you fly stand-by, and you don't even know your destination in Europe until you board, I got to spend eleven hours Thursday at DFW airport without getting on the plane to London. I had only three hours of sleep the night before, in anticipation of sleeping on the plane, so I fell asleep twice at the gates. I spent the night with my college friend, Sheri in Dallas and started again this morning at 6:00 a.m. They were now putting me stand-by on a flight to Madrid the next day. Interestingly, however, while trying to find a ride to the Sheraton near Sheri's apartment, I met a man named Kevin. He was going in that direction, so he drove me to the Sheraton. Kind of dangerous, but I did it. I was so tired. Anyway, when I told him that I was going to Madrid the next day, he told me that he had a nephew named Bill that lived there. How lucky is that? He called his wife from the car phone and got his nephew's phone number for me. Too strange.

This time, Friday, I got a flight to NYC, then on to Madrid, Spain that evening. On the layover, I met a Spanish girl named Rosa who was twenty. She had just spent one year in Philadelphia being a nanny, and was going home. She was neat.

We landed at 6:15 a.m. I decided to stay my first night at a hotel with my own room for $27. What the hell, I needed the sleep. I met a guy named Jchong something something from Africa who traded cab fare for knowledge of a good cheap hotel. The scenery from the bus and cab rides were indescribable. I was looking around not believing that I was actually in Spain! My first impression was that their trees are different. They have more Juniper trees, but Palm scattered here and there. I found Oleander and the tree with the big leaves and ball fruit that is not Sweet Gum. The next thing that stuck out was the architecture. Some of the buildings were very modern, but as we got closer to city central it was like going back in time to ancient Spain. Many cathedral-type buildings with sculpted designs and figures every square foot. All the cars have ugly, flat butts—Peugeot, VW, Ford, Porsche, Benz and some Beamers. I actually saw a red 3000GT, though.

Jchong invited me to breakfast. He told me to be ready in one hour. I did not want to wait that long, but agreed. It was a free meal. I decided to use the time to call Diego. I met Diego in college. He was my roommate's friend's sister's ex-boyfriend from Geneva, Switzerland who stayed at our apartment a few times while visiting in the States. I let him know that I was coming to Europe, and could he return the favor by allowing me to stay with him. He surprised me by offering to be my guide through Europe! That is his profession, but he explained that he is between jobs and would guide me for free. How lucky is that? I went to the phone company one block away, but they did not open until 9:00 a.m. I went back to my room to wait for Jchong, but he never showed. I walked to a café across the street and had the best cup of coffee that I have ever had. It was very strong and half of it was steamed milk. I think it was called a cappuccino. It reminded me of CDM coffee, but with no chicory. These Europeans know how to do a cup of coffee! I then went back to the phone company and finally got through to an AT&T operator. It took forever, even with a very nice girl who helped me, and cost me over $11 for three fucking minutes! I told Diego I would be in Geneva on Tuesday.

I then walked to the Museo de Prado. I loved the buildings on the way. They are so ancient. When I got there, I called Bill and we made plans for dinner. The Prado was huge and beautiful, but the paintings just weren't my taste. Most were religious. All the angels were nude and had the same body—fat with small tits, and either she or some guy was holding one of them. Goya is okay. I spent a couple of hours there and then walked to a nearby café for tapas, which is the Spanish version of hors d'oeuvres. I had a tuna sandwich with red pepper and a sausage something with green pepper and mineral water. I then went to the post office, which really looks like a cathedral both outside and inside. Why are our post offices in the shape of a boring box? I posted Mom, Dad and Marissa. Went back to my room at 4:00 p.m., slept till 6:00 p.m. and got ready for my "date" with Bill.

When I talked to him I got scared because he sounded like a pimply geek. He picked me up at the hotel, and to my surprise, he was actually kinda cute. We got along immediately. We went to a Spanish restaurant and ordered paella—rice with saffron and meat. It was okay. And wine. We then parked the car at his penthouse and walked to a nearby pub. I met his friend bartender named Gregory. Very nice. Balding, but nice looking. And his friend Domingo who kept calling me a Yankee, much to my protesting. We both got pissed (as Bill says) on beer and tequila shots. I got bold enough to tell Bill to tell Gregory that if he wasn't married I would take him home with me. Geez! I don't remember much of the rest of the evening. I was so tired from my flight.

Sunday, October 24, 1993—Toledo, Spain

Bill woke me up in his bed with no clothes on kissing me down there. We made love for a long time. I enjoyed it very much. I especially liked the way he sucked on my breasts, kinda hard. He got up to shower and I went back to sleep for two hours. He woke me up and made love to me again. I checked out of my hotel, back to his place to shower, and he drove me to Toledo.

Even more bonita than Madrid. The city, which is 3,000 years old, is surrounded by a river and a wall. We visited several very old cathedrals that were breathtaking. St. Thome had the painting by El Greco, The Burial of Count Orgaz. Then to the monastery of San Juan de los Reyes (Cloister of St. John of the Kings). The architecture of this place was magnificent, with a courtyard in the center which had an orange tree and two tall Juniper trees. Bill and I had a picture taken there. We went to the cathedral with the Retable of the High Altar Cathedral. Fascinating. We went to a hotel across the river with a gorgeous view of Toledo and took pictures at sunset. We got a tortilla (which is somehow eggs with potato and onion here in Spain) and drove home. We vegged for a while at his penthouse. It is on top of the seventh floor and has its own balcony. So beautiful. I cannot imagine living like this. He works for Boeing, introducing new airplanes to customers all over the world. He is obviously very comfortable. Bill and I went to an Italian restaurant for dinner. I had fish lasagna with spinach noodles and wine. Very tasty and cheesy, but it was not lasagna. It didn't even have tomato sauce. A wonderful day.

Monday, October 25, 1993

I woke up at 8:00 a.m., and so did Bill. "Guess what I have," he says to me. Anyway, after he got up to shower for work, I tried unsuccessfully to go back to sleep, so I got up and had coffee and cereal. I found the subway, called the Metro and went to the Royal Palace. (The doors of the subway stay open for only seven to nine seconds so you must push to get in or out if it is crowded. Oh my God, the palace was exquisite. They still hold state functions there and parties for 160 guests. It has 2,008 rooms, of which our tour showed seven: the throne room, the porcelain room, the dining room and others. Wow. What amazes me about every place I have been to so far is the details in the many marble and rock carvings on the inside and outside walls. Other things—the Spanish look and dress no different than North Americans. Everything is in Spanish (duh), even the captions to the paintings. I then walked the three miles to the Museo Nacional Reina Sofia. I shopped and ate a tortilla on the way. The Plaza Mayor was impressive. I almost bought a black studded halter, but it didn't fit right. The Sofia is a very modern building and had artists like Picasso (who must have been insane, I am convinced), Dali (my favorite), Miro (kinda weird, some plain), Gris and Solana plus many others. Even though my feet hurt and I was harassed by the tenders, it was much more enjoyable for me than the Prado. The walk back to Bill's was very long, but so many people are on the street. And window shopping was fun. At one point I was very lost, so I ducked into a pharmacy to ask for directions. I was so surprised that the pharmacist, who knew very little English, got me going in the right direction with help from my map. What struck me was that he was so nice, and he helped me even though there were people waiting for their prescriptions.

Thoughts—light switches (which are push-in) are on the outside of the bathroom. The toilet flushes many times and have huge handles that you push in. The girls in Spain wear pants or skirts and shirts with two different prints—yuk. Their shoes are always black and nice, no tennis shoes or hiking boots. Some look like they would fit the wicked witch of the west, they are huge with two-inch heels and a buckle. No one wears T-shirts or sweatshirts with writing of any kind on it. Everyone dresses nice to go anywhere.

Bill and I went to a restaurant called Hollywood for dinner. It had American movie posters all over the wall. I had a cheeseburger and fries and a Spanish beer. We stayed up, drank beer and talked until 12:30 a.m.. Bill is a fascinating person, but he is also an arrogant asshole who is very big on himself. He is very money smart and has purchased two houses and an apartment in Seattle. And he invests. Boeing pays a shitload for him to live like a king wherever he goes. His parking space alone was a one-time cost of $200,000! He says, "they get what they pay for." Bill is pleasant enough, but I was ready to leave his company.

Tuesday, October 26, 1993

Bill dropped me off at the train station at 9:30 a.m. I spent a semi-hectic twenty hours on the train to Geneva to meet Diego. I met a London couple who shared half of a sandwich and an apple with me. Very nice. I am not used to bringing food onto trains, and the dining car wanted $18 for a hot meal and $4 for a small sandwich.

Wednesday, October 27, 1993 — Genève, Suisse

Arrived in Geneva, Switzerland at 7:20 a.m. Rang Diego, woke him up of course, and told him to meet me at the Café de la Gare (Station Café). I drank coffee, again mixed with steaming milk. So good. We went to Cathedrale di St. Pierre and climbed 400 steps to the top to look out over the entire city. There are two rivers that wind through the city: Le Rhone, which is green, and L'Arve, which is gray and the prettiest. They intersect at Le Junction and you can watch the colors intertwine and mix on a bridge right over the junction. Then went to see the Le Jet D'Eau (the fountain in Lake Geneva that shoots water 460 feet into the air). We must have walked ten miles. We stopped three times for a hot tea, hot coffee, then hot chocolate throughout the day. This is a very popular thing to do here. We had lunch at La Boursiere. God, I was so hungry! I had eaten half a sandwich and an apple on the train the whole two days. I had something that looked like roast beef, fried potatoes that were between fries and tater tots, and peas. Mom, I even ate my green peas! (I hate green peas.) The meat was scrumptious. We came home to shower and relax, then went to eat fondue (fromage) that tasted like brie with garlic pieces. Mmmm. Then to Carouge (a nearby small town) to a couple of bars. The walk home was about forty-five minutes. I slept like a log.

Thursday, October 28, 1993

Slept until 10:30 a.m.! Went for a two-hour boat tour. Met Luciana from Brazil. She changed her thirty-five-minute tour to hang out with us. She was touring Europe before starting a one-year chef course in London. She owns a restaurant in Brazil. We toured the shores of Lake Limon from the boat and saw Lennon's old cottage, several castles, the UN building, the place where Reagan and Gorbachev signed something, Eisenhower's retirement place, and other places dating back to the 13th Century. We then went with Luciana to the train station because she wanted to change her ticket to go to Barcelona the next morning. Her English is very good. She spent her high school senior year in the US. She was very nice.

We then went to a bar for a drink, where she met her friend. Diego and I then went to an excellent Bombay Indian restaurant. I had lamb curry that was just way too spicy but awesome. Then to an underground festival with many young bands at a huge place called L'Usine. The band that was on when we arrived was horrible, so we went upstairs to this huge warehouse-type room with another bar. There was no band, but two Africans were playing a big drum with their hands. It was pretty cool. We sat down next to a Rasta dude with dread locks. He was selling these bracelets he made of leather with white and black paint and dark red background. Diego bought me one.

The dude wanted ten franks, but Diego got him down to five. He is really good at that. At the flea market the other day, he bargained for everything. I got a small porcelain flower basket, a pot that said Genève (this is the correct French spelling and pronunciation), and an Italian porcelain shoe with flowers in it that looked like Maw Maw's.

Then this guy started to dance something I have never seen to the rhythm of the music. The guys in front of us shared their hashish (very weak) with me. I started to see the cultural diversity in this one room. It seemed like the whole world was represented in 200 people with no racism. I was in awe. Then we went back downstairs and a new band was playing called Restless Marshaits. I loved them. They played music somewhere between Reggae and rap in French, Spanish and a little English. They did not stop. I could not understand a word they said, but I could not stop laughing at them. There were at different times five rappers, one bass, one guitar, one drum machine and one synthesizer dude. That makes nine people on the stage at one time. And they were all colorful in their own way. One with dread locks . . . no, two. Two with tall, flat top colorful hats. Two that jumped around everywhere. They kept asking rappers in the audience to come on stage and join them.

We then went to a different room and sat with an American and her stinky French friend. We talked until the next band came on, and I was introduced to the wonderful world of Ska! There were four horns, real drums, a very cute lead guitar and one absolutely colorful yet loco lead singer. He was dressed in a black and white checkered blazer and red t-shirt. He had very short, straight, brown hair and blue eyes. I know because he bugged them out every minute. We were standing very close to the stage. His expressions and body language were remarkable. He reminded me of the lead singer of the Talking Heads. They were great! I wanted to buy their t-shirt so bad. Gotta say no sometime. They sang about Ska, a dead dog named Spot, and his girl leaving him. I will never forget the band Ska Pig. My funnest night ever.

Friday, October 29 — Barcelona, Spain

Woke up at 11:00 a.m.! Waited for Luciana to call, but she never did. Oh well. We showered, went to buy our train tickets to Barcelona (leave tonight at 10:00 p.m., we got a sleeping car), went grocery shopping for the train ride, ate at Pizza Hut, came back home to pack and relax before the train ride. I am now en route from Barcelona to the southern tip of Spain to catch a boat to Morocco, Africa! It seemed like a cool thing to do, and I can go anywhere I want.

I am four days behind on my journaling. I will ask Diego, who is watching me as I write, to help fill in the days. Got to Barcelona around 9:00 a.m. on October 30th and took the subway to the youth hostel. I did not sleep on the couchette very well, but the hostel closes from 10:00 a.m. to 3:00 p.m. for cleaning. So we checked in and then got kicked out. Walked to a major street, Las Ramblas, to look for cheap hotels, went to the flea market, walked and walked. Went back to hostel at 3:00 p.m. and slept until 6:30 p.m. Showered, dressed, ate and went clubbing. We went to a disco with very old rock, Fine Young Cannibals, Prince and other stuff I liked. Left and went to a bar that made their own beer. I did not like it, but it was okay. The atmosphere was cute. Got help from very friendly locals beside us and went to an all-night discothèque. They played mostly techno stuff, but some of the older stuff I liked. We switched to hard alcohol, gin and tonic for me of course. They actually put more gin than tonic here. But they also charged almost $9 per drink. We danced until 6:00 a.m., mostly because the hostel is locked from 12:00 a.m. to 7:30 a.m. Then we had to walk all the way back because the subways stop at 12:00 a.m. My feet are killing me. Back at the hostel, desayuno (breakfast) is included, but was disappointing. A sweet thing and a muffin and ONE cup of coffee. We slept from 8:00 a.m. till 10:00 a.m. and got kicked out again.

We went to Sagrada de Familia, a beautiful and very old unfinished cathedral. It was designed by the famous Gaudi and has been under construction since 1882! The religious carvings are very modern, they showed a Jesus on the cross with no cloth. The castle has nine very tall steeples jutting out into the city. So tired. Went to bed early.

Thoughts—Diego has a watch that runs on the heat of his wrist. The McDonalds and all other American fast food joints have a bar!

Monday, November 1

It is a holiday. All the museums are closed, so we did not have many options. We went to the mountains where Gaudi made lots of structures with mosaic. Nice view of the city. Then up to the tallest mountain where there was a very old church and an amusement park at the top. We sat on a wall for a long time to watch the beautiful vista. Back to the hostel to shower and change, then to the playa (beach) to eat at a very expensive (but didn't look like it) restaurant. We got a grilled variety plate ($30!) with shrimp, mussels, crawfish, a filet (maybe shark?) and some weird shellfish that I did not know but had no taste. I got a picture with Andre, our waiter. He wants me to send him a copy. Went to a plaza for a final beer and made it back to the hostel by 12:30 a.m.

Tuesday, November 2

Rose early and went to the Picasso Museum. Fascinating and not so weird. Very different from his stuff that I saw at the Sofia in Madrid. Saw Toros, Matadors, woman with candles, his poking fun at Velazquez' Marie Margaret and his very horny stuff in his final years of the late 60's. I bought a poster of a man courting a woman in a garden patio,' but lost it at the train station. Shit. Train left at 5:30 p.m., did not get a couchette this time. Big mistake, but funny because we were in a compartment with nine people with luggage with seats for eight until 7:00 a.m.! One psycho woman, two young men, an older man, another older woman and a younger woman with her six-year-old daughter. At some points—no, nearly always—they talked and laughed and laughed and no one knew a word of English. I felt sad sometimes that I could not laugh with them. Diego translated very little—as should be. I picked up the motif of most of the conversations, but very few words. I knew the bad words, ha ha. I read a lot, and caught hell for it from the psycho. She kept talking to me, and was clearly frustrated that I could not understand her.

Wednesday, November 3

Three-hour layover in a little village called Bobadilla. Very quaint and very Spanish. Now I sit in first class. So far, we have the whole compartment to ourselves. The difference is night and day!

Thursday, November 4

Arrived in Algeciras (they pronounce the "c" like a "th"), the port city on the southern tip of Spain. The train ride to get here turned into part bus ride because it rained like Texas for almost two days and part of the tracks were under water. The scenery was bonita through the rain-soaked windows. And there was no non-stop psycho to listen to! It was still raining when we arrived. We ate some bread, ham and cheese that we had bought in Barcelona at the train station. Got a hotel room for $21. We walked the streets of Algeciras, and stayed at the bars until 2:00 a.m. and talked, and had a Frangelica. Made love for the first time. Enjoyable. He is big for such a skinny body!

Friday, November 5 — Morocco, Africa

Day 13. Arrived in Africa today. The ferry took us to Puerta de Ceuta, a Spanish port on the northern tip of Africa. We took a bus and taxi to Tetuan. On the bus, we met Abdul. One of my small bags broke, and three rolls of my 35mm spent camera film canisters went rolling down the aisle as the bus was making a turn. It was so embarrassing. They were very important to me, as they were all of my pics of my trip so far. Abdul was sitting near the back and caught them as they rolled his way. Abdul was tall, lean and neatly shaven. He wore a very nice dark blue silk suit with a flowered silk tie, white socks and black shoes. He brought me my film canisters, and sat in the seat across the aisle. I was very grateful for his kindness. We talked with him, and he offered to share a taxi to Tetuan. The taxi driver turned out to be his nephew. He said that all the taxi drivers overcharge the tourists getting off the bus, so we were lucky. It turns out that his family owns a pension (small hotel) and he took us there. We dropped off our stuff and took his invitation to eat with him and his friend, Mohammed. They are both Arab Muslims, but Mohammed is much darker skinned than Abdul. Mohammed was much shorter and stockier than Abdul, and he enjoyed the scruffier face. For dinner, I had couscous, which is boiled wheat, with onion, carrot, lamb and yummy spices. It was excellent. Several times during dinner people came up to Mohammed to say hello. He is the mayor's son.

Mohammed then invited us to go walk around the city with him as our guide. We stopped at an outdoor shop where they dressed me in a hiyak for pictures; a thin, white, wool or cotton fabric covering from head to toe with only the eyes showing, the traditional costume for Moroccan townswomen.

We ended up at his father's tapestry shop where they made and sold exquisite tapestries. Mohammed introduced us to his friend, who showed us the hand-machines that they make them on, and two unfinished carpets on the machines. He and Abdul then left. His friend said that students make them and that this was the last day they would be in the shop selling them. He then invited us to sit and drink sweet mint tea, and we talked a while. His friend brought in a helper and they began to lay out about thirty beautiful carpets, explaining the differences between the wool, mixed and silk weavings. He said that each girl (only girls) made the designs from memory from family designs. I then got the feeling that they were trying to sell carpets to us. It took a long time to lay them all out. He asked that, as he folded them up, to tell him which ones that I liked. He said that he would teach us two Arabic words: *la* means yes, I want to know the price and *wahah* means no, I don't like that one. If I said *la*, he would set it aside and *wahah* he would put away. He said to choose six or seven. I chose five. Diego did not say much. I later figured out that this is when they hook their fish, me. We went into another, bigger room to lay them out and deal. I was still convinced that I was not going to buy, but not as strongly. He asked me to choose my favorite one. I chose the only silk with dark greens and burgundy. It was beautiful. Then my second favorite, a big, beautiful dark and light blues with a natural wool background made of cashmere. He gave me a price of $2,400 for both of them. I say I can only bargain with one. He says, Okay, $1,200 for the one silk. I hesitate, say I can't. He then decreases to $1,000 and not start payment for eight months. After much time, I finally agree. I was reeled in. I paid with my credit card, of course. Then, he introduces me to Mohammed's uncle, who somehow gets me to buy my second (cashmere) and third choices for $1,000 more. I chose a wide variety, convenient for them. I think I did pretty damn good, considering I can sell the cashmere one for maybe $4,000 in the states. But man, was the process intimidating. I think they possibly drugged the mint tea. He gave me a gift of a large blue cloth and a beautiful carved bone necklace.

We then went to tour the city some more: the court, one of the king's palaces, the cinema, as he was explaining the history of the city. We always walked in twos with Diego and I apart. It was like they wanted to talk with us alone and find out what we were like, and also talk about themselves. We ended up at a café that did not serve alcohol, and had a coffee. I had juice, already too much caffeine in one day. Mohammed's brother and another friend found us and joined us. Very popular, these two. Abdul rolled a cigarette with hash, and we went to the back room of Mohammed's brother's video store to smoke it. Actually, only Abdul and I smoked three hits off of it.

We talked, then two more friends showed up, then two more. They mainly talked amongst themselves, but Mo and Al talked with us. Mo talks a lot, mostly about his religion, his country and his people. I found him fascinating. He talked a little about the horrors in Israel and Palestine. How they kill innocent people for their land, but not many at a time. And how they must return each death. He said they were harder people than Europeans or Americans because they have had it bad all their lives, and their parents', and their parents' . . . I have always wanted someone from their sides to explain what was going on. I was fascinated. I felt so lucky to have met these fine people who would look out for us and teach us about their culture first hand. I also felt lucky to be amongst a small party of friends in a country as exotic and unusual like Morocco. They are no fucking different than anybody else. And very different in some ways. I hope that makes sense, it does right now.

Thoughts: They pee in porcelain holes in the ground with raised foot holders and no toilet paper. The pure Arabs don't drink alcohol, but some youth do. Several times the first carpet dude said that he does not think that all Americans are rich, implying that many Arabs do. So much more to say, but I gotta sleep. The women all wear the long gowns and scarf on their heads. There are very few overweight people here in Africa and Spain and Geneva.

Saturday, November 6

Woke up and had an ice-cold shower. Such a horrible experience. What can I say, I am soft, like Mo says. I just cannot get under the cold water or wet my head. Mo came and got us and we met the carpet dude at the post office to get insurance and see my new carpets off—bye. We were there almost two hours. Ick. Abdul met us and we mailed all my post cards, only $0.53 each. Not $0.29, but not $0.80 like in Spain. We finally got coffee and breakfast at a very nice and new café—crepe squares with chicken and curry inside, and crepe things with honey and fresh squeezed orange juice. We somehow convinced Diego to delay our trip to Casablanca for a day so we could spend the day together with our new friends. I feel like I have made some very good friends here. They spent the whole day with us. The feelings were very mutual all around. In just one day we grew to love each other. We went back to the pension and paid for another night and soaked some clothes in a wash tub. We then walked all around the "old city." The markets here sell everything. We went to wedding reception halls. Then we went to a place where they wash and dye leather in many cement basins built into the ground. It smelled of decay, but was so interesting. No tourists are allowed there without knowing someone. Abdul explained about the seven gates that surround the old city and how many years ago the Muslims had to lock themselves in every night from attack. We ate soup and an omelet. We brought a bottle of wine back to our room and drank and laughed. I can't wait to see my pics from today. Mo and Abdul left, and we washed our dirty clothes on a washboard and hung them to dry, knowing full well that they would not be dry by 7:00 a.m. tomorrow morning. They came back at 9:00 p.m. and we had a juice, then said our goodbyes. We exchanged addresses. Abdul says to call him in a week, but it was still very sad knowing we may never see each other again.

Sunday, November 7

Woke too early and caught the 7:30 a.m. bus then train to Casablanca (about six hours in transit). I was in a bad mood this morning and cold to Diego. Partly because I wanted to spend Sunday with our new friends. I found the most adorable, yet sexy, Arab man on our train compartment. Smile, eye lashes, dimple, too cute! I wanted to run away with him. His wife (I assume) was not pretty enough for him. I watched him sleep and smiled at him often. Stupid, but I felt sorry for myself for not being able to try for him. I think I hurt Diego's feelings, he left the car for a while. Not fair to him, since I had just made love to him the night before. You can be a real bitch, Della. But then again, I love Diego, but I will never fall in love with him. Abdul asked if we loved each other. I said, "as a friend very much." I guess it was good that he knows not to hope. My trip would be so much worse without his guidance, companionship and friendship. I do love him for that. But he stinks in the pits and feet sometimes. Somewhat of a big turn off. I don't think he uses anti-perspirant or even deodorant.

Anyway, we arrived in Casablanca at about 2:30 p.m. and walked with our luggage to find the only youth hostel till it hurt, about thirty minutes. It was supposed to be only 315 meters from the station, but we got off at the wrong stop. We finally got a cab fucking four blocks from the hostel and checked in. Very nice place. Lots of colored tile, like in the mosques. I paid for a hot shower, and it felt so good! I have never enjoyed washing my hair more. Had spaghetti Sicilia for dinner, different but good. They put long strips of bell pepper and a lot of cheese. Walked some, we are lucky that the hostel is near downtown. Neat city, but not overwhelming. I crave English conversation, and I miss Abdul and Mohammed. The owner of this hostel is very nice, and kinda cute. I love the French language.

Thoughts: Everyone in Europe and Africa smokes. Young boys sell cigarettes all over the streets. Women do not go to the bars here. None. I feel a little lonely about that. A man sang in my ear tonight at La Comedie. Glad I could not understand him. Mopeds, older ones, are everywhere. Silver is cheap, must go Christmas shopping tomorrow. Want to call my family, but no one has heard of AT&T.

Walked through the old town toward the beach where the most beautiful mosque was. It was huge! We wanted to walk to the water, but military men would not let us get too close to the mosque. We detoured through a bad part of town, where many kids were playing football (soccer) and many spectators were watching an adult game. We were walking parallel to the beach, trying to get to it, when four boys approached us and shook our hands. I would guess they were ages twelve to fifteen. They seemed friendly enough until they asked us to give them money. We told them no, and they went away. Then, the biggest one came back with another big one. Diego saw them and told me to be careful. They asked Diego for his watch and $10. They started to try to trip both of us and pushing us into the wall. We kept walking and somehow managed to duck into a café. We drank a coffee, but we could see them waiting for us to leave. We asked the staff to please call us a taxi, but he said that we could just flag one down. Asshole. He knew what was happening. We had no choice but to hail a taxi and get the fuck out of there. We were very lucky that one was driving by. In the end, they only got Diego's cigarettes.

We got dropped off at the Hyatt Regency, where they filmed the famous scene in the movie *Casablanca*. There are pictures of Humphrey Bogart and Ingrid Bergman everywhere. We went into "Rick's Bar" and ordered a juice ($11) and a coffee. The bartender wore a trench coat and hat. We left there and started walking. We got harassed again, so we went directly to the train station to get tickets to get the hell out of this city. We walked back to the hostel for a nap, I think I am catching a bug. Then went to the silver shop, I got twelve gifts for only $30. We had a lovely dinner at a nice restaurant.

I had some excellent veal couscous and Diego ordered a shrimp cocktail, but the sauce was not like home. We got stuffed and stole the picante sauce, which was more like a hot tomato paste.

We then walked into the rain. I laughed my head off. We have been trying to wash our clothes and get them dry for three days, and they were hanging outside back at the hostel. On the way back to the hostel, we got harassed again. This time, the man wanted Diego alone. I got some courage from somewhere, or maybe it was just anger. I grabbed Diego, put my arm around him and yelled at the bad man that Diego was mine and that we were married. We started to walk off and the man grabbed my ass. I lost it. I told him to fuck off and he said the same to me. He grabbed Diego and told him where he was going to bed with him. I grabbed Diego's arm where he had a hold of it, yanked it towards me and yelled "No!" Thank goodness, a few guys saw what was happening and ran to our rescue. They followed us most of the way to keep the bad man away. We brought our wet clothes in and went to sleep.

Monday, November 8

I was very relieved to be on the train back to Tetuan. Glad to be out of that fucking hell hole. Things have changed a lot since Humphrey was there. We go to the mountains.

Friday, November 12

Many days to catch up. When we got back to Tetuan, we stopped at a café and had a coffee. I suggested that we call Abdul to see if he can join us for lunch. Diego would not call, and I was too shy. Man, these mountains are so beautiful. We decided to get a cab to the bus station and catch a bus to Chefchaouen in the mountains. Well, it was fate that Abdul happened to look up from his breakfast and watch us go by in the cab. He chased us down and we got out. We went back to the café and ordered some breakfast. He introduced us to his friend Said, who could not speak English. But he was signing us in conversation. He said that he lived in Hiram with his seven wives. He wanted me to be number eight, and I said, "no way."

We were walking to Café Paris and talking when Said busted out laughing. It turns out that he did know English. That night we hung out at the video store and drank beer. Said read my fortune. He said that I would meet my husband in the States soon, that we would have twin girls, and that Mom and Dad would get back together if I bought Dad a "hand" pendant and Mom a carpet. I kind-of knew that they were roping me in again to buy more, but I didn't care. He said that the five fingers keep bad spirits away. He said that I could tell no one, and he would bless the carpet himself to make sure. Well, I knew that was not going to happen, but I played along anyway. This was very important to him. He, Abdul and I went to get beer and the gifts. The pendant was only $3, but the carpet was $350. I hesitated a lot, but he somehow talked me into it. I cannot believe I have spent so much money on carpets. It is hard not to believe that these people are out to get my money.

Anyway, we got the beer and talked until 12:00 a.m. I told Abdul my relationship woes and he did the same. Said sat in a corner because he did not like to mix with alcohol. He is a professional soccer player, but was injured. We stayed at the same pension.

The next morning, we left Diego at the Café Paris and went to the post office to see my new carpet off. We still wanted to go to the mountains, but the guys said that Chefchaouen had a very bad drug reputation, and if it was stamped on your passport, that Spain would look through all of your luggage for drugs. They were right about Casablanca, so we believed them. Back at Café Paris, we met Mohammed, who had been out of town. After breakfast, they made some phone calls and took us to another mountain town on the beach called Oudlau.

The taxi there was so pretty with the mountains jutting out of the sea so blue. We met more of their friends there at restaurant Grenada. They seem to be very popular. I ate a fish fried whole, that was a first. I bet they don't sell frozen fish sticks here. Then we drank a warm beer at a bar patio. We then walked up on the mountain where Rachid lives and met his kids coming out of school. They got such a kick that Diego had three earrings, they could not stop laughing. We chatted with them for a while, such beautiful children. We toured Rachid's farm and I got a picture with his outdoor oven where they bake bread. We call them an horno. We saw his goats, and then watched the sunset on the mountain. So bonita! We went back to the bar and talked, and decided to stay the night. We rented one hotel room for the five of us with two beds and a couch. The hotel was very basic, but it was right on the water and we could easily hear the waves break hard on the beach. We ate fish again, drank wine, and talked politics and war until 2:00 a.m. One of my most favorite nights. As I watched Diego play Rachid at Dramar (like checkers), I fell in love with him deeper. I felt so lucky to have Diego and our new friends. I like Abdul's friend, also Abdul. He teaches Tai Kwan Do, plays the loud (a guitar) and sings very well. Abdul number two sang two songs by a popular, but outlawed, Arab singer about being born during a war and the love for your mother.

We came back to Tetuan on Wednesday, Nov 10 and met everyone at Café Paris. Mo started to convince us to stay another night and Diego got fed up and walked out. I had never seen him like that. But his motto is "we need to see more" and we had been in Morocco for seven days. It was time to move on. Diego offered that I could stay if I wanted to, but I would never be without him. I have grown to care about him very deeply, like I knew I would. We were in a cab for Puerta de Ceuta in thirty minutes. I cried the whole way. I surprised myself. We did not speak a word, but he held my hand to comfort me. We stayed the night in a very nice pension.

On Thursday, Nov 11 we took the ferry back to Algeciras and had a six-hour layover before we could board the train to Bordeaux, France. We left at 9:00 p.m. and arrived at 5:00 p.m.

It is now 2:30 p.m. on Friday, Nov 12. I am actually thankful for this long train ride, as I caught a cold and have a fever and needed the rest. As I look out the window now, the mountains are so beautiful. Diego and I have been very fortunate to have this compartment to ourselves the whole time. We eat our bread, meat, cheese, fruit and cookies, and we made love while traveling at 55MPH last night.

Saturday, November 13 — Bordeaux, France

Arrived in Bordeaux late last night and checked in to the hostel. Pretty nice, but guys are separate from the girls. I think Casablanca was a rare exception. They have a dining area where you can buy coffee and bread cheap, plus a kitchen with many gas burners for all to use. Got kicked out at 9:30 a.m. for cleaning and went to the flea market. We each got a sweater for about $5, and Diego bought me a hat for $8. He also bought himself two scarves. We went into what reminded me of a Wal-Mart. I tried on a pair of jeans that were $15, but they were too short. I decided that I did not need jeans, but a large back pack. I was so miserable carrying everything on my shoulders and arms with straps. Diego, of course, played the "I told you so." What do I know? I am an amateur traveler. I found one that I liked, but it was $91. I decided to think about it. Bordeaux has two very nice McDonalds, much nicer than the States, and they sell beer! The toilets are especially nice (they use the word for the whole room). I had to have a big mac for $3.20. It tasted exactly the same as the States. We passed them all the time walking around, and they were always full of clients. That night we bought a large bottle of Belgium beer (after each having a glass) and drank it outside of the McDonalds. Diego actually bought food there (he hates McDs and all American fast food). It was only an apple pie, but it was unusual none-the-less. We went to a café/bar (brasserie) where two English dudes with one electric and one acoustic guitar played all American music, such as Tracy Chapman and Jim Croce. They played *The City of New Orleans* song. I had a ball singing all of the songs. We each got a rather tall beer. We got back to the hostel by 12:30 a.m. (even though they locked the doors at 11:00 p.m.). Diego, having not eaten that day, was drunk and uncomfortable. He does not like the feeling, and he does not like it when I drink a large amount either. I was not sleepy, though, and happy and did not want to go to sleep. Luckily, I found two girls from Ecuador talking in the ladies' bathroom. They were both nannies and very nice. We talked until 1:30 a.m.

Sunday, November 14

Slept until 9:00 a.m. but stayed at the hostel until 10:15 a.m. We found out that the wineries for wine tasting are closed on Sundays. So we walked a little and had a coffee and croissant (as we do every morning) and heard church bells. I asked if we could go to mass, partly for the lack of something better to do. The French mass was neat and I followed pretty close. And the church was gorgeous. It was called St. Andre. We then walked to the bridge over the River Garonne. We ate a vegetable pie, bread, cheese and yogurt sitting on the river bank. We stayed in that night to save money.

Monday, November 15

We planned to go to Sete, a small village in southeast France Diego had heard about, so we lugged our luggage to the train station and stored it in a locker. We went to the House of Wine for the wine tasting, but it was not until 3:30 p.m. So to kill time, we hung out at coffee shops (the first was very expensive and plush, with live jazz) and I read my newspapers. I read *USA Today* and *The European*, which is neat because it has unbiased views of Clinton and the USA. Diego wrote post cards. A cup of coffee was over $2! We were there the better part of an hour and then went to another coffee shop and sat outside in the bright sun with a beautiful church to gaze at. My hormones were going nuts that day (maybe too much caffeine) and I had to masturbate in the bathroom. It worked. I felt better.

The wine tasting was interesting. First a twenty-minute video then we tasted three wines from very dry to very sweet. My favorite, of course, was the sweet. It was called Sainte Croix-du-Mont which is the mix of grape varieties from a region, not a brand. The place was called Mason de Vin du Bordeaux (The House of Wine of Bordeaux). We decided to stay one more night, so we went to buy my backpack so we could hitchhike the next day.

Tuesday, November 16 – Back to Genève

Woke very angry. I could only fit the Moroccan bag in the backpack, so I was not much better off than before spending $91! I said I wanted to take the train to Geneva to drop off all unnecessary shit. Diego obliged. Mi consuelo. He sacrificed Sete for my comfort. We opted for a six-hour layover in Paris and went to a huge, beautiful church on a hill called Sacre Coeur and then to the Eiffel Tower. But we did not go up because it was $9. We did a huge circle of Paris on the subway. I love Diego for being so knowledgeable about touristing. I know it is his profession, but still. We arrived in Geneva at 11:00 p.m., and went back to L'Usine for a beer, DJ and Reggae. His kitten, Esmee, has grown so much. I am growing very attached to her, and her to me.

Wednesday, November 17, 1993

Walked and shopped all day. It is pretty cold here, almost 1°C. Listened to lots of music, went to a Thai restaurant, but they did not serve Thai food. Bought salad fixins for dinner and ate with rice at home. Had a dry red with dinner. Diego gives me his bedroom while I am here, and he sleeps on the couch in the living room. His mother has a bed in there. I wanted to ask Diego so bad how he felt about making love in his room when his mother is home, but I was just too scared. I was sure he wanted it when he said, "Let's go to your room." We listened to more music and looked at books. Then he said he wanted to go to sleep. I am fairly certain that he saw the disappointment on my face, but I said nothing. He kissed me good night and left.

I am unsure of my feelings, and confused. And, I am more unsure of his feelings. If I know that he is not the "one" for me, why do I want him? My sexual appetite surprises me. I even got jealous when he introduced me to his friend, Maria, today. Grow up, Della. Diego is your friend. Sometimes—no, all the time—I wonder if he is growing tired of my company. My self-esteem has always been so low. Why? I told him once, "in many ways we are alike, but in some ways, you are more like I want to be. I worry too much about everything. You are so care-free. Can you change yourself without changing yourself?" He had no answer. Why do I feel like I have to be loved by everyone? Why is it so important that he like me? I used to think from his post cards that he sent to me in Texas that he was in love with me. Now I know, he is just a wonderful person who can share his feelings on paper. But not verbally. I told him once that sex would inevitably bring us closer. It did. I told him this also, that I love him more now than I ever have. He said nothing. My feelings may be back-firing. He cuts me down a lot more lately, "Come on, think" and "I know more about your country than you do" and "I told you . . ." What is happening? Fight back! Don't worry, be happy. Try not to lean on him.

Thursday, November 18, 1993

On the train to the southern tip of Italy. Diego had an English copy of *Harold and Maude*. Very short book. Some of my favorite quotes: "The Earth is my body. My head is in the stars." "Vice? Virtue? It's best not to be too moral. You cheat yourself out of too much life. Aim above morality." "As Confucius says, "Don't simply be good, make good things happen."" "And this too shall pass away." "A cliché today is a profundity tomorrow, and visa versa." "There is a little bit of God inside us to show us where we have been, and a little

God outside us to show us where we are going." "Everyone has the right to be an ass. You just can't let the world judge you too much." "It has been my experience that it is kindness that matters, and kindness is what the world sorely lacks." "But—as everything will—the foe has changed. We have met the enemy, and he is us." "One laughs. One cries. Two uniquely human traits. And the main thing in life, my dear Harold, is not to be afraid to be human." "Oh, don't get officious. You are not yourself when you are officious. But then, that's the curse of a government job." I finished the book in a little over two hours, just as we crossed the frontier to Italy. People I know, places I go . . .

Tuesday, November 23, 1993 — Greece

Behind again. This journal is beginning to feel like homework. We got to Southern Italy on the 19th, a city called Brindisi. It felt like I was home, that part of me belonged there. I suppose it is my Italian heritage. Diego thought we should go to Greece first, then through Italy on our way back to Suisse. Got a ticket for a couchette on the ferry for $22 with my Eurail Pass. It was an eighteen-hour ferry ride from Italy to Greece. The couchette was nice, but too hot. They had the heater on max. We ate our sandwich stuff in the dining room. They had a cafeteria, but the meal was $10. Diego was sick, so he went to bed around 9:30 p.m. I watched *Trading Places* and then partied with the Greeks until 1:00 a.m. I met three French truck drivers—Jacky, Pierre and Bartoh—who got very drunk and repeatedly asked me to sleep with them. No, of course. On the ferry, the guys way outnumbered the girls, and the Greek boys acted like they never saw girls. Well, as truck drivers, maybe they don't. I got a lot of attention and paid for very few of my drinks. It was hard for me to be friendly because I knew what they all wanted. But I did my best.

While I was sitting and drinking with my truck-driver buddies, I asked a cute Greek boy to sit down and join us. Jacky said, no way, that there was friction between the French and the Greek. I should have left them then, but instead I tried to explain that people are just people, no matter where they are from. That night after I went to bed, the seas got very choppy. The waves must have been over ten feet, because I was awakened about twenty times. One time, my entire body was lifted off my bunk. Oh, by the way, they put Diego and I in separate rooms, each with four beds. Each of us was alone in our room. Strange.

Landed in Patris on the 20th and went to the youth hostel. We ate at a home-house and I had excellent beef and veggie soup. Diego got a Greek salad. It surprises me that the restaurant owners dress in warm-ups and always watch TV when they aren't attending to customers. The next day we took the train to Olympia for $5. This is where the Olympic games began in 400 BC. In 1829, they discovered the ruins. It is an awesome place. The next day we tried to hitch a ride to Tripoli, 100 kilometers away. We got a ride in the back of a truck after waiting an hour and got almost halfway there. We then waited two-and-a-half hours and finally caught a bus there. We then took a bus to Sparti.

Today we walked six kilometers to a beautiful little village in the mountains called Mystras, which means mistress—how suiting. I think about Leo a lot. It has many ruins, a whole village, from the 14th Century. Palaces, cathedrals, homes. I fell in love. I got very upset with Diego because not only did we not stay in Mystras, but Sparti, because his precious guide book said it was cheaper. But he had already bought two tickets to Tripoli for 3:00 p.m. that day. And Mystras was the most beautiful place I had seen yet. I cried.

Thursday, November 24 — Happy Thanksgiving

Today Diego is 29. Happy Birthday, Diego. Or, Joyeaux Anniversaire! I sit now on the balcony of our house where we rented a room in Mystras. It is a beautiful day, sun is shining, and we have a wonderful view of the mountains. Today is a day to relax. I will explain, but let me back up first.

For the first three nights in Greece, we slept in the same bed because there was no heat in the rooms and I used his body heat to warm me. On the nights when we had separate beds, I would go to his bed and he would wrap his arms around me so I could thaw. He is the best spooner I have ever slept with, preferring to be on the outside. So gentle and loving. But no sex yet. He is still sick. Maybe tonight. Anyway, yesterday at the ruins he said that he was impressed at the mountains, which you could not even see in Sparti because of the buildings. I said that a few hours were not enough to appreciate them, and he agreed and said we could stay the night and leave at 10:00 a.m. the next day. Well, given how upset I was, that just wasn't good enough. I told him that two people would never always want the same thing, and that we had been traveling every day since Italy. I can't travel like that. I told him to go to the coast without me, that I needed a rest in my beautiful city of Mystras, and that we could meet in Athens. After a long silence, he asked if I wanted to stay two or three days. I said yes. I was kinda surprised that he wanted to stay with me. I must ask him why. Today, we took advantage of the 70°F sunshine and hiked up the mountain next to a small river for two hours. We then took a two-hour rest on a hill facing the ruins. It was absolutely gorgeous. I was so happy. He thought to bring his book, though, so I left him there to hike home. I took a small dirt road instead of the one we took to get there to be adventurous. Like Diego says, "never take the same route twice, we need to see more." I liked being alone for once, and leading the way. The road ended abruptly and I was walking through a field. There was a lot of tall grass with stickers, but I didn't mind. I started to worry that I was getting lost, but then I heard the river and I knew how to get home. I found another walking stick, which saved me many times from falling. I came across some ruins and decided to investigate. There were three rooms, one with a three-foot ceiling. A large bird took off and scared the shit out of me. I walked the river some more and finally found the rock Diego and I sat on before going up the bank. One kilometer later I found Diego watching me from a bridge crossing the river. Butthole did not believe that we had taken two separate roads. I met him in town, waiting for me on a curb. He didn't have a room key.

Thursday, November 25, 1993

Left lovely Mystras. Although the Greeks in general are friendly enough, they don't pick up foreign hitchhikers. They love to use their horns, and they have no respect for their beautiful land as they throw trash everywhere, even in the historic ruins and rivers. Arrived in Nafplio by bus. We passed it because the stupid bus driver did not tell us to get off and we had to buy a ticket back from a close town. The ride was nice, though, down the mountain and around the coast. There is a castle in the middle of the inlet with no land going to it. Pretty cool. We got a hotel room with heat finally. We bought a cake each at the bakery and a candle and went to a bar to eat them with a shot of Ouzo for Diego and Amaretto for me. I sang him Happy Birthday and he blew out his candle. He told me that he wished to travel his whole life.

Friday, November 26, 1993

Gray day. We didn't want to risk walking up 900 steps to the ruins with the chance of rain, so we shopped and walked the streets all day. We got another room at a pension for $13 for tomorrow night. A whole $4 cheaper, but it has no heat. We stopped into a liquor store. It was family owned for 130 years. They make their own brandies, ouzo and some wines. The owner's name was Dimitri, and we talked a long while as we warmed ourselves with his space heater. He offered us one of his ouzos, and I bought a little bottle of Frangelica. At 9:30 p.m. he closed his store and invited us to go see his friend, Frances, who does mosaic art. Really good stuff. We all went to a jazz bar for drinks, then to an American music bar. There were no songs in English, but then not all of the music was American. Dimitri and Frances left at 11:30 p.m., but Diego and I drank and talked until 1:00 a.m.

Saturday, November 27, 1993

Rained all day. Yuk. We shopped and ate and walked all day in the town. We went to visit Dimitri, who suggested we go to museums and art galleries. We went to a museum that described the art of cloth-making in Greece's history, then to a gallery. Diego did not want to go back to Dimitri's store, but would not tell me why. I started today, so my hormones are not flaring. He taught me how to play chess. Now we are back in this freezing room at 9:45 p.m. I have been reading a lot, *Weaveworld* and now a Koontz novel called *Dragon Tears*. I have been having weird dreams.

Wednesday, December 1, 1993 — Athens, Greece

I am sitting on a ruin wall on top of the Acropolis. I must write anything. I am getting to know myself more and more every day, and so much of it I do not like. My emotions get so strong, and I cannot control them a lot of the time. So I cry. And then I get angry with myself for crying, and I cry more. Why is it so important to me that Diego like me? No, love me? Why does he make me feel so rejected? He did not want to make love to me last night. It blows my mind. He refused me. Somehow, I know it was more than just the last day. I fear that he is getting to know me—knows me—and likes me less because of it. I don't want to dwell on it anymore. I should never fuck him again, for me. God, he drives me crazy. What is important is that I love myself. Yes, there are things about me that I will try to change. To grow emotionally. But I refuse to be a different person for anyone. I should not have to. I want to enjoy the rest of my trip without all of these emotions in my head. This is a once in a lifetime chance for me. I have been gone close to sixty days now. Not many days remain before I enter the "real life of working in a career" world. How can I push these emotions out of me? They are a part of me. Part of the person I love, but I do not love them because they make me feel sad and many times angry. But on the other hand, maybe it is those same pools of emotions that allow me to love people, places, the sunshine, flowers, animals, all the wonderful things that God has given to us. Geez, I am crying again. I have an emotional pool bigger than anyone I have ever met. God, I cannot push them away. The good ones or the bad. I must love every part of me. All of me. Even the bad emotions. And deal with them as best I can. When I am in times of hurt, maybe if I write, it will go away. To go all the way through it. Let it live its course. Get in touch with it, know it and try to understand it instead of pushing it away.

Okay, so why is it so important to me that Diego want me? Because I love him and want him? If so, then the solution is to not want him. But there again, I can't change the way I feel. I can't push the good feelings out any more than I can the bad ones. Maybe there is no answer. Maybe analyzing is the wrong thing to do. I have gone full circle, and still want to cry.

So do something else. In learning and discovering and analyzing my own feelings, and hence, my own mind, I realize how little I know myself after twenty-six years of life. I picture that my mind is like the Earth, and if you travel from land mass to land mass, you learn more. But most of the time, you stay in one spot and live day to day. Not traveling. Not learning. So like a traveler in Europe, I am being a traveler of my mind. But there is too much to see in one lifetime. So I will possibly and probably never learn all there is to know about my inner self.

So with that knowledge, the hardest thing in the world must be to get to know and love and be with another mind (and Earth) for a long period of time. It is like trying to make two Earths live in harmony. Sometimes we sing and sometimes we make war. Because, after all, that other Earth-mind is traveling and discovering his own Earth-mind. And we are four billion Earths!

Thursday, December 2, 1993

Wow, my birthday is in a few days. We just spent four days in Athens. It is beautiful, but huge. Four million people live here. The air pollution is terrible. They say in summer, there is no blue sky. We stayed in an okay hotel with a TV room and a bar for $13 a night. And heat in the rooms. But we still snuggled every night. It rained for two days, then it was sunny and 70°F. Then cloudy, but no rain. The ruins and museums were awesome. Acropolis with Parthenon and four ladies. The National Archeology Museum was great. Wow. Then the National Park, Byzantine Museum and Mount Likavitos where the view of Athens was spectacular. Diego and I played cards in the hotel bar to save money. Met a pretty boy from Sweden named Peter there. He was the first man I really wanted to sleep with. No, second, there was the Moroccan train boy. We took a bus from Athens to the island of Corfu, and twice the bus got on a ferry. Pretty cool, man. We traveled all night and got to Corfu at 6:00 a.m. Ugh. We got a room at the Hotel Cyprus and I went to bed.

Monday, December 6, 1993

I am sitting on the ferry to Brindisi watching the islands and mountains of Greece go by. I can't believe this is the fourth day of sunshine and blue skies in a row. The afternoons go so warm in Corfu. I loved it there very much. I have to go back in the summer. Money is running very low—only $200 for Sicily and Italy. I hope it lasts five days. We had planned to stay in Corfu one or two nights, but it was too beautiful. The ferry left only Saturdays and Mondays at 9:00 p.m. We originally planned to take the Saturday, until we found out on Friday night that it was Friday night, at 11:00 p.m.!

Vacation is fun, but I keep losing track of the days. I must be doing it right. We had been to a café/bar called Espresso where they had MTV on in the bar downstairs and English-speaking patrons, so I wanted to go back. It was very small, so I asked if we could join two guys sitting at the only table you could see the TV. We ended up talking all night and getting fairly pissed. Larry, Dave and Al are all Canadian sailors who were in Corfu for ten days. There are 313 Canadians on their ship and their job is to sail around and if a boat looks suspicious they board it and look for weapons. They are part of the UN peace-keeping mission for Croatia. Pretty damn neat. They were very friendly and they wanted to take us on their ship, a destroyer I think, so Diego and I decided to stay the weekend. We met Al and Dave and eight others at Café Espresso the next day. We decided to meet at 6:00 p.m. to go to the ship.

Diego and I walked the beautiful city of Corfu. It has the largest square in Greece called Esplanade (Spianada) which overlooks the port. We sat on a bench and I wrote post cards. We ran into Dave and Al again as they were joining more sailors at an English pub called the Mermaid Bar. We waited until 7:30 p.m. at Café Espresso playing Scopa, then went to check the Mermaid Bar. Dave and Al had just walked in. They felt bad, but they had forgotten. They also had bad news, they could not have guests on the ship because it was not parked at the jetty. They also said Larry was sick. We stayed at the pub till it closed and had a ball. I met several more Canadian sailors, Charlie, Dave and others. Diego went back to the hotel to get his chess pieces and played with Dave. I met an older couple from Scotland, Margaret and Robert, who were not married but lived on a yacht and had been traveling together for six years. They spend their winters in Corfu. Must be nice. Robert played guitar and we sang. They introduced me to Nagib from Tunisia. Margaret wanted to set me up with him, but Robert said she couldn't because I had a boyfriend. I just smiled and agreed. Funny thing is Diego had also told several people that I was his girlfriend. I guess I really am, since sex implies a relationship. But mutually temporary/strange. I enjoyed talking to Charlie a lot. We discussed racism and life in general. He is very nice and down to Earth. Diego was challenged to a game of chess by a Greek local dude named Spiro (as common as John back home). Diego refused to play another game with the noise of the bar, so they went outside. It was humorous because they had a crowd watching them, including Dave who was quite pissed by then and had knocked pieces over several times. I got bored and talked with Nagib for a while. I missed Larry. He was the one who gave me my Canadian pin.

The next day, Sunday, we went to the new fortress (only 600 years old) because the old one was being remodeled for a summit. It was really neat. I shit in this one room full of soil. Cool. I don't think I had a choice in the matter. We sat at the top and read a while in the sun. We went to the archeology museum, but it had closed twenty minutes earlier. I had a small fit. We went to an old church where some saint was buried. It was beautiful, but the people all kissed the coffin in the same two spots. Ick! We then went back to the Mic Mac for a Greek salad (last one) then to the port to buy our ferry tickets. We stopped to buy condoms, but didn't? Diego and I made love the night before, only the fourth time not counting Mystras when he lost his hard-on, and we used my last one. It was definitely the best and very enjoyable. I got to drive.

The ferry office was closed, but we watched the end of a beautiful sunset sitting on the dock. By chance, the taxi to the Canadian ship stopped right where we were sitting. The big leprechaun we met the day before got on and told me that Larry was in the Hotel Atlantis right on the port. I went to say hello, and what luck, a Dutch ship had arrived that day, so they were allowed visitors! Yippy! We took the 7:00 p.m. taxi to the ship. We took a long tour and partied with Larry, Al, Dave and met Terry. We got pissed and smoked, all for free! I started with rum and coke, switched to beer, then in the upper hangar, drank Bailey's and milk. Yum. We stayed on the boat till 12:30 a.m. and took the last taxi back to shore with all the drunk Dutch and sang Sweet Chariot. I kissed Larry goodbye. What a beautiful and memorable night.

Saturday, December 11, 1993—Sicily and Separation

Wow. Five days since my last entry. From Brindisi, we took the night train to Palermo, Sicily. Finally, home after four generations. My ancestors from both sides are Sicilian. We did not get a couchette, but there were only three in our compartment and the chair reclined on both sides. We slept fairly comfortably. Diego and I even managed to spoon. We got a room at a pension. Next day we spent in Palermo and ate at a Chinese restaurant for my birthday. Tension was pretty high between us. Diego is tired of me leaning on him and having to make all of the decisions. I don't get it, since that is his job. We went to a neat museum that day with films, in Italian of course, but the scenery was bonita. The people in 800BC carved their village of 5,000 out of the rock in the mountains and there were many ancient artifacts found in the tombs. Diego chose to ignore my questions, so I was pretty depressed. He left me in the middle of a fight sitting on a street curb in Palermo. I was pretty upset. But he came back with a cupcake with a lit candle in it. I could not help but smile.

The next day we woke at 5:30 a.m. to catch the 6:15 a.m. bus to Bisaquino to find my family. That is where my mom's side is from. But December 8th was a holiday, La Madonna, and the busses were not running. We watched the sun rise and spent the day walking and shopping. We found a family pension and got the largest room with a nice view, four beds and a TV. We argued a lot that day. That evening we watched a PBS special on Chagall. Diego went out alone without a word.

The next day we rose again at 5:30 a.m. and caught the bus to Bisaquino. We sat at opposite ends of the bus. The two-hour ride in the mountains was awesome. We kept picking up students in uniforms at every stop. By the end of the ride, it was like a high school party on the school bus with laughter and singing from music blaring from a boom box. I was cracking up. [I found out the artist was Eros Ramazzotti, and later purchased his CD. Decades later, I feel like I am back on that city bus turned school bus with those kids whenever I listen to his CD.]

In Bisaquino, we went directly to the town hall and spent two hours there while two nice ladies looked for Maw Maw and Paw Paw's parents. I had to call Mom to get all of their maiden names. In the end, they could only find Maw Maw's father, but there was no record of marriage as she got married in the States. So no possibility of finding family relatives. Oh well, I tried. I did get a certificate of his birth and his parents.

We walked the beautiful little mountainside village. Population is only 5,000. We stopped at the cemetery, which was really neat. They bury their dead in huge family structures above ground. Most had pictures of the deceased and built-in vases to hold flowers or candles. I took pictures of some family names I recognized, Pizzitola and Salerno.

We had two hours to kill before the bus back to Palermo, as there are no hotels here. So we sat at a restaurant and talked. Diego blew my mind. He got an Italian newspaper and I asked him to translate our horoscope. It said to resolve conflicts and that no love would be found. I said, "Let's do it then." He told me that he was tired of "supporting" me, that he accepts the way I act, but that he did not like it, and that he wanted to separate. Of course, I was very hurt and close to tears. He did not want to go to my beloved Venice. He wanted to go to Nice to a Chagall museum alone. I told him later that I was not ready to separate, which is funny to think back to Mystras. We compromised and decided to separate after Rome. The bus ride back to Palermo was even more beautiful. Again, we sat separately. We took the train to Rome that night. The train got on the ferry!

Mainland Italy

Rome was exquisite. We went to the Colosseum, which was very cool. We walked around the park and ruins nearby. At another beautiful but modern park, we sat in the grass in the sunshine. We walked by the Vatican, but it was closed. That night we ate at a semi-nice restaurant and drank wine.

The next morning, Diego went to Florence alone while I stayed in Rome. I went to the Sistine Chapel and met a man from Atlanta who went with me and stayed with me part of the time. His name was Tom and he works for Coke. He travels all over the world, but gave himself the day off. The Chapel and museum were beautiful—no, beyond! Michelangelo's ceiling was awesome. The basilica, or church, was also awesome. I then went to Castel Sant'Angelo and saw a beautiful view of Rome. I walked to the Pantheon and it closed ten minutes before I got there. Oops. I walked all the way back to the train station, about forty-five minutes, and caught the last train to Florence. Diego met me at the station all smiles. He took me to the hostel and then we went to an Irish pub for a beer. He kissed me goodbye in the pub, as he had to catch the 6:00 a.m. to Nice. I was shocked. I met a nice boy from Suisse working in Florence and we had a nice conversation. I left at 11:30 p.m. because curfew at the hostel was at midnight.

Sunday, December 12, 1993

Went to the Bargello Museum where Diego said Michelangelo's "David" was. I bought a guide and spent three hours reading and admiring. This was a splurge, because even though the museum is free on Sundays, the guide was $10. It turns out that Donatello's "David" was there, not Michelangelo's *David*. I sat in the sun a while at a plaza and ate a yummy eggplant dish, then shopped. Back at the hostel, I washed socks and underwear and talked with my four new roommates Samantha, Marica, Saski from Australia and Kate from the States. Very nice.

Monday, December 13, 1993

All the museums are closed today. I hung out with Saski and Sam. We shopped a bit and went to Il Duomo di Firenze. It is one of the largest cathedrals in the world and is made of gorgeous white, green and purple marble. The outside was way more beautiful than the inside. I got a caricature made of myself with my long, curly hair flowing out of my European hat that Diego bought me. It was a gray, cold, drizzly day though, so we hung out in the train station for three hours, as the hostel was closed until 4:00 p.m. I bought a cool brown and blue leather belt. The blue part is silk. Diego got a belt for half the price, but I hate bargaining.

I ate at the hostel, bread and spreadable meat stuff from Geneva and instant broccoli soup. I ate with my four new friends and met Marica's boyfriend, Greg. We played a game of spades, then all six of us played a very fun and laughable card game of spoons. We laughed so hard that people in the dining room asked us to be quiet several times, so we moved to the kitchen table. We broke Greg's pen twice. So fun. Tomorrow, Marica, Kate, Greg and I travel to Venice together. I am having a great time without Diego. Maybe we should have separated long ago. I am not as dumb as I think I am traveling alone, and I can meet more people on my own. I am very happy that I get to spend a few more days with my new friends in Venice.

Tuesday, December 14, 1993—The Statue of David

In the morning, all six of us went to the train station at 9:30 a.m., deposited our bags in a locker, and went to the bakery where we bought yummy bread and sweets. I went to the Academia to see Michelangelo's *David*. He was truly a masterpiece, and I stared at him for almost half an hour. I loved his expression and his curly hair. And the way his right hand rested on his thigh. And his ass was perfect. Also loved his curly pubes. What was he holding, though, a towel?

I was disappointed, though, because he was the only piece I really enjoyed, and I paid a lot to get in! They had four unfinished statues by Mickey, and they were pretty cool because it looked as though the figures were trying to escape from the marble. But the rest was Christ on the cross stuff, and if I see one more Madonna and bambino I think I will puke.

I then wanted to go to the park, but it was still sprinkling, so I went to the department store and spent over an hour buying one bra. It is really pretty, though. Medium blue, silky and plain with darker blue flowers. No lace! I paid too much, almost $20, but I put in on my credit card. I swear that card must be maxed out. I feel very scared going into so much debt. Anyway, I got out at 1:00 p.m. and I had to meet the gang at the train station at 1:30 p.m. But dammit, the sun was out. I went to the river and sat on the bridge, ate my apple and bread and fed the pigeons until 1:20 p.m. I did not want to leave Florence, but my beloved Venice awaits.

David Comes to Life

The three-hour train ride was nice with the four of us. We talked a lot, read and popped our ears when the pressure changed from all the tunnels. We finally hit the sea, then the one hundred seventeen small islands that make up Venice. Even though it was cold and drizzly, I was in awe and wonderment. We caught ferry #82 to the hostel, and met David on the ferry. He was going there too and asked if he could tag along with us. We rode for eight stops on the outside, brrrr. The hostel was the best I have stayed in yet. It is on a different island than the main ones. It is very modern with a very large dining room, kitchen where they cook good, hot, savory meals. And they serve a bowl of coffee in the morning with a strange roll included in the fee. The rooms are nice and have only two to four beds per room. The hostel also has a very nice bath/shower room with endless hot water! The girls have to climb eighty-eight stairs to get to their quarters, though. Why are the girls always on the top floor? The staff is also very friendly, as opposed to Florence where they sucked really big donkey dicks.

We ate at the hostel then walked in the sprinkles for forty-five minutes on our island. Everyone went to bed, but I stayed up and drank two tall beers. Even though drinking alcohol is prohibited inside the hostel, you can buy it here, go figure. I talked with Sylvester, Barry and Steven. We talked about guns in the States, football, and each of our professions. Sylvester is a successful and very lucky sculptor of wooden boxes. Steven is a designer of clothes and belts. But mostly we talked about relationships.

All three had fairly recently broken up from a long relationship or marriage. All I could add to the conversation was that I had had seven major heart breaks in nine years. It made me realize that that is pretty fucking sad, and that just maybe I am doing something wrong. But I am me, damn it. There has to be someone out there who will accept and love me for who I am and want the same things I want! That night while lying in bed, I tried to remember the order and reasons for my heart breaks: Fred was unavoidable. Ray, he got too serious, and was not meant to be. I suppose none of them were. Jacob graduated. Aaron was an immature butthead, but I scared him. Adam was such a babe, but I scared him too. My beloved Ricky, man I loved him, but we each refused to move cities to be together. My beloved Leo, I have never loved anyone more, but a wife and kids tend to get in the way. Jim I loved very dearly, but he wanted to go back to his fucking French ex from Paris. Jonathon, who wanted a serious relationship but was not ready for one, so he dropped me cold. Each of these men brought me to tears. Four of them had broken my heart beyond repair.

Wednesday, December 15, 1993

Woke, lovely shower, lovely coffee, but not comparable to the $1/cup cappuccino. The four of us plus David took the ferry to the main island and went to St. Marco's Square where there is a lovely and very large church. I guess Venice takes the cake for detail in carvings on churches. The high tide was at 10:00 a.m., so they had planks everywhere since it was too deep to walk. Pretty neat. David and I went off together, Kate by herself, and Marico and Greg, of course. We decided to meet at 1:00 p.m. for a cheap lunch at the university. I am starting to like David. We spent the whole day together. He reminds me a tad of Jim in the eyes, smile, attitude and profession; but he does not wear boxers. I had to ask. I think men who wear boxers are a bit more relaxed. David said he would stay one more night if I would. I said okay.

We shopped all day. I bought a Santa candle, a sweatshirt and a gorgeous mask. I found an ATM, but counted my money and decided I could not buy any more souvenirs if I wanted to eat. David, me, Marica and Greg played spades at the hostel that evening.

I feel myself already wondering what it would be like married to David. He is thirty and he likes Austin. But what the fuck is my problem? He turns me on. We massaged each other's shoulders. He opened up to me, and I opened up to him, but hell, I will open up to anyone. We drank a coffee. He wanted to know more about me. I definitely sense a mutual attraction, but what the hell is my problem? I gotta stop thinking this way. Tired.

Thursday, December 16, 1993

David and I ferried to the main islands with Marica and Greg, separated from them, and again met them at 1:00 p.m. to eat at the university cafeteria where meals were super cheap. David and I shopped a little, went to an aquarium and went to the campanile in the church. I took an elevator this time. We stayed there a long time while viewing the beautiful city. We took pics and video, David has a camcorder. We fed the pigeons and had a Japanese girl take our picture. It was the first time we put our arms around each other and it felt very comfortable. Then, we both jumped out of our skin as the huge tower bell inside the campanile began to ring right beside us.

It was so loud! We also saw some pretty cool stuff at the basilica of St. Marco.

After lunch, we all went to the Peggy Guggenheim Museum, which has modern art. But we somehow lost David ten yards from the museum and he could not remember the name. The paintings were very enjoyable. I loved Dali. But I was worried and concerned about David the whole time. We met him back at the hostel. Greg and Marica left that evening. David and I ate and showered. We tried unsuccessfully to find a bar on our island, so we talked at the hostel until 11:30 p.m. He asked me to travel with him until he had to go back to the States. He lives in North Carolina. I told him that I was completely out of money, that Venice was my last stop because of it. He said that he would pay if it meant that he could travel with someone. I was flattered, and agreed. We decided on Munchen, Germany. We call it Munich. Why the hell do we butcher European names? Why can't we pronounce it the same as they do? I mean, how did Firenze become Florence?

Friday, December 17, 1993 — Germany

We left our bags at the hostel and spent the afternoon in Venice. I bought Diego a Christmas / thank you gift, a green, wooden music box in the shape of an acoustic guitar. It was expensive, but he is worth it. David bought a belt and a kit to build a gondola, good wood. We walked along the boardwalk to a park and sat on a bench facing the water. But we could not see it because the fog was way too thick. We talked and listened to all the boats communicate. After a while, I asked if we could go for a coffee because my feet were very cold. He said no, and kissed my lips oh so softly. He held me in his arms and we kissed for a very, very, very long time. I looked deep into his blue-gray eyes and saw his affection for me. God, it was so completely romantic! Venice, cold, fog, the sound of the boats all around us, and beautiful David kissing me on a park bench. I can't remember a truer heaven. From that point on, we were lovers, kissing and touching everywhere we went.

When we finally left the park, we drank our last (and most expensive) cappuccino and went back to the hostel. We showered and ferried to the train station. We tried to get a last view of the grand canal from the ferry, but we got on the wrong one because of me and missed the grand canal. David was so disappointed. I was too happy just being with him to mind too much.

We took the overnight train to Munchen. We both slept poorly. The guy in our cabin was kinda strange. He was in a blazer and tie and had a very long ponytail. He liked to talk to both of us. He was friendly, but only when we were separated. We laid down, and when we kissed in front of him, he would leave the carriage. Worked for us! David mentioned that the tracks were old because we were being jerked around a lot. I said that it could be thrilling. He said it would be. I knew at that point that we would make love.

Saturday, December 18, 1993

We changed trains in Klatenfert at 5:46 a.m. Our next carriage was more comfortable and we were alone. We reclined all the seats to make a big bed and fell back to sleep. A couple of hours later, David woke me up to see the snow on the mountains, trees and buildings. It was beautiful. He started to film it and take stills. But I went back to sleep, awakening every once in a while, to see the awesome view. We got to Munchen at 10:30 a.m. We sat on the floor of the train station to try to figure out what the heck to do. Should we find the hostel? Lock up the bags and eat? Five minutes later a pretty blonde with an English accent approached us and said that there was a hotel ten minutes-walk away for $37 including breakfast because business was slow. We were both so tired, sleepy, hungry, and in dire need of a cup of coffee. David did not want to make any decisions. I wanted it because I wanted privacy with him, no curfew, and close by. We got directions from her, locked our bags, and went in search of food and coffee. We found her again and she led us to a stand-up deli near the hotel. We ate, and decided to see what it looked like since we were so close. I knew that was all it would take.

The room had a nice view, nice bath with shower and was a nice treat! But still no shower curtain. And the TV did not work. The windows were huge. We pushed the twin beds together, I did not like that. We slept for three hours, then woke up and made love for two hours. I was completely correct in my assumption from his massage and soft kisses that he would be wonderful in bed. We kissed for almost an hour before our shirts came off, and man can he kiss good! His attention to detail was amazing. He was so gentle, yet so passionate. He made all the right moves. But what impressed me more than anything was that there was no oral and no penetration. He said that he wasn't ready, and that he had already gone too far. He said that he hoped I wasn't offended, and I told him it was quite the contrary. It made me love him so much more. We showered and took the S Bahn to the Hoffbrau House Beer Garten. But it was 11:40 p.m. and they were closing. We found an open bar with pizza. We drank a beer called Export draft and it was awful. But the pizza was good and spicy.

Sunday, December 19, 1993

 We got out of bed just in time for the 7:00-10:00 a.m. all you can eat breakfast. It was scrumptious with cold cereal (oh, how I missed it, Cornflakes, Cheerios, Cocoa Krispies and a muesli with small chocolate pieces), yummy yoghurt with fruit pieces, rolls with butter, marmalade, honey, Nutella, bologna, swiss cheese, other cheeses with white crusty stuff on the edges, orange juice and coffee. It was definitely worth the price of the room (even though I wasn't paying). We went back to Marienplatz where there was a gorgeous church with a clock that had dancing figures at noon. We made it there one minute before noon only to find out that it only "performs" at 11:00 a.m. So we decided to return Monday to watch it.

 We spent the rest of the afternoon at the Deutche Museum. It was a technological museum with different departments including automobiles, trains, planes, ships, astronomy, chemistry, physics, musical instruments, ceramics, glass, porcelain, computer science, hydraulic engineering, electric engineering, technical toys, agriculture and many others. Each department had its history to present day. The automobiles were my favorite, as I took about twenty photos. We then went back to the Hoffbrau House to eat and drink beer, but David did not like the menu or the music. So we went to another nearby German place affiliated with Lowenbrau. I had a mixed sausage plate with Vienna (yup), German (excellent) and bacon with sauerkraut and mashed potatoes. David had a beef steak with onions, potatoes and then apple strudel with ice cream, which was scrumptious. We talked about his hang-ups with getting carded and people stereotyping other people when they look like they don't have any money, which happened to us until David brought out his gold card.

 We went back to the hotel then out to a nearby bar for

two more beers. We brought one back to the hotel and drank it and smoked the last two cigarettes. I confessed to him that I wished we had more time. He said that there would only be a pause before we saw each other again. That made me very happy to hear. We made love again and again without penetration. God, he got me so damn excited, I was dripping. I wanted him so bad. When he let me drive I tried to let him enter, but he stopped me and said, "I am not sure about going in, just rub." Frustrated, I said, "You have more self-control than anyone I have ever met!" But I came anyway. For the tenth time since we met, he asked me what I was thinking or why I was smiling. I asked, "Why are you always analyzing my face? You are just going to have to find out the hard way." When I came out of the bathroom, his comments made me realize that he had taken offense, and he admitted it. But he said he knows he shouldn't, and that I will tell him when I am ready. I could not tell him that I held back to try not to get too close to him, so that I would not hurt as bad if he dumped me, or if I never saw him again. Thinking this made me cry and he held me tight until I fell asleep.

Monday, December 20, 1993—Back to Geneva

As I gazed in awe at Michelangelo's *David* in Venice just six days ago, I wanted to hold and caress and kiss him. My David came to life. Same curly hair, same chest, same arms, but twice the member. I have known him barely a week, but I have fallen . . . again! I am scared shitless that my fragile heart will be broken again. But I am willing to take that risk if it means I have a chance to spend my life with him. I know that sounds ludicrous, but when you have a gut feeling, you have to take a chance.

It is dark on the train now. I am on my way back to Geneva, alone. Germany is beautiful with the cute A-frame houses and rolling hills. I have been crying on and off (mostly off) all day as I journaled and watched Germany speed by. David took the 10:44 a.m. to Berlin to see the Berlin wall for three hours, then another eight-hour train to Frankfurt where he leaves for North Carolina tomorrow morning. He begged me to go with him to Berlin, but I could not because I only had one last trip left on my Eurail Pass and I can't travel past midnight. And it would have cost $165 to rail from Berlin to Geneva. Plus, he was only going to be there for three hours. If only I had changed the number to make it look like I had one more day. Fate? Or bad luck? I tried so hard not to cry as we hugged and kissed goodbye near his track. It didn't work. He sniffled too.

I know that I will see him again. We talked about me going to North Carolina on my way home from Europe if I don't find a job here. He also wants to come to Texas sometime next year. I know that I love him and I know he loves me. He is like me in many ways, casual and affectionate. He had no problem kissing me on the subway. And he says I make him laugh, which is something I noticed our first day together in Venice. God, I have been fatally wrong so many times before. Please don't let me be wrong about my David. He left me with a liter of water, seven Dutch Marks, a package of chewing cough drops, and his phone number in North Carolina. Did I will this to happen? Is it fate? Is there another broken heart in store for me? I am also scared that if we do give it a whirl, I will grow tired of him. Will I break his heart? This is just as bad. But I do know that right now, at least I think I miss him. Damn, we didn't get a chance to know each other. Or, should I be sure now? No, how can I be? Oh, my David, my statue come to life, are you for me? Am I for you?

OFF TO EUROPE, BACK TO MYSELF

Tuesday, December 21, 1993

David got to NC today. I spent time unpacking in Diego's room, organizing and washing. Then, Diego's Italian friend, Dario, came over and played some electric guitar. We went to some unemployment office, then for a hot chocolate (chocolat chaud in French), to a store, then back home to bake a carrot cake and play more guitar. Diego went out and could not take me, or would not take me and would not say why. So Dario and I went out for a beer, then to his friends' apartment for another beer. The fun part was that he could not speak English. We took a dictionary and had slow conversations. I had a good time with Dario. He is a genuinely sweet-natured person. No wonder he has a girlfriend. She lives in Italy. Lucky gal.

Friday, December 24, 1993 — Merry Christmas

Joyeaux Noel, as they say in French. It is very strange being away from my family at Christmastime. When I woke this morning, I wanted to hug Mom very badly. I guess I miss her most of all. I should tell her. I will. Our family is so much more affectionate than Diego's. I didn't even get a "Merry Christmas" in any language, even after I said it. I need a hug from someone. Anyone. But I have learned the hard way not to show any affection towards Diego. He has shown me zero affection since I arrived in Geneva. He is still his mean, old self, always finding fault in everything I do and say. Sometimes I really hate him. But at the same time, I do love him dearly as a friend. It is humorous to think back to the time when he told me that I was his girlfriend, in Morocco, I think. Ages ago! I am pretty sure that he suspects something romantic happened between David and me. I told him the truth when he asked me if we stayed at the youth hostel in Munich. I do not lie. Also, when David called me two nights ago at 12:30 a.m., I offered no info; which says more than if I had. There goes the old saying, "you say more by what you don't say." I am sure that he is not heart-broken. The way he treats me sometimes, I wonder if he even wants me as a friend. I feel like such a burden to him living here. On our trip, I told him several times that he hurts my feelings when he treats me like a child. He never apologized or even offered any explanation. Well, only in Bisaquino. He is singing now. He always seems happy. So strange for such a mean person. Maybe part if it is just the European attitude, on top of the Diego attitude.

Anyway, enough about that. It is Christmas, damn it. We had a wonderful day yesterday. Diego was gone for an appointment when I woke. I had fun getting lost in the snow for an hour. The flakes were so big! Diego came back at 2:00 p.m. and we made another carrot cake. Well, he made the cake, I shredded carrots. Dario came to visit at 5:00 p.m.. We went to St. Pierre's Cathedral (with the tall steeple that we climbed) on my request for a wonderful Christmas concert by the Trinity Choir and ten bible readings about the birth of Christ. They sang Christmas songs in English and part of Handle's Messiah, which I know from my days in high school choir. We sat very close and I sang my heart out. Oh, how I miss choir with four-part harmony! I was in pure heaven. And I miss my choir director. I even dreamed about him and a high school choir friend last night. I should look her up.

When we left the church, it was snowing again with even more humongous flakes. We walked all the way home in the snow and threw some snowballs. We talked, and I was happy being with him. We got back to the apartment, prepared and ate a lovely Christmas Eve dinner with his mother, Preciosa. We had these small, flat cheese pancakes with a martini for appetizer. Then whole fried trout stuffed with ham and garlic, boiled potatoes with ham and onions, a salad I made with oil and vinegar, and white wine for dinner. Then mocha-vanilla ice cream for dessert. Mmmmm. Diego had to take my bones out for me. He had also removed my bones in Oudlau. "You never learn," he says to me. We burned my Santa candle I bought in Venice and listened to Christmas music, Handel and various other classical selections. It was so nice.

Then, Diego and I took the car to see his friend Adriana, her boyfriend Hussain and their daughter Michelle. We had champagne, and Adriana made us eat ham and duck pate with bread and cheese. She was very sweet and did not seem to care that we were stuffed from dinner. Then Cognac with Black Forest cake and Amaretto cookies. Mmmmm. She speaks a bit of English and we had a very nice two-hour visit. I was very surprised when Diego asked me if I wanted to go have a drink and hear a band. Why not? The place was called a "Squat," in a very old building of subsidized apartments where bands play in the basement. Wow. Sometimes I am so attracted to him. Diego told the door man that I was from the States, we were traveling and didn't have much money, so he let us in for half price. Always the bargainer. The first band was awesome. Five guys: a stand-up bass, a violin, an accordion, a saxophone and a banjo! Only in Europe. They played Russian dance stuff and sang in English, Spanish and Italian. Very enjoyable. The second band was pretty good, but I hated them. Heavy metal and screaming. Two songs were good. The evening ended perfectly when on the drive home (yes, it is my home) at 4:30 a.m., Pink Floyd's *Wish You Were Here* was on the radio.

Saturday, December 25, 1993

We spent Christmas evening with Diego's mother, aunt, brother, Jose and his brother's wife, Patricia. Jose and Patricia both speak English, and Patricia was very kind to summarize much of the French conversation. Diego got me a pocket French/English dictionary and a novel. I gave him his music box that I bought in Venice.

Tuesday, December 28, 1993

I am starting soon, any hour now I think, and my emotions again are going crazy. I yearn so much for a friend. Someone to talk to who actually wants to talk to me. Diego got me so angry Christmas Day that I decided to leave the very next day. I called my former roommate's sister, but she lives in the boonies and I would have no way around. I finally talked to Diego about it that evening. He said that I got on his nerves, but that he would try to be more gentle with me. We had a good, long talk over three beers (well, Diego had one). But I was foolish to think things would change. We spent all day apart, yet now he still won't talk to me. He doesn't want me here, and I detest being where I am not wanted. And it hurts. He seems sincere when he says that he wants me to find a job, and not to worry about the living arrangement until then. And I am aggressively seeking an au pair (nanny) position here in Geneva. But in the meantime, I am so unhappy. My only friend in Geneva is not a friend to me. I want the States. I want someone who will love me. I want David. But most of all, I want away from Diego. But why should I let him make me not want to find a job here? It is not fair. He stayed with me plenty while he was in the States. I am sad and unhappy, and the next few days will only get worse because of my mood swings and out-of-control emotions that come with my period. Yet, I don't want to feel sorry for myself. But is it so wrong to want to be happy? Is it so wrong to want to be away from someone who ignores me? WE NEED TO SEPARATE!

Saturday, January 1, 1994

Happy New Year! Wow, have things turned bass ackwards and more complicated, and it has only been three days. Wednesday was good, we did not see each other at all. He babysat his niece and I walked back to the old town to visit the oldest house in Geneva, called Maison Tavel. I enjoyed it very much. It was like a tiny, wooden castle. They had a lot of the original stuff—stove, tableware, beds, chairs, paintings—and also models and old photos of Geneva from the 1860's and on. I saw one photo from the 1890's where Lake Geneva was completely frozen over and people walked across it. Cool. I then went to a museum nearby with an African exhibit—masks, jewelry and ceremony stuff. It was really cool. I bought Liza, Diego and myself a postcard. Then I went to the Manora Restaurant at the Placette to an English-speaking club meeting called Six to Eight. I had a lovely time chatting with people from all over the world. It was so nice to speak my language with someone other than Diego. I met Leslye from London who is 55 and we went to have a couple of beers and talk. I told her all about my problems with Diego, and she told me her men problems. Then another lady from 6-8 showed up and complained to us how hard it was to find a single, Suisse man. She seemed desperate and sad. When I came home, Diego was already in bed.

Thursday, I went to the UN. An intern showed me around. Then, Diego took me to his friend's apartment. We smoked some hash and listened to music. Then Diego, Dario and I went to a café, then to a restaurant to eat. Dario and I got a pasta dish to share that was divine. The walk home was very long. I loved spending time with those two. They are both good-looking in their own way. Dario is extremely Italian and has hair like mine. What cute kids we could have. And he is genuinely sweet. And Diego was being his funny self, and being very kind to me. He talked and translated a lot, and didn't seem to mind. I began to fall in love with him again. Oh Shit! We still argue, but I don't take it personally anymore. I just tell him he is full of shit and argue my case. Things are going well and I don't want to leave. How I wish I knew if he thinks of me romantically at all. He never even kisses me on the cheek anymore. I am fairly certain he thinks we are better just as friends. So why am I feeling this way towards him? Damn it. We never agree. Funny, I even enjoy arguing with him now. Help! Dario was too tired to walk home, so he stayed with me in my bed. Diego gave me a look of warning, which I resented, like I would start something. If I only knew how I felt about him. Dario and I did not even snuggle. We both slept very little, though. He rubbed my elbow, but I did not respond.

Next day, Friday, New Year's Eve. Yippy Skippy. I did not even know until Diego told me. We hung around the house all day. Then, Maria came over and at 7:00 p.m., the four of us went out. It was raining and gross. We walked for almost four hours. My black shoes I got in Barcelona are actually water proof! We tried several places and finally ended up at a pub in Carouge, the next town. I can say that it was one of my funnest NYE celebrations. Bonne Annee! The people got drunk and crazy. At midnight, there was a tiny countdown, then everyone in the place kissed each other. Diego hugged me tight. I drank Adelscott, my newest favorite beer. It is a sweeter beer made with peat-smoked whisky malt. Dario and I smoked some hash before midnight. I was feeling happy. Poor Diego had to translate all evening. Maria did not have as much fun. She never drinks and was very tired. Also, her shoes were not waterproof, so her feet were wet. We stayed out until 3:00 a.m., then took a taxi home. Dario stayed over again, but tonight I was in for a surprise. We snuggled all night. He woke me up at sunrise kissing me. He even felt me down there when I was on the rag. He wanted to make love to me, but I told him with the "bible" that it was too fast and too soon. Earlier that night I had asked when his girlfriend was coming to Geneva. He said that he didn't know, and told Diego to translate that girlfriends come and go. I had no idea till sunrise that he liked me so much. I am in BIG TROUBLE. He just came into the living room and kissed me. I am very confused and sad:

1. I do NOT want to be the female to come between a friendship that is over twenty years old.
2. What about this alleged girlfriend?
3. The fact that he made a move on me leads me to believe that he asked permission from Diego first, who obviously said that Dario could have me, which means that Diego does not want me romantically.
4. What the hell am I? Someone to trade?
5. I am definitely still in love with Diego. This is a biggy.
6. What if I do fall in love with Dario? I am just setting myself up for yet another heartbreak when I leave.
7. What about David? How do I really feel about him?
8. Do I want Diego only temporarily until I leave? Are we all pawns?

No answers, only questions. I am only certain that of three men, two want a relationship with me, but I want the one who does not want me. Of course, it has to be that way. Murphey's Law says so. God, how I want to talk to Diego. But what the hell do I say? I am fairly certain that it would be a big mistake to tell him how I feel about him now. And what do I do about Dario? Do I pursue this relationship or nip it in the bud? What will happen the next time he wants to make love to me? What makes it even more difficult is that we can barely communicate. How can I tell him how I feel? And how do I feel? I keep thinking about how David would not allow penetration, and how I did. I was so impressed with that. But Dario wanted to and would have. He did, however, stop to make sure, and even got up to get the bible (our dictionary, so dubbed). I know in my head, not my heart, that I would not be happy married to Diego. He gives no public affection. Scratch that, there was the pub in Florence when he French-kissed me. For the last time? Probably. Yes, definitely. This makes me sad. Is he breaking my heart? No, he is not even aware of my feelings. I am breaking my heart because I want him. But want him how, Della? As what? A temporary lover? Well, that was the agreement two months ago. Yes, I want to be his lover again, while I am in Geneva. But for what? No good will come out of it. We will inevitably separate in the end. Or am I unconsciously thinking long-term? I do have to admit that I was toying with the idea of marriage. Am I fucking crazy? We are so different. I hate him sometimes. But I saw last night that he treats Dario the same way he treats me. And I told him so.

And, again, what about Dario? And what about David? Is my future husband going to be decided by a job? Is that bad or wrong? Or, if it is all up to fate, then why am I so worried? I must also keep in mind that it may not be any of these three. It takes two to tango, Della. You can't have someone who does not want you. Diego! I know you the best. Is that why I want you? Am I in true love with you? Or, do I just love you? The answers are within.

Diego, we need to talk. Will you let me in? Can I tell you how I feel? Doing that may kill my chances with him and Dario. If you find out that Diego has NO desire to be with you, is it wrong then to consider Dario? Would Diego tell Dario of my feelings towards Diego? Of course, Della. Maybe I should tell Dario of my feelings towards Diego, just as I told Diego of my feelings towards Leo over three years ago when he was staying with us in Texas. Maybe the best answer is to not become lovers with Dario or continue with Diego. Who the hell am I to choose between them? Is it unfair to choose one? I think that I secretly want both of them, at the same time. But not at the exact same time! Funny, Diego and I have talked about a ménage-a-troi with Peter, and Diego told me that he was looking for someone, a third, with Dario. Of course, this is all just fantasy. Isn't it? No, I can't do them at the same time. I want them both, separately. Whenever I want! FANTASY! But it is ok to dream. I am fairly certain that David would be the best lover of the three. But can I have fun while I am here? Then choose David? People do it. Is it me? Can I make it me?

Sunday, January 2, 1994

Diego and I talked alone last night. It was good. I told him that I felt awkward about the affection that Dario is showing me. He had no idea. He asked me if Dario wanted to make love to me. I nodded. He told me that I was free to do what I wanted and that he would not care if we became lovers. Asshole. But I suspected that. These damn Europeans.

I said, "But you two are so close. I can't jump from being your lover to Dario's. I can't. Ya'll think that girlfriends come and go, like a piece of cheese. Well, that is not me." I paused, then to my surprise, added, "Plus, I feel awkward because I still have feelings for you."

He said, "But it is impossible for us." Question answered. I figured as much. He said, "I want you to do your own things, to not always do what I do. I was glad when you went by yourself last week." *Je sais.* I know. But he got angry at me again for mimicking him while he was playing with the phone books at the phone place. God, he is such an ass! How can he get so angry over a stupid thing like that and not even flinch if I fuck his best friend? God, I don't understand these people! He added, "It is good that we communicate. And I am learning to control my anger."

I said, "Good, because it will probably happen again."

Then, he shocked me and said, "You never know if things will work out between us." Wow!

I said, "I can't help but keep that at the back of my mind."

"Why do you still love me?"

"I will always love you, Diego."

"Yeah, but do you still think we have a chance?"

I hesitated, but told him the truth, "The possibility is very small, but it does exist. I don't think that you think we have a chance. Do you?"

I got that "I don't know" face, then, "Yeah, maybe. We need to know each other more. It would be difficult, because we always argue. Ppppppt. I don't know."

I left it at that. Then he asked me, "Did you make love to David?"

"No, but we did other things."

"Kiss?" I nodded. Why did I lie to him? And I did lie, because even though there was no penetration, David and I did make love. For hours! Della, why did you lie? Especially when you know how these Europeans are—how Diego is. It would not have made a difference in our chances together. But I am American, and it would have made a difference to me. So I lied. I think I really do want to try to be with Diego. He really is a beautiful person, when he wants to be. And, perhaps, I did not want to give him any more ammunition to criticize me.

Monday, January 3, 1994

The tables have turned, again. I am positive now that I could NEVER be with Diego. And yes, it breaks my heart. I have been crying all damn day. I only hope that my period has something to do with that. Last night was a night to remember, always. Dario spent the night again, and he and I talked until after 1:00 a.m., using our bible of course. He asked me if I was shy. I said no. Then he asked why I was scared to make love to him. Oh boy, trapped. But we did not need to discuss it. I told him about my fears of his closeness with Diego. As I suspected, he said that he and Diego don't discuss women. I asked about his girlfriend, and he either said that he only makes love with her for pleasure, or that making love to me was only for pleasure. I got it, no strings. So I said okay, mostly because I ran out of excuses. And because I was on my fourth beer. We talked and practiced French and English for another hour. I told him that I loved Diego, that he was different and special. Dario disagreed about the "special" part. He told me that Diego is not confident about women.

Anyway . . . Dario was beautiful in bed. He shocked me twice. First by going down on me with Betty in town. Then by rotating and doing 69 with me on the first time. He came too quick (rotated) but continued for a long time after we cleaned up. His chest is hairy! I told him, not knowing if he understood, that he was going to make me fall in love with him.

    Surprisingly, I did not feel awkward at all over coffee with Diego. It was none of his business. Plus, he would not care if he knew. After coffee, he told me that he and Dario were going to get a newspaper. I missed my US news, so I asked him if he would pick me up a *USA Today*. He said, no. I asked why. He said that I had to get it by myself. Shocked and still dripping from my shower, I asked him, "if you saw a *USA Today*, you would not get it for me?" No, he said. "I don't understand!" "Don't try to understand." "Okay, I will not try to understand." "Thank you." And they left. I was so shocked and hurt that I started to cry. And, nine hours later, still am. I cannot believe that he can be so blunt, cold and mean to me. Or anyone. And, I do take it personally. *Je ne sais pas*. Maybe he heard Dario and me last night. But damn it, that is no excuse. Dario left and I started to cook my lunch. He came into the kitchen with his coat on and asked me if I needed anything. I said no without looking at him. He told me to have a nice day and left. I have been gone for four hours how, and plan to stay out four more. I have walked all over this beautiful city. I will call David at 11:00 p.m. I called Mom, who suggested that I may not be happy here. I have hung out in coffee shops and walked by the river and cried and cried. And I did not have any tissues. I had to blow my nostrils into the river, one at a time. I wish I knew why I am so upset. Maybe because I had made up my mind to try to make it work with Diego. And now I am positive that it will NOT work. I guess my big heart is breaking again . . . .Almost Della. Perhaps I will put that on my tombstone. "Here lies . . . Almost Della." But damned if I am going to put up with that fucking, total bullshit. I don't deserve to be treated that way. So I guess I am leaving Geneva. And I don't want to! Because I lose Dario as well. And my dream of working overseas. Damn you, Diego, damn you. Just when I was getting comfortable with you, Dario and beautiful Geneva with its beautiful rivers.

Saturday, January 15, 1994

This will probably be my last entry, mainly because the pages are running out in this journal. Also, because I need to leave the "travel mode," as David puts it. A lot has happened since my last entry, but more of the same shit. Diego made me bawl again yesterday. The night before, he told me that I was always around, like a piece of furniture stuck in a corner. For a while, things were going good. He made me feel like I was wanted. He told me that he hadn't wanted to strangle me in over a week. But I saw differently. Last weekend we went to watch a band at a very nice night club. The guitarist was Diego and Dario's guitar teacher. I had a great time dancing with Dario and Diego. Damn, he is so fun to watch. But mostly, I danced by myself. The whole time it felt sad that Diego did not want me around and that I would have to leave Geneva to save what was left of our friendship. Of course, the next day, I changed my mind, like I do every day.

The next week I hung out with Diego and Dario every day. Big mistake, but I love being with both of them because I love them both so much. I realized yesterday that I am still very much in love with Diego. For some reason, it does not matter that he can be such a dick. The other day, we were out walking and it started raining. I did not have my hat, which he has told me is not nice. He had two, so I asked if I could borrow one. And he said, "No, it's mine." He has also told me that my hair looks like an Apache Indian, and that he hates my fucking Texan accent.

I also realized that I am very jealous of Maria. She is his "little angel" while I am his "little pest who won't go away." He has started to give her a lot of attention, touching her in front of me. Ugh! He never held hands with me or put his arm around me, even when we were lovers. It hurts so damned much. I cannot be around them anymore. I cried for three hours yesterday by the river. He says that I don't talk to him about my ideas anymore. True, but only because I am scared of his reaction. I am scared that he will find something to disagree with or argue about. Which he has figured out. Butthead. Now he has grown more tired of me than ever. One time, Dario told me that my face was pretty, and he covered it with both hands. He says things to me like, "you are stupid when you . . . ," "you are wrong," "we saw you drinking beer at the club" and "Dario knows more English than you know French." At a restaurant once, he refused to tell me what he ordered because, "you cannot do what I do." And once he told me, "I need three months to cure myself of you."

I have to leave this apartment next week. I have an interview for a live-in nanny position. If I don't get it, I will ask to stay with my new friend, Liliane, until I can get my plane ticket home. We met a few weeks ago, at a pub, and really hit it off. I was sitting at a table reading the newspaper and drinking an Adelscott when she and her group of five friends came in. I had the only open table, and she asked me if they could join me. They were all so nice, and we enjoyed the rest of the evening together. Liliane and I exchanged phone numbers, and have hung out several times. I was pleasantly surprised that all of her friends have invited me in to their group. I have been getting to know them all, and have been hanging out with them ever since. They have invited me to go restaurants, home parties, and dance clubs. Liliane has even invited me to her home to meet her father and brother. I have to get used to every person giving me a kiss on each cheek every time we greet each other. Kind of nice, since I have no other human contact. Liliane and her friends have been a Godsend to me here in Geneva.

I spent very little time with Diego this past weekend, and he invited me nowhere. I studied my French verbs alone last night. Today, I went to the Red Cross Museum, saw Clinton's caravan leaving the UN, and went to a mass in English at the Basilica of Notre Dame. Tonight, Diego cooked me dinner and then did the dishes, shock! If he had any heart, he would realize that I am acting this way, always being around him, not because I don't have my own ideas, like he says, but because I am in love with him, and I can't fall out until I leave this apartment! But I also realized tonight in mass that Jesus is within everyone, and that I have to forgive Diego.

It is so hard to be around him now, because I know that I am not wanted and I know that I love him. I am so scared that I will say the wrong thing or something that he will find an argument in. I barely say anything at all, which makes him want to be around me even less. Catch 22! Dario, on the other hand, has spent the night with me every night for the last six nights. And he bought me a single red rose. He calls me his dolce fiore (sweet flower).

What I Learned in Europe—And What I Didn't

I did end up getting that au pair position in Nyon, just outside of Geneva, caring for a newborn and a three-year-old. I was there for about six weeks before they had to let me go. I was getting ill every week, and they could not count on me. Sometimes I was violently ill, with vomiting and the runs at the same time. My head ached. It seemed like I was always fighting a cold. This may be in part because my room was in the attic, and it was winter. And part of it, I believe, was divine intervention. God was telling me to go home. I did visit David in North Carolina on my way home from Europe, but the spark was just not there. The romance of Venice was gone. I was not upset about David. I guess that was not meant to be.

I learned a lot about myself. I had gone to Europe by myself for five months. I stayed in hostels and traveled by train to eight different countries. This was the beginning of a lifetime of world travel, one of the few truly satisfying feelings that comes from my soul that would turn out to shape my life for the better. Traveling to other countries, learning new cultures, and meeting new foreign friends kept my heart alive. And it was so much fun. Well, the traveling part.

However, I was still allowing men to walk all over me. It seemed Casey used every man she came across to repeat the love-and-pain cycle. But all I could see was that these failures were my fault. Here is a poem I wrote upon my return titled We Need to See More. It was inspired by my travel experiences and Diego's constant nagging to get to the next town.

We need to feel more
To understand others
We need to love more
To be loved in return
We need to cry more
To cleanse ourselves
We need to laugh more
To enjoy life
We need to see more of the world
Get out of our comfortable corner
Little fantasies
We need to hear more
And listen to the needs of others
We need to share more
And own less
We need to look more
And realize that we are not so different from one another
We need to create a world where
Everyone can peacefully live the life they choose

Chapter Seven

CALIFORNIA

DICK THE CON ARTIST

A few months after my return from Europe in summer of 1994 was my ten-year high school reunion. I was twenty-seven. The evening after the reunion, many of us went to a bar where a good friend from high school was bartending. While there, I met Dick. He was also in our graduating class and a good friend of my bartender friend. I did not know him at all in high school. I knew of him, but he hung out with the popular crowd. We dated for several weeks. I kept thinking, *There is nothing wrong with this man, everything about him is so good. He is absolutely too good to be true.* We had fun together, and were both interested in drinking and occasional drugs.

But my career was about to take off. I was finally offered a job at a seed company in California after sending off what seemed like a hundred resumes. I was not head-over-heels in love with Dick, and I thought that we would just say goodbye as I moved. I had been through a long-distance relationship with Ricky that did not end well, and I had just gone through hell with Diego.

And I was excited about my first job in my new career! To my surprise, Dick revealed that he wanted to move to California with me. We had only been dating several weeks. That should have been a red flag. But, as I have mentioned before, I did not even know that flags of red existed. He wanted to be with me, and that was enough for me.

Moving to California was huge. I was the first in my family besides my father to leave Texas. And California did not disappoint. It was beautiful. My job was on the central coast near San Luis Obispo, and so I made that cute little college town my home. I got a cute little apartment and rescued a tiny Calico kitten from the SPCA. I named her Calley, which referenced both her breed and the state where she was born. Little did I know that she would be my only constant companion for over fifteen years. I soon found a great bar near my home that had a few pool tables. I quickly developed a friendship with some fellow pool players who also frequented the bar. And I was grateful for that.

I loved my new job, and things were going well. I was finally in the workforce! The seed company had hired me because of my plant research expertise, which involved treating seed. The seed company crossbred bedding plant seeds, which they then cultivated and sold to wholesale plant companies. They had a dozen pounds of seed in storage that was recently bred and cultivated, but that did not meet their standard of quality. One of them was a beautiful white and purple Viola, which is a bedding plant. This seed was a particularly difficult variety because some genetic traits in its seed coat made it very difficult to treat. I designed an elaborate experiment and came up with a recipe to treat the Viola seed so that it germinated with vigor. This was a huge accomplishment, and to this day, Viola is my favorite bedding plant. I treated the entire seed lot and saved my new employer a lot of seed inventory that was previously unsellable. I succeeded in several other seed treatment accomplishments, and I was very happy.

Meanwhile, I talked to Dick frequently on the phone. He was still living in Houston, and we finally made a plan for him to move in with me in California. However, there was a six-week delay. His story was that he had a DWI, and needed to take a state course before he could leave Texas. The first date that he planned to leave Texas came and went. And then the second, and yet a third.

I remember being a bit suspicious that he was lying to me, and told him that he could really just stay in Texas if he wanted. This was a huge clue that I was not really in love with him at all. But he convinced me that he wanted to start a life with me. Again, I was missing red flags and signs.

Two months later he showed up on my doorstep unexpectedly. He told me that he had taken the bus. I was surprised, but we resumed our relationship where we had left off. I had made some friends at work, and I introduced him to our IT tech, Bruce, who had invited us over to dinner. Bruce lived on several acres out in the woods on a very winding road. He gave us a tour of his home, which he shared with a roommate. Bruce was very proud of his guns, and showed us several of his antique rifles that his father had given to him. We even shot a few rounds with his pistol at a sock in the woods. That was a first for me.

Dick got a job fairly quickly at a local second-hand store. Things between us had not gotten off to a good start in California, but we were working on it. He would not come home many evenings and I was beginning to be very suspicious of his excuses. I could not afford to go home for Thanksgiving or Christmas, so Dick and I spent the holidays with just the two of us in my two-bedroom apartment. I was not very happy with Dick, and I missed my family greatly. This was only the second time that I had ever missed a family Christmas.

About a month later, my suspicions solidified and I caught Dick in a lie. I started to piece things together, and realized he had been lying to me from the very beginning of our relationship, as I had suspected. I wish I had listened to my gut. Back at home in Texas, he had watched me hide some cash in my room. When that cash went missing, I immediately blamed Mom's boyfriend, Lukie. Mom was furious at me that I would accuse sweet Lukie, as was my sister. Dick watched my relationship with both my mother and my sister deteriorate as we had one horrible phone conversation after another. Then my neighbors complained to me that Dick had gone to their house without me, and had gotten in to some drugs and become belligerent. Things were beginning to add up. Dick was not the man I thought he was.

Dick and I got into a really huge fight, and I told him that I needed to move to a cheaper apartment—and that he needed to find somewhere else to live. Two weeks later, I got a call from Bruce. His antique rifles had been stolen. His roommate said that someone in a red car fitting Dick's description had been seen leaving the property. But Dick did not have a car, I pleaded. Bruce convinced me to let him come over to my apartment to look for his rifles. It did not take long to find two of them in the storage space under the stairs, hidden amongst a bunch of stuff that belonged to the landlord. I remember being a bit relieved that it was over between us. Bruce called his friend in the law and had Dick arrested. Two more of the rifles were found at a nearby pawnshop. So at least Bruce got his property back. The stolen red car with Texas license plates was then found parked a few blocks from my apartment. Dick was charged and put away.

I went to visit him once in prison. He asked me for some money to be put in his account so he could buy extra snacks and cigarettes. At one point, I said something that he did not like. I felt a chill as he glared at me with his cold, steel blue eyes. I felt the hatred emanating from deep inside of his soul. I sensed the evil that lurked within him. At that moment, every cell in my body told me to get as far away from this man as possible. I got up and left immediately. I knew at that moment that I did not want to ever have anything to do with this evil man again.

It was after Bruce and I had put Dick in prison that I discovered that my period was almost six weeks late. I went to the nearby Planned Parenthood and got a pregnancy test. My worst fear had come true. I cried hard when the nurse told me. Dick had lied and told me that he was sterile, so we never used birth control. The thought of adopting a child with a partner had never scared me. I thought back and knew the exact moment on Christmas Eve when we conceived. We were watching movies on the couch in the living room. Afterward, it was a feeling of knowing that we had conceived a child, but that something was very wrong. That premonition would become very real.

I felt mortified that anything could tie me to this cold-blooded individual with his hard steel-blue eyes. I sensed that someone who lied to people as the norm, and stole from people, and who used drugs daily, could not be in a stable state of mind. I sensed that Dick had a chemical imbalance, and was most likely dangerous. That is what I saw in his eyes. I wanted no ties with this man. Plus, I was on my own with no support. I had only a few new friends, and my family was so far away.

I still had many child-bearing years left. I deserved a family with a good man! Plus, I had seen first-hand how hard single parenting was. Even though it was an agonizing decision, I knew the instant that the nurse told me that I could not have Dick's baby. And so, I made the appointment and aborted it on Valentine's Day, 1995. Little did I know that this pregnancy would be my last.

I called Daddy and told him everything in a long conversation. A week later I received a letter from him:

February 25, 1995

> Dear Della,
>
> Sometimes I wonder about my sixth sense. You had been on my mind for days. I wanted to call but the time was never right. It was either three o'clock in the afternoon California time and you would be at work or it was five a.m. there. I am sorry I didn't listen to my gut and call anyway.
>
> For almost everything you talked to me about, I've been there. I know what you feel and my heart went out. I had a flashback to when you were in the hospital for your second eye surgery. You were just five years old. It was about three a.m., I was sitting there watching you when you awoke and said, "Daddy, it hurts." I wished and wanted so much for some way to transfer the pain to me. I feel like that now again.

Sometimes I am blown away at the similarities between us. I know exactly where you are coming from, I know what you want, what you need. I know it is possible to close both eyes and not see what the whole rest of the world can. You have so much love to give and so much capacity to receive it that it makes you so vulnerable. Been there—done that. The only real danger now is that you may learn from your mistakes too well and begin not to trust anyone with your heart, when all that it really takes is to learn to make some different choices in people. Easier said than done. If I could sum it up simply—and there is nothing simple about it—I would say: If you always do what you always did, you'll always get what you always got. That's something I heard years ago, and when I looked back on my life and found myself saying "Why is this happening to me—again," I sat up and took notice.

I am going to go way out on a limb and suggest to you that you go and talk to a professional. I bet your insurance will pay for it, or most of it. You need some support right now and I hope you seriously consider it. You have had some tough decisions to make. And if you are human, you are probably kicking yourself pretty severely for letting yourself get into this predicament.

I love you. I understand how difficult it was to even have that last conversation with me. I admire you. And I want you to do whatever is necessary to take care of yourself. We are both survivors.

Forever and ever, Amen

Dad.

I did not seek therapy, and I cannot even really say why. Perhaps I thought what most people think: *I don't need it. I am strong. I will get through this.* I wish now that I had sought therapy. I also did not learn from that lesson that Daddy was trying to get into my head. I continued to make poor choices and pour my love and trust into men who were not right for me. What I did know, and what Daddy validated with his beautiful letter, is that he and I have the most special bond in the world. He was so wise. My love for him seemed endless.

I suffered greatly through my relationship with Dick. More suffering came from the horrible dilemma and decision of the abortion that I was forced to make than from losing another man. Yes, I was back at square one in finding that mate that would fill my heart and make a life with me. But this time, the ending of the relationship was quite different. I stood up to Dick. I did something about his treatment of people. I held Dick accountable for his wrongs by putting him in prison. Perhaps, in the end, this decision helped him with his own growth.

The other very difficult decision that I made was not telling him that he had conceived a baby, much less that I had aborted it. I fantasized about telling him that I terminated our pregnancy, just to get him back. Did he have a right to know? Probably. But I felt that his rights were taken away the first of one hundred times that he had lied to me. And stolen from me. And stolen from others. I just knew deep within my heart that the best thing for me and my safety would be to completely sever all ties with this man. And so I did. And I felt no guilt. I knew I had made the right decision. But that decision would come into question down the road.

Marriage to Harry

Earlier, I mentioned my band of new friends that I played pool with at the local bar. There were seven of us, and we saw each other regularly. After I moved out of my apartment, three of us rented a house together. Harold, one of the seven, was a student at Cal Poly and had a nice apartment nearby. We all called him Harry. He had a good sense of humor and was fun to be around.

Harry and I would regularly be pool partners. He had

become a good friend while I was still reeling from the ordeal with Dick and the weight of the abortion. I was drinking quite heavily by then to cover my pain, and trying to move on with my life. Harry was a stable man doing well in school. I enjoyed being around him, and he, along with the rest of our "band of brothers," comforted me in a time of great need.

A few months after Dick went to prison, Harry dropped a bomb and told me that he could no longer just be my friend. He said that if I wanted to continue to see him at all, we would have to take our relationship to the next level. Coming out of such tragic events, I could not imagine losing the rock of his friendship in addition. So that night, we got drunk, and I spent the night at his place for the first time.

The next morning, he said, "Are you going through that, 'oh no, what did I do last night' feeling?" We laughed about it. But I kept my good friend. Except, now, just like that, he was my boyfriend. And I played very little part in that decision. About two weeks later, I discovered to my horror that I had contracted genital herpes. It was so easy to blame it on Dick, and so I did. I could not conceive that Harry had given it to me, even though Harry had confessed to me that he had sought a prostitute at least one time while in the military in the Philippines. But, it must have come from Dick. He was the bad man. Well, whomever it came from, it was with me for life . . . Almost Della.

You may be thinking that any relationship based on an ultimatum is doomed to failure. And you would be right. And somewhere deep down inside, I knew it, too. But I pushed that thought away, and told myself, *After all I have been through, I deserve this good man. He will never end up in prison.* Being with Harry seemed like a solid idea. Unlike the man I had just left, Harry was smart, financially secure, mentally stable, and a high achiever. And he loved me. And he was determined to marry me. He was just what I needed in my life at the time. I buried any doubt I had with the bottles of wine that we drank almost every night.

After Harry graduated, he got a job right away in Livermore. So after much debate and deliberation, I quit my first job out of grad school, and we moved up to the Bay Area. We got married in

Texas a year later. It was the spring of 1997. I was thirty years old.

My Texas wedding was a blast. It was outside, on a few acres adjacent to the restaurant where we would have our reception. In the beautiful exterior gardens was a well-manicured field of green grass surrounded by blooming Azalea shrubs, man-made ponds with coy fish, a beautiful bridge, and half a dozen loud peacocks in residence. The ceremony took place on the steps of a beautiful, white gazebo decorated with pink ribbon. My white dress was perfect, the weather was perfect, and the peacocks called to their mates during the ceremony. We got our scuba certifications and spent our honeymoon on the romantic islands of Tahiti. I was inside a fairy tale. I was finally going to get my good husband, white picket fence and raise 2.5 children.

But reality set in soon after we returned from our honeymoon. I remember sitting on the edge of our bed crying while Harry was at work, knowing I had made a huge mistake. I could not spend my life with this man. Unlike my past relationship failures, this one was quite different. The chemistry just wasn't there for me. It never had been. We were good friends, but for me, that was all. I no longer wanted to jump his bones, and sex became an act of duty. I realized that Harold had caught me on the rebound from a relationship of lies, emotional abuse, and an abortion. I tried for several months to make my marriage work. I truly hoped that my feelings for him would grow and that the chemistry would magically appear within me.

I finally came to the irrefutable realization that this was never going to happen. One night I began crying in bed while lying next to him. I quietly got up, went to the living room, and cried my eyes out. My marriage was over, and it had barely begun. I had failed, again. About half an hour later, Harry surprised me and joined me in the living room. There was no way I could lie to him.

"I can't make this work, Harry. I am so sorry."

"I have known for a while that you have been unhappy. I could see it in you." Harry said.

I was a bit relieved, but I knew that some hard times were ahead of us. The next day, I moved into the spare bedroom and began looking for a place to live. Harry became increasingly devastated, and made me feel guilty every chance he could. About a week later, I found a place to live, and showed up to the house with a moving truck with my new roommate. Harry had gone through all my photo albums and removed all of the pictures of him. Several weeks later, he called me and admitted to me that he realized that he had coerced me into the relationship while I was in a very hurt state. He told me that he understood that it was mostly his fault. We filed for an amicable divorce with no lawyers, and were divorced within a year. I say to myself that I cannot regret this marriage, because Daddy was there to walk me down the aisle. When I look at my wedding pictures today, I see a happy couple. There were no lasting ill feelings, but we did lose touch with each other.

AFTER THE MARRIAGE

I decided to remain in California. I had a good job in plant research, although it was low-paying. I thought, *Hell, if I am going to work in the Bay Area, I am moving to San Francisco!* So I did. Of course, I could not afford to live alone, even in the tiniest apartment, so I found a house in Japan Town with three other roommates who needed a fourth. I fell in love with the city, and I had a great time. I marveled that at the top of every hill was a park. A cool city ordinance stated that hilltops were banned from development. I learned to master the art of parallel parking and avoiding the street cleaners. The owner of that house wanted a bit more from me than just being a roommate, so a year later I moved into a house in the Mission District, again with three roommates needing a fourth. It was a light blue Victorian home, and I got the dining room with a crystal chandelier, at the back of the house.

I loved wandering around my beautiful city by the bay. Each neighborhood had its own look and feel. And the homes were so beautiful. On Saturdays, I would bring a blanket and a book to Delores Park and gaze at the stunning views of downtown and the bay. You could see the Golden Gate Bridge as well as the Bay Bridge from the rolling hills. Mom came to visit me, then Marissa, then my niece and nephew, and even Dawn made a trip. I got in to bicycle riding with some work buddies. I hated work commute traffic (and still do) and discovered that I could bike-ride to the train station in San Fran and take the train south to get to work. I loved it. I had an hour train ride with a twenty-minute bike ride on each end. The train had cars with bike racks specifically for bikers. So cool! Each bike was required to have a tag declaring your stop. It took a little longer than the car, even with traffic. But I got to work out, be outside, listen to music, and read on the commute. I was in heaven, and I soon developed biker legs. I got a gradient street map from the bike store, and would go a mile out of my way to avoid the steep hills. On Fridays, a bunch of us from work would pick a brewery in the bay area and ride or commute there. I had to remember to get on the rapid transit by midnight to catch the last train home to San Fran. I also got really good at biking under the influence, a skill I'd first developed in college.

Unfortunately, in the two years that I lived there, I did not make any close friends in the city. Plus, I went through two more boyfriends and two more rather harsh breakups. Both were heavy into alcohol and one occasional cocaine use, which I gladly took part in. To make things worse, one of them was a work colleague, and that is a nightmare I highly recommend against. There was no escaping him at work with his blue eyes and curly brown hair. And the other was a friend of a work colleague. I cannot count the number times I cried at work or in my car to or from. Or how many times I walked the streets of San Francisco in tears. I just could not escape my pattern of heartaches! Even for a few months! Was this my destiny? I just wanted to be at peace and happy.

Chapter Eight

HOME TO TEXAS

RETURN TO EUROPE

As time went on, I grew tired of having to always deal with roommates. I decided to look for a place on my own, but on my salary, it was just impossible. I craved connection to good people, and I eventually got super homesick. So to the delight of my family, I moved back home to Texas in February of 2000. I was thirty-three and had been in California for six years.

I believe my strong desire to move home was divine intervention, because one month later, Daddy found blood in his urine. He made it a point to tell us not to worry about it until tests were complete. I remember thinking, *I am not worried. Why would he tell us not to worry? There is nothing to worry about. Daddy will be fine. Why would he say not to worry? Well, now I am worried. No! I am not worried! Really! Nothing can happen to Daddy!*

That March, Dawn and I traveled to Europe together. I was so happy when she called me at work one day the previous December and asked if I wanted to go to London and Paris. The funny thing was, I had already told Helen (my longtime friend who lives just outside of London) that I was quitting my job and returning to Europe, and asked if I could stay with her for a few days. As travel was in my blood, it had become a habit for me to travel in between jobs. Now, I would get to travel with my best friend!

On day one, we dropped off our luggage at the hostel and went straight to the Eiffel Tower. After the tour, I was about to collapse from jet lag. "I need a coffee! A French coffee!" I remembered well how good the coffee is in Europe. We walked into the nearest coffee shop and ordered a cappuccino. Somehow, the US had never gotten that one right. Turns out the gentleman who took our order was named Dino. We got to talking. And flirting. And within the hour, he had invited us to dinner that evening with his friends and his cousin, Cristiano. I remember thinking how dangerous it was, but I said, "Well, this is Paris! Let's live!"

CRISTIANO

Cristiano was a sexy, Portuguese-French man twelve years my junior. He was full-blooded Portuguese, but was born in Paris after his parents immigrated. He had light-brown dreadlocks, beautiful yellow eyes, long and curly eyelashes, and a laugh that would knock your socks off. He was foreign, sweet, and passionate. The sexual attraction between us was tangible. Turns out that Dino was also smitten with Dawn. And vice versa. I will never forget, after I walked out of the lady's toilet, Cristiano was standing at the end of the long hallway waiting for me. I thought it was so funny that he had followed me and was waiting for me to come out of the bathroom. And I was a bit flattered. So I smiled really big. Next thing I knew he was rushing toward me and passionately kissing me! By the end of the evening, there was no need for translation. Years later I learned that, in France, smiling at a man in a bar or club is an invitation to sex. No wonder the French ladies never smile!

Dawn and I never made it back to the hostel. I stayed with Cristiano. And his parents . . . and his sister. It is not unusual for unmarried offspring to live with their parents until marriage. Needless to say, I extended my stay in Europe after Dawn went home.

After the Ricky-New Jersey fiasco, I had sworn I would never do a long-distance relationship again. But alas, here I was again. I will tell you, sex with this one was a blast. However, Cristiano was also immature, unambitious (he had no career goals), and a pothead. And he regularly stole from his employer and sold the goods on the side to make some extra cash. I could not condone this behavior; I don't care if there is a cultural difference. But he did have one interesting talent. This man could drive through the busy streets of Paris, talk on his cell phone, and roll a cigarette mixed with hashish, all at the same time. And driving in Paris is akin to driving in New York City.

Upon my return home from Paris, our major form of communication was email using an online translator. We were so in love. I was truly in heaven. Again. The distance, and the fact that he was French and actually living in Paris, was so romantic! Back home, I got temporary jobs from a temp agency in administration. This allowed me to work for ten weeks at a time, then take off again.

In June of 2000, me, Marissa, nephew Joey, and niece Alexa drove to Florida to spend three weeks with Daddy. He did not have health insurance. The VA had done a multitude of tests on his bladder, but was taking forever to come up with a reason for the blood in his urine.

In July, I went back to Paris to spend two months with Cristiano. He planned a camping vacation and we drove from Paris through France to Portugal, to visit both sides of his family. We made several camping stops with his friends in France before driving to Portugal. It was beautiful, and I was having the time of my life. One side of his family lived in north Portugal, and one in the south. However, I have never been so tired of being in a car! In one driving leg, we spent twenty-four hours in the car. Before I headed back home, Cristiano gave me a promise ring.

I flew back to Paris right after Christmas and stayed through New Year's 2001. We then started planning my move to Paris! It was scary, but so exciting. I had always wanted to live in another country! But I was so close to my family. It was a hard decision, but I had finally found my Mr. Right. Or so I thought.

That February Cristiano came to visit me in the States. I brought him to Mardi Gras in New Orleans, then on to Pensacola, Florida to meet Daddy. We had a great time. But then, Cristiano threw a wrench in our love engine. He wanted to change our plans and move to Texas instead of me moving to Paris! And live off my tiny income. I asked him about getting a job, and he said that it would be very difficult without a good mastery of the English language. When I asked him about enrolling in an English course, he was not very enthusiastic about that either.

Well, that was a wake-up call! Thank goodness, I recognized that red flag right away. It suddenly became clear that he wanted to live off me without getting a job. It was funny how fast I saw the true Cristiano. My heart just flipped a switch, and I was no longer in love. It just didn't feel right anymore. I chalked it up to the fact that he was just too immature, being twelve years my junior, and too unstable. I knew that we were not meant to be together. By the end of March, our relationship was over. Worse, Daddy's situation deteriorated, and became paramount.

In April of 2001, I brought my good friend Liza to Pensacola. We had a great time visiting with Daddy, taking boat rides and swimming in the bay. But Daddy was visibly frustrated when I told him about the breakup with Cristiano. "Do you see a pattern here?" he asked me. His words stung me like a thousand wasps. I had disappointed Daddy with yet another failure. I had no idea of the lasting effect his words would have on me for years to come. In my mind, the question meant that he judged me for all of the failed relationships I had had. And from that moment on, I judged myself for every single one of my failed relationships. And I blamed myself. After all, I had chosen all those "bad" men. Who else could I blame? It was my fault. A heavy weight called *blame* had been added onto my existing shame for sleeping with my sister's boyfriend/fiancé. And I kept all this inside. With Daddy's comment, Casey had a lot more ammunition against me now.

Chapter Nine

DADDY

In May of 2001, I was hired by a Montessori school as a middle school science teacher. I was thrilled to have a real full-time job with benefits again. And I was excited to teach again! I had done a little as a teaching assistant in graduate school. But this was full-time. Pre-Algebra and Algebra 1 came with the job. I was sent to training that summer.

That same May, Daddy turned sixty-five and was finally covered by Medicare. He finally went to a real doctor in a private practice. He had been going to the VA to save money, because he was not covered under any health insurance. Where the VA had found nothing with their dinosaur equipment, the real doctor immediately found a tumor in his bladder. I was angry that money had prevented the true diagnosis, and I hated the government for having faulty equipment at the VA. A surgery date was set immediately to remove it.

In July of 2001, my nephew Joey and I headed back to Pensacola to see Daddy. Marissa and Alex would be following the next week. Daddy had had a doctor's appointment the week prior to find out the results of the biopsy to see if the tumor they had removed was malignant or benign. I did not want to find out the results over the phone. When I walked in, I hugged Daddy tight. We parted, and I said, "Well?" One look and a nod from Daddy brought the ugly truth to the surface. He didn't have to say a word. His tumor was malignant.

"Well, we are just going to have to beat this thing!" I said. "Lots of people go into remission from cancer! We are going to kick cancer butt!"

The next day, Daddy, his friend, Rob, Joey, and I went fishing on Daddy's boat. He had a boat house over the canal right in his front yard. Daddy loved taking his boat out on the water. He named his boat *My Tern,* after the tern, a bird that dives into the water to catch fish. It was a play on words, as he had waited his whole life to have a house on the water with his boat in his own boat lift in his front yard. It truly was his turn!

Every trip, we would take the boat instead of the car to run errands or go out to eat. We always made a trip to Joe Patti's World Famous Seafood Market. They had their own fleet of boats, so we always bought pounds of freshly caught shrimp and fish, and two baguettes of bread. One was for the ride home. We discovered at one point that we needed two, or we would have no bread with our meal. Resisting the bread on the boat was like trying not to dive into the French fries on the drive home from a fast-food hamburger joint. Nearly impossible.

Our plan was to cross Pensacola Bay and fish at a sunken ship in the Gulf of Mexico. That spot was known as a big fish hangout. And if that didn't work out, there was another good spot in the Gulf that Daddy wanted to try. Well, the sunken ship produced no bites. We got bored, and started to head out to the Plan B spot at a fast speed. Suddenly, two dolphins caught up to us and began to ride the bow of the boat. They jumped for joy as the boat propelled them. They must have called their friends over, because soon there were several dolphins riding the bow. I quickly grabbed my camera, carefully scooted on my butt to the bow rail and started shooting. We were all feeling joy at the dolphins' presence and fun. At one point, we must have gone farther than the dolphins wanted to go, because the dolphins turned back.

"Daddy, turn around!" I shouted.

We made a wide circle and started going back the way we had come. It worked. There must have been fifteen dolphins at one point trying to get in those two sweet spots on the bow.

"This is better than catching twenty fish!" my nephew, Joey exclaimed. And we all agreed.

We must have spent close to an hour providing their propulsion before they finally tired of the game. It was an hour none of us will ever forget. Too bad Marissa and Alex were not there to witness this historic and joyous event.

In August, the doctor went in to remove the tumor from his bladder. "Will you do a scan after the surgery to make sure you got it all?" I asked him.

He claimed that was not standard procedure. He said that he did not see any more spots, and had high hopes that he had gotten all of the tumor.

Within weeks after the surgery, Daddy began having pain in his tailbone. The doctor initially said it was from a bruise that happened while transferring him to the table during the surgery, and not to worry about it. That sounded very unlikely to me, because the pain he was experiencing was quite severe and getting worse. It got so bad that in October, Daddy went back into the hospital. Tests revealed the unimaginable. The dreaded M word. The cancer had metastasized to his coccyx before they had even removed it, and was now spreading throughout is bones.

"This is just horrible bad luck" the doctor told me.

"I think getting you as a doctor was the bad luck. I asked you after his surgery to check for more tumors. You said it was not standard procedure. But the tumors were there!"

I was so angry. Angry at the VA, and angry at his new doctor. It was all so unfair! The VA could have caught it in time! We begged Daddy to transfer to Houston, where there is tons of excellent cancer care. But he flat-out refused. He would not leave his precious house that he had waited his whole life to build.

I stayed in Pensacola for a week. I remember Daddy telling me in the hospital, "I don't know how much longer I can take this pain." We talked about a plan to hold back some of his pain meds to take care of that, if it came to that.

But Daddy held on to his humor. One time he looked down at the hospital bed where there was an obvious layer of dried skin all over the sheets. Daddy had always had an issue with eczema. Skin would constantly flake from his legs if he didn't use lotion daily. "There is a lot of my DNA in this bed," he joked.

Daddy spent the next six months in and out of the hospital. We all returned at Thanksgiving and then again at Christmas break. The day after Christmas, Daddy began having trouble breathing and went by ambulance to the ER. They admitted him into the hospital immediately. This time Daddy was in a severe decline. I will never forget that New Year's Eve Marissa and I spent at Daddy's bedside in the hospital. He was on a breathing machine, and the doctors did not expect him to make it through the night. They sent two cots to the room so that Marissa and I could stay with him.

We put Cat Stevens' *Tea for the Tillerman* in his portable tape player and put the headphones on his ears. "He may as well go out with his favorite music," I said. This was one of Daddy's favorite albums. He even had it on 8-track back in the sixties, and left us with a few tapes and the player all those years ago. We did not know if he could enjoy or even hear the music, but he did lift his eyebrows once.

Marissa and I brought in the new year holding hands over Daddy's frail body and talking to him. And comforting each other. A few hours later, Ron came to relieve us. Ron was Daddy's best friend. They had started out as partners when Daddy first moved to New Orleans in the early seventies and they stayed together for eight years. But it had turned into a lifelong friendship. After he moved out, Ron would visit Daddy often and stay for months, both in New Orleans and Pensacola. I used to tease him and call him my "stepmom, Ron". He was an odd one. He was abandoned on a farm by his parents at five and was raised by another family. He suffered from severe depression, but he was mostly jovial around us. He liked to joke, and he called our painted toenails, "candy toes". He worked for many years as a waiter or bartender in the restaurants of New Orleans. On Saturday mornings, he always made us French toast and served it to us, lining all of the plates on his arm. He was wonderful, sad and difficult at times, but his bond with Daddy was strong. Ron stayed with him in the hospital during the nights, and Marissa and I spent the days with him. That New Year's Eve night, she and I left the hospital exhausted and emotionally drained. We had said our goodbyes.

By some miracle, and to even the doctor's surprise, Daddy made it through the night to bring in 2002. And then he made it to January 2nd. Then, day by day, he actually got better! We asked him if he remembered opening presents on Christmas day, and he said no. So, we rewrapped his presents and Marissa, Joey, Alex and I brought them to him in the hospital the next day so he could open them again. We all really enjoyed that day. They sent him home from the hospital on January 10. I left for home the next day. As a teacher, it was hard to be away from my classes for so long.

We all returned in February for a long weekend. My aunt, a devout Catholic, had asked Daddy if he would talk to a priest before he died and while he was feeling better. Probably something about last rites and all. My father was not involved in any organized religion. He was raised Catholic, and even spent some time in the seminary before college. But I think the Catholic church's disdain for homosexuality was a sore spot for him. He had to live the way he was born. But to please his sister, he agreed, and the Catholic priest came to the house for a visit.

The next day, I asked if he wanted to talk about the visit. Daddy was surprisingly very open about the conversation. Daddy had asked the priest if he could be absolved of his homosexuality so that he could go to heaven. The priest said no. Homosexuality was a sin. That priest had basically told my Daddy, on his death bed, that he was going to Hell. Let me say that no human on this planet has the right or ability to make such a claim! I personally do not believe in Hell. I believe that we all go to the same place when we cross over. We are met by loved ones that we wish to meet with who have passed before us. For those who do believe in Hell, that is great. But make no mistake, the place that your soul will finally reside is between two entities only, you and your Higher Power. This Catholic priest had told my beloved Daddy that whom he chose to love is a sin worth spending eternity in flames. Well, I believe that this priest was conforming to his own human agenda. Not the spirit world's, and certainly not Daddy's. He was politely asked to leave my father's house.

Daddy had asked me during that trip to go with him to a chemo treatment, which he went to every day. I kept finding excuses not to. On the last possible day that we were there, I went to the mall with my sister instead. We left for Texas the next day. I had a feeling that there was something important that he wanted to discuss with me. I still hold guilt that I never would find out what that was.

On March 24, we got a call from Ron that the end was near. So we quickly packed and left for Pensacola the next day. My aunt (Daddy's sister), uncle, and cousin also made the trip. They had set up a gurney in Daddy's living room so that he could see his canal and his boat. Hospice was with him around the clock, and we were grateful for that. Daddy was mostly out of consciousness and on a morphine drip. I had brought the book *Tuesdays With Morrie,* about a journalist visiting with a man dying of cancer every Tuesday until the end. Marissa and I would lie on a blanket in the front yard next to the canal and read aloud to each other. Appropriate, and we got some comfort talking about death. At Daddy's request, my cousin gave us each a framed, beautifully bordered printout of the lyrics to Simon and Garfunkel's *Bridge Over Troubled Water.* She told us that Daddy said that he hoped that he was our bridge during hard times, and had asked her to make them for us. I had never really listened to the lyrics before. And like a bridge over troubled water, this simple request of Daddy's eased my mind.

In the next few days, Daddy had a few lucid moments. Whoever was at his bedside would yell "Daddy is awake" so that we could talk to him. At one of them, we put his beloved Yorkie, Charlie, on the bed with him. They had been together fifteen years. Charlie was an old man himself, and had been on heart medication for years. Apparently, Daddy had made a deal with Charlie that they would leave the living folk at the same time. Charlie went straight for Daddy's face and licked him. Daddy laughed that beautiful laugh, took him into his arms and held him tight. He suddenly had a thought, and pulled Charlie away from his chest and looked him in his eyes, "I beat choo, Charlie," he said lovingly. Daddy was leaving first. We all had a good laugh.

Daddy went to Heaven on March 29, 2002 at 10:55 a.m. It was Good Friday. I like to think that Daddy chose that day as a final "gotcha" to the Catholic priest who told him he was going to Hell for being gay. Daddy was a child of God. He was going to die on the same day that Jesus did. I knew he was going to a beautiful place with unending love to be with his soulmates.

Peggy, the hospice nurse, had been monitoring his bowel noises. Apparently, when one is close to death, the bowels begin to shut down first, so we had about a ten-minute heads-up. She lightly said, "It is time." Good thing we had the heads-up, because Marissa was in the shower. I quickly ran into the bathroom and told her the news. She got out and quickly threw on some clothes and put a towel on her head.

We all gathered around the gurney and began saying our "goodbyes" and "love yous": my aunt, uncle, cousin, Ron, Marissa, and me. I remember there being a sense of urgency, knowing we only had a minute or two. Marissa and I were at the head of the bed, each holding one of Daddy's hands. Those moments were incredibly sad, but full of relief at the same time. Daddy had hung on for five days after we had arrived. He obviously wanted to take his time and spend a few more days with his family.

I got near his ear and spoke softly, "I love you so much, Daddy. You have been the best Daddy a daughter could have hoped for. You are going to a beautiful place! Marissa and I are going to be okay. It's okay to go."

Finally, Daddy started to struggle for air. We could feel his fear and his tension as he squeezed our hands. Peggy told us to tell him to relax and go to the beautiful place that he was seeing. We did. And then we felt his body relax. He was looking directly into my eyes. I fought so hard to keep the tears back and smile. He took his last breath. And then his eyes lost their focus.

I had read somewhere that the hearing continued even after the last heartbeat. It was the last sense to go. When the hospice nurse with the stethoscope on Daddy's abdomen shook her head, I said into Daddy's ear, "You made it, Daddy! I will see you in Heaven."

For the next few minutes, we all cried in silence. We were in shock. I had never witnessed any being cross over in person. And this person was the most important man in my life.

Marissa, with tears streaming down her face, reached up and closed Daddy's eyes with her hand. "Bye, Daddy," she said.

Peggy told us to take as much time as we needed with him before she prepared his body for transport. We all starred, held each other, said silent prayers, and cried for quite a while. We then placed Charlie on the gurney so that he could see that Daddy had gone and say his goodbyes as well.

When we were done, Peggy asked us to bring her one of Daddy's T-shirts. She asked us to step out onto the front deck so that she could remove the various tubes and dress Daddy with dignity for the hearse. Just then, the Blue Angels flew overhead. Daddy lives just across the canal from the navy base where they live. We made a comment about that as we held each other. Marissa held my hand tight.

A few minutes later, we heard a splash. We looked toward the canal in front of his house and saw a group of dolphins surfacing. We were all amazed and delighted, and this brought us momentarily out of our grief. This could not be a coincidence! Dolphins are Daddy's totem, and they had come to say goodbye and pay their respects personally. Well, dolphinally? Perhaps they had come for us, too. To ease our grief just a little. Or, just maybe, Daddy had sent them for us.

The dolphins brought me up a bit, but soon I went into a dark place that lasted for hours. I cursed the entire world, the entire body of angels and God. I was angry that they had taken him away so young. He was only sixty-five. And I was angry that they had taken him away from me. They sent Daddy a white hearse that day, and they took him to be cremated. Daddy had already planned and paid for everything.

We then had to prepare for Daddy's service. Daddy had requested that we have a "party" instead of a funeral in his front yard with the canal in the background. He asked that we include music, and to not call it a funeral. The next-door neighbors, Molly and Paul, offered to bring pounds of shrimp and have a shrimp boil. They had an outdoor pot which they put right in the front yard. The smell of the crab boil was so fitting. Daddy's friend Rob, the one who went on the fishing/dolphin trip with us, offered to put some chosen songs onto a CD for the service. Daddy had told us months before that Charlie was to live with Rob after his death. He said that Charlie had chosen Rob, and that prevented us from fighting over who was going to keep him. Charlie died just four months later to join his lifelong friend. Ron, Daddy's friend of over forty years, died a few months after that. Daddy was the most important person in both of their lives.

We all got to pick a song or two that reminded us of Daddy. *The Way Old Friends Do* by ABBA, Bocelli's *Time to Say Goodbye,* and *Forever and Ever, Amen* by Randy Travis were put in at Daddy's request. Of course, we also played Simon and Garfunkel's *Bridge Over Troubled Water,* which Daddy had dedicated to Marissa and me, and *Cecilia,* which was a favorite of his. I can always picture him singing that song in his living room with his eyebrows raised and a hop in his step. Many songs from Cat Stevens album *Tea for the Tillerman* including *Miles from Nowhere, On the Road to Find Out, Moon Shadow, Morning Has Broken,* and, fittingly, *But I Might Die Tonight.*

Two of my good friends came to Daddy's funeral. Liza drove in from Texas, and my roommate from college, Camille, coincidentally already lived in Pensacola. Liza brought her famous deviled eggs. Fred and his wife brought my niece and nephew, who were thirteen and seventeen, and a neighbor graciously put them up. Marissa and I wrote eulogies, and read them at the service. My eulogy follows:

> *Because Daddy moved to New Orleans, and far away from us, Marissa and I had an extra special relationship with him. Every visit was special. Every minute, precious. Every arrival, full of tears of joy. Every departure, tears of sadness. We would cross out the days on the calendar before every summer visit to Daddy with a big, black marker.*
>
> *Upon arrival to New Orleans, because we were young children, the flight attendant would walk with us to greet Dad so she could check his ID. She never had to,*

because Marissa and I would take off in a run as soon as we saw him to hug him. When leaving New Orleans, he used to wait at the window of the gate after we boarded and wave to the plane until it took off back to Texas. During our month-long summer visits, we would fill our days with sun, swimming, boating, crabbing, or visiting with his friends. Our nights were filled with watching Daddy cook dinner, conversation, listening to music and hugs. Daddy always seemed to find reruns of M*A*S*H to watch, but he also loved Star Trek: The Next Generation, as did I. He must have moved residences over twenty times in his lifetime. But each place was filled with Daddy's things, Daddy's pets and Daddy's love. I can remember the smell of each home.

Daddy had a funny way with discipline. As most of you I am sure know, he never raised his voice. He was an expert at giving a look worth a thousand words. He taught us solid morals, which basically said, above all else, "Be true to yourself."

Daddy's life was filled with great accomplishments, of course, Marissa and I being the most important. He was a very successful businessman. And even more important, he had common sense. Even until his death. He was always a very smart man. A source of wisdom. It seemed that he knew something about every subject. Whether it be just how the moon revolved around the Earth, how the Earth and other planets revolved around the sun, or how to completely rinse the toothpaste out of your toothbrush by holding it under the running water while you run your thumb down the bristles. He taught us so much. But I stumped him once when, as a seven-year-old full of questions, I asked him, "Daddy, why are there trucks?" He brought that one up often so we could all get a good laugh. He was educated, and he did his part for the environment. He had a compost bin for his garden, he recycled his plastic bags, and even now he is even giving his body back to the Earth.

Daddy was a stubborn man, and he always wanted

to get the most for his money. If he did not get total satisfaction out of any product, say for example, too few raisins in a box of Raisin Bran, he would write the CEO describing the problem and get a coupon for free product or his money back. Get this: he never gave in to liquid detergent. To this day, he still has a huge bucketful of dry powder detergent in the laundry room.

Daddy lived for the carefree way of life. He gained joy from cooking at home. But he also loved a good restaurant, especially Mexican food, which Pensacola does not have. He loved sitting at the piano bar in the French Quarter, singing with the crowd and drinking a beer. And he enjoyed an occasional game of pool. Memories I will always treasure.

He so loved this house he built. He loved cleaning his pond, planting a garden of vegetables, and a garden of flowers. He loved his boat. He loved fishing. Yeah, he really loved fishing. He loved pulling Marissa, me, Joey, and Alex on the innertube, riding down to Joe Patti's for three pounds of shrimp and a fresh-baked baguette of sourdough bread (we always bought one extra for the ride home), or just anchoring near an island and getting in the water for a swim. With Charlie, of course. But most of all, Daddy loved hanging around the house that he built and enjoying it.

He never complained. He always gave people the benefit of the doubt. And he never judged on hearsay. He always looked for the good in people. We could all use a dose of that.

Daddy always gave more thought to the other person. He never put himself first. He cared about the lives of those he loved more than his own, and that is why his life was full and complete. He lived for happiness. He lived day to day. A coworker recently told me that I was "incredibly optimistic." I could get this from no one but Daddy.

I want to blame someone or some being for taking my Daddy away from me. He was so young, and he barely *got to enjoy his retirement, this house, or that boat. But that would only cause me more pain. So why bother?*

Daddy would say, "I got the best life that anyone could have. I have a loving family and friends who love me. I named my boat 'My Tern.' Now, it is my turn."

You will always be my guide, my inspiration, my true hero. Goodbye, Daddy.

Marissa read her short eulogy, and then I read mine along with the letter he had written me after my abortion in 1995. Of course, the crowd did not know the real reason for the letter. Ron, always shy in crowds, did not share. I knew that I had to keep a straight face to keep from breaking down, so I tried to think of anything except Daddy's death. *Breathe deeply. Focus on the breath.* During my reading, I was doing fine until my eyes met with Joey's. He was crying. I had never seen him cry except as a child, and I started to tear up. *Don't look at Joey, don't look at Joey*, I repeated in my head, and I got back on track. After I finished my eulogy, we asked if anyone in the audience wished to speak. My aunt said a few words. Rob said a few words. Then my friend Camille said a few words. That really meant a lot to me.

Then, Marissa and I held hands as we walked the short distance to the canal to scatter Daddy's ashes, at his request. We had gotten his ashes the day before. They came inside a plastic bag inside a box. Picture a large shoe box. To all our surprise, the box weighed over five pounds. You don't really think about how much a person's ashes weigh. I quickly realized that we could not scatter all of them at the service. It would be several large "clunks" into the water, rather than a windy scatter. So we had to divide Daddy for the service. Marissa and I had to rush back to the crematorium and pick out a small urn to spread his ashes at the ceremony. Plus, we wanted something to keep a small part of him in for ourselves. We found an urn that was gold, turquoise, and pink with flowers and a big heart. It was kind of girly. But considering Daddy's sexual preference, it seemed perfect. We had to laugh about that one.

Dividing Daddy seemed grotesque, disrespectful, and like

a complete violation to him. But I reminded myself that Daddy was no longer in physical form. This was not Daddy. In fact, he was probably right there with us in spirit. The thought of separating Daddy's ashes recoiled me, and Marissa certainly was not going to do it. We did look at them, though, and were quite shocked to see parts of teeth. Some things just don't burn. Graciously, Fred volunteered to do it. Then, that evening after the ceremony, they had to be divided again so that Marissa and I could keep part of him in the small urn forever. We each would spend time with him, then pass him to the other sibling for a year or two. Again, Fred volunteered to place some back into the urn. We then put the rest of the ashes into the canal where we had scattered his ashes during the ceremony. At least those parts of him would be together.

After the service, I think I decided that I just could not handle his death. I thought that I could, but I could not. But I had to go back to work with my students. So I buried any unfinished Daddy business. I just could not be in a state of grief. So I stuffed it all deep inside of me. Casey would take care of that grief. She would just add it to the rest of my blame and shame. I never thought about how all these bottled emotions might just erupt.

When I returned to work, my co-teacher had all of the students sign a card for me. One of my students, who had also recently gone through the death of his father, said simply, "I know what you are going through." This meant the world to me. When school was out for the summer, we returned to Pensacola to go through all of Daddy's stuff. Marissa and I took what we wanted, someone came to pick up his clothes for some charity, and the rest was going into a garage sale. One of my cousins on my Dad's side bought his boat. Then we had to get the house clean and ready to put on the market. Before they took his clothes away, I wanted to pick one or two of Daddy's t-shirts to keep. I sat in the garage with the open box of t-shirts in front of me. When I brought one of them to my nose, I could smell and feel Daddy on them. I felt his death once more come over me in a wave of emotion, and broke down and cried all over again. After all of the emotional pain that I had gone through with my various "men," nothing compared to losing Daddy.

Chapter Ten

MORE TRAVEL, MORE MEN

JEFF

In 2003, at the age of thirty-six, I began dating an alcoholic with seven DUIs. Of course, I did not know about the DUIs at first, and he withheld this little nugget of information for many months. We were on a vacation in Peru and he began acting very strangely when the subject of our future arose, like he was hiding something. I finally cornered him into telling me what was up. He confessed that he was soon going to prison for drunk driving, and was feeling guilty about keeping it inside for the past several months. This should have been a serious red flag. But I was drinking heavily too, and taking drugs with him. We were well into a serious relationship by then. But when he did tell me, he lied about the number of DUIs that he had, saying he only had two. A few weeks later, a friend with connections got hold of his criminal record and discovered the true number. Even with this unbelievable criminal record, Jeff was still drinking and drugging heavily. Really, who does that?? After all of this came out, again I thought, *I must keep this one, because he is THE ONE. I have failed so many times before, I can't fail again. Besides, I have been guilty of drinking and driving at least seven times, I have just never been caught. How can I judge this man for something I am guilty of?*

I really cannot believe that I put up with this news. Plus, there was his behavior. You can imagine someone who was arrested for drinking and driving seven times may not really be a whole person. He was mean and disrespectful to me a lot of the time. But he proposed to me while on a trip to Miami a few months later, and I accepted. I then waited fourteen months for him to get out of prison, a sentence that he assured me would only be nine months. I was committed, and I visited him in prison almost every other weekend. I could not wait to finally be married and have children. I knew deep down that I would have to stop drinking when he got out of prison, so that he could stop drinking. I resented this. He had the problem, not me. I would not stop my drinking. It was my only escape from the pain that was festering so deep inside of me. Besides, all my friends drank. What would I do without them? Who would I hang out with?

When Jeff finally got out of prison, it was a nightmare. He was incapable of respecting anyone, especially me. His temper was downright scary. He projected a superiority over me that was condescending and hateful. One Saturday I invited him to a youth event I was working, at an educational land institute an hour outside of town. When I got a break from the students, I sat down next to him. He refused to even talk to me. I just shrugged and went back to work. On the way home, he projected his anger with me for "ignoring him" by driving around cars in and out of the highway lanes at high speed. I was terrified, but I said nothing. I just sat there and took his shit. I guess I felt that this was just him. Can you imagine? How could I just ignore so many signs and red flags? One of my best friends, Lora, kept telling me that true love should not be so hard! Still, I persisted.

We planned the wedding, and I put a deposit on the venue. Many months later, I caught him in a huge lie. I had begun therapy for my misery, and my therapist suggested that I write and have him sign a contract stating that he would not take any more drugs. Of course, alcohol was not in the contract. Before he went into prison, he had been abusing prescription pain medications and shooting steroids. I did not want him to go back to prison. He signed the contract that I had created on the spot, with no discussion. This surprised but appeased me.

Then one day, I was looking through his gym bag while he was in the shower and I saw a recently-filled prescription bottle for more pain meds. And it was empty! In that moment, I finally saw Jeff for who he really was. He had never intended to comply with my contract. And I finally saw that he held no respect for me. I remember feeling relieved instead of sad. I broke up with him that night. I gave him back his ring. But he would not give up so easily, and dragged out the breakup process over many months, making it hell for the both of us. Of course, I allowed this. I thought that maybe I could believe him when he said that he would be able to stop the drinking and drugging. I remember being in tears one day at work, telling my co-worker, "I gave that man everything!" And, emotionally, I had.

TRAVEL

In 2004, I continued my passion for travel, and went to Hawaii with my sister. You might be saying, "Ummm, that is part of the United States." Yes, it is, but they retained their Polynesian culture, even if I can't put another notch on my country count. I flew out first and visited Kauai for a week alone, then Marissa joined me in Honolulu. Kauai is one of the most green and natural places I have ever been to. We had a grand time. One of my old high school buddies was stationed in the military there. He lent us his jeep and told us the best parts of the island to visit. We even got to go up to his barracks, where he gave us both our first tattoos. It was a hobby of his. The barracks were not anything like what I had pictured. The building was about fifteen stories tall, and was open to the outdoor environment. There was no AC, and they benefited from the natural wind that almost was almost always blowing.

At the end of that same year, I bought a cute little condo near the school where I taught. The complex has a New Orleans flair with courtyards of green and units of different color and style, some with balconies (including mine). In the summer of 2005, I took Mom to Sicily to fulfill her dream of seeing the land of her grandparents. We did a lovely seven-day tour of the island with a hot Italian driver guide named Ivan and four other participants. Two of those participants were Italian sisters my age, and they became part of our Italian family. We ended the trip by taking the city bus to Bisaquino, where my maternal great grandparents were born. It was the same city bus I had taken with Diego twelve years earlier. Upon arrival, we stopped in the closest coffee shop and somehow secured a free personal tour of the majestic mountain village from a native who spoke English. It turned out that his wife's maiden name was the same as my mother's. No way we were not related to our new friend. It was very special.

In 2006, India called to me, so after I quit my middle school science teaching job of five years, I left for India for two months by myself. Thanks to a fellow teacher from India, I had a home base with a family in New Delhi and traveled to Rajasthan, the foothills of the Himalayas, and then flew south to Goa. I loved having no schedule and immersing myself in the culture by hanging out with the locals. That same year I got my dream job as an informal environmental educator, with the official title of education programs manager, at a local environmental nonprofit.

In 2007, I went on a cruise to Belize with my then-boyfriend. I remember being so drunk that we spent a lot of the time in our cabin nursing our inebriated bodies. I swore I would never do a cruise again, as we could only spend eight hours in Belize. In 2007, a friend's family gave him an intervention, and he went into an alcohol program. He raved about how it had changed his life. I thought, *What the hell, I drink a lot too, maybe it will change my life*. After two unsuccessful months, I convinced myself that I was not an alcoholic and quit the program. I just could not stop drinking. In 2008, I went with a group of seventeen to Australia and New Zealand for three weeks. The trip was organized by a teacher at one of the schools I worked with at the non-profit. She had become a friend. My love and passion for travel and culture immersion was solidified, as this made nineteen countries that I had traveled to so far in my life.

From 2005 to 2009, I had three serious boyfriends. Each was controlling, always offering a mix of selfishness, meanness, dishonesty, and/or alcohol abuse. I continued to allow men to walk all over me, emotionally and sexually. After each breakup, I could not escape the words that my father had said to me after my breakup with Cristiano, "Do you see a pattern here?" Those words continued to haunt me. I did see a pattern: I was a failure. I was still single, miserable, and I had an alcohol problem. I felt trapped in a vicious cycle, spiraling ever downward. And it was all my fault. One way or another, I would come to face that truth.

A Reason for My Broken Picker

Finally, at the age of forty-two, I began to think that perhaps my relationship and emotional turmoil with Fred and his subsequent marriage to my sister was behind my destructive behaviors and lack of ability to find a healthy relationship. I wrote a letter to a friend who was a natural healer and whom I completely trusted, and we did some work together. It summarized a litany of failure and despair, much of which I have described above.

September 10, 2010

Rosanna,

I am going to tell you things about my life that only one or two people on this planet know about. No one knows all of them. They may be the reason for my destructive behaviors and the lack of ability to find a healthy relationship. This is hard for me, but I feel it is important for my healing that I completely open up to you. I trust you completely.

I want to tell you about a relationship that I had with an older man when I was fifteen through seventeen. He was my first love. I was so impressionable. It was so powerful. This may or may not be the reason why I have chosen unavailable men to be in a relationship with since that time. For almost thirty years, I have chosen alcoholics. Two criminals (I waited fourteen months for one boyfriend to get out of prison for seven DUIs, only to find that he had no respect for me). Mental abusers. Men who need to be in control. A married man. A womanizer. A cheater. An old man who was an employer who gave me money for sexual favors (but no intercourse, I was nineteen). Liars. A thief and con artist. One with a mental illness. And those who just didn't want me, but didn't let me go either. And the good ones, I just fell out of love with. Or it was never there to begin with.

My sister and I met Fred when I was fifteen and she was sixteen . . .

[This portion of the letter repeats The Fred Diaries, so we'll jump to the end of the letter.]

Marissa eventually got pregnant and they got married. Joey is my godson. Alexa, my niece born three years later, I adore. I must have been in a constant state of hurt. But then I went off to college. Perhaps I still have some shame and guilt from that time period. Perhaps I still feel second best.

He stayed part of my life, as a brother-in-law, for seven years until their divorce. I was away in college, but he was still part of the family. He was there at holidays, and family gatherings. I really can't remember when or how I forgave him. Perhaps I never did. Perhaps I just buried the whole damn mess. But we were amicable. And I didn't hurt when I was around him. At least, I don't think I did.

He has remarried. He moved away many years ago. And now, more recently, I hate him for what he did to me. What he did to us. At such a young age.

The reason he moved away is that a friend of Alexa, age

nine, accused him of sexually touching her. Her mother filed a lawsuit against him and threatened his life. I even lent him $3,000 of my own money for his bail, since he had none. He lost his job. He had to leave town by court order. No one in our family believes that he did it. Not even I believed it at the time. But I do now.

So there you have it. Maybe this has nothing to do with anything. Some women are beaten by their husbands for years and come back healthy. I don't know. I do know that this hatred for Fred cannot be good for me. And I have kept it secret for so long.

MENOPAUSE, THEN DEPRESSION

In March of 2010, within six months after the horrific breakup with Levi, my last boyfriend who turned out to be bipolar, my periods started getting irregular. Six months after that, they stopped completely. I had reached menopause. But I was only forty-three years old! Women could still conceive at that age! The hormone swings and hot flashes were extremely uncomfortable. But they were nothing compared to the devastating realization that I would never have my own children. I had stopped producing eggs. My lifelong dream of having my own babies sometime in the future was shattered! It was too much to bear. I remembered the belief I held as a child that babies start as the size of a pinhead in all girls, and when they got bigger, they popped out. As a girl, I could not wait for my baby to come into this world. I could not wait to be a mother, and I had waited my whole life, knowing that I would be a mother someday. But I would never be pregnant again. My one and only pregnancy in my life, I had terminated. I was beyond devastated. I was shattered.

I fell into a dark depression with thoughts of suicide. Every aspect of my life suffered, even my education job at the nonprofit that I loved. One night I cooked dinner for a friend, and I began to have a pain in my chest. It started out dull, like my bra was too tight or something. But the pain slowly increased in severity, and my anxiety level rose with it. I had never felt anything like it before. I thought that I was having a heart attack. After my friend left, I called my doctor in horror and left her a voice message. I was lucky that my doctor was my friend before she was my doctor, so I had her cell number. When she finally called me back, I had already vomited everything in my stomach. After I described my symptoms, she assured me that I was experiencing a severe anxiety attack, not a heart attack.

"Do you have any valium?"

"No," I replied, in a tone of, *Does everyone?*

"Do you have any muscle relaxers?"

"No," I said again.

"Your fear is increasing your symptoms. You need to try to stay calm. Think of something calm." After a couple of agonizing hours on the couch, I finally went to bed in exhaustion. I writhed in pain for another hour, then finally went to sleep. The next day, my chest ached, and I spent the day on my couch watching movies. My chest was incredibly sore from the attack, I was weak, and I could not stand to be in my own skin.

My alcohol intake increased with my sudden and drastic increase in self-pity and disappointment. A few months later, my California calico Calley, who had gifted me with her presence and had been the one and *only* constant in my life for the past fifteen years, passed away suddenly. When I arrived home after visiting a friend after work, she was very skinny and listless. I took her to the vet immediately. I waited in the waiting room for an hour. Finally, someone came out and told me that she was a very sick kitty. She said that they had given her a shot to feel better and a shot to help her diarrhea. They told me to take her home, but that she would not make it past two weeks.

I brought her home and placed her on a towel on my bed. I somehow knew that she was going to die that night. I laid awake with her all night long, stroking her fur and talking to her. I finally dozed in the morning, and she took the opportunity to jump off the bed. I woke, and placed her back on the towel. She arched her back, took one last breath, and died. I cried for days.

My life and my outlook on life spiraled down and out of control as I dove into a deeper depression. I began to contemplate suicide. I didn't want to live in this life anymore. Honestly, I believed in reincarnation. I remember thinking, *If I am going to get a new life after I transition, then I would just rather start that new life right now. Because this one sucks! I have failed. This life is a complete failure.*

I drank every night to drown in my sorrow. In all honesty, I knew that I would not actually commit suicide. But it certainly filled my thoughts. I hated my life, and I hated myself more. I loved my job, but hated my disrespectful, dismissive, micromanaging, rude boss. I was the only one in the office that he treated so badly. But I thought about my family, and what my suicide would do to them. I also thought of my first cousin, who we had lost to alcoholism just the year before.

In May of 2010, I finally came to the realization that I desperately needed help, and went to a psychiatrist. He immediately put me on antidepressants. They made me feel great, but in the back of my mind was, *Oh good, just what I need, another drug.* The drugs did not get rid of the underlying cause. Hell, I had tried that method on my own already. But they did pull me out of that suicidal spiral I was in.

That shrink did not work out. There was definitely a personality clash between us. But he did get me to admit that I was using alcohol to self-medicate. No doubt there. So what was so wrong with that? Well, alcoholism is wrong with that. I had to admit that I was an alcoholic. But I couldn't believe it. I didn't want to believe it. I could not imagine my life without alcohol. Especially not right then. *Hey, I never black out*, I thought, *So that must mean that I am not an alcoholic! Right? Right . . .*

One morning in November of 2010, I woke up with a red, swollen, itchy rash all over my face and neck. I didn't know what it was. A week later the rash broke out all over my inner thighs. It was extremely painful, and I could not go to work. In addition to depression and severe anxiety attacks, the stress and emotional pain I felt were surfacing and being released as painful hives. *Shit!* I had never experienced hives before. *What else, God? This is even worse than poison ivy!* I could not believe the amount of pain they were causing. I had to take some time off work, and I just knew my boss, James, thought that I was making the whole thing up. So I took pictures of my swollen face and neck and sent them to him. I was so down on myself. And I had no cat to love me at home.

My severe anxiety attacks continued. They felt like someone was shoving a fist-sized rock into my chest for three hours. In total, I had eleven anxiety attacks that year. They often coincided with vomiting. Gone was my lifelong dream of a happy life with a husband, a house with a white picket fence, and our own 2.5 children. I felt like I had wasted my childbearing years on losers. I had wasted so many years of my life. And it was my fault, because of the poor choices I had made in men. Over and over.

FIRED

In June of 2011, I was fired from the job I loved by a boss who had been a constant source of emotional torture for me for the previous year. I was an emotional wreck. To ease my physical and emotional pain, I increased my alcohol intake even more. I was drinking five to six nights every week and continuing to self-medicate. I felt that I had no other choice. I just could not live with the reality that I had failed at every chance of a happy life with Mr. Right. Plus I had just lost a job I loved. In the eleven years since I had moved home from California, I had witnessed all my friends get married and have children. I was the only single one left. And in those eleven years, every one of my failed relationships was another added layer of blame for me. I counted fifteen unbearable heartbreaks in my life, including Fred and a failed and loveless marriage. And I blamed myself for all of those failed relationships (except for Fred), as well as my addiction to alcohol.

Following is my journal entry from that period:

Friday, July 1, 2011

Last month I was fired from my dream job in informal environmental education at a nonprofit. Well, officially, I was forced to resign, as the boss had recently fired two others, and it would make him look bad if he fired a third. He had tried really hard to get me to quit on my own. But I refused. I wanted that package.

For the first few years, I loved my job. And I was very successful at it. I had built up the education department to five student programs, with over fifty participating schools and twenty volunteers. Plus, education played a big part in all of the organization's public events. In the five years that I was there, I had never once received a bad review. And I had earned a raise every year. But tension between me and my boss had escalated in the past year. Near the end, he called me from his home and asked me to bring a proposal that was sitting on his desk to his house. While looking for it on his desk, as it was not sitting on top of the strewn pile of papers, I found a document containing a list of reasons why I should be let go. One of the items was the fact that I had used the lemonade stir spoon that was being served to the public to taste the lemonade. I believe that he wanted me to find that document. And quit. But I refused. I received a small package in exchange for staying three more weeks to help the education department transition. That was pure torture, because I was not allowed to discuss the true reason for my departure with my colleagues, who were my friends. And the hot flashes from my menopause were at their peak.

Deep down, I knew that the decision for me to leave the nonprofit was the right one, but I was nevertheless devastated. It never occurred to me that my hives might be a sign that I needed to leave my very unhappy place of employment. I had never been unemployed for very long in my life. And I didn't know what turn my career should take. I felt like I was lost in the dark and swimming upstream at the same time.

My career was uprooted and my hopes for a happy marriage and family were diminishing. For the past thirty years, I had thought that I was happy. I had even told Daddy once that if I died tomorrow, that I would have lived a happy life. But there was so much hurt intertwined with my amazing travel to so many countries. Happiness and pain were embraced in a hug, twirling around, and then weaving together to create the fabric of my life. And Casey was the director of every scene. As soon as it was clear that my future with a man was uncertain, she doubled her efforts to drag it out and inflict emotional pain on us. She was part of me. Something had to change, or I was going to die.

Chapter Eleven

INDIA CALLS AGAIN

IN JULY OF 2011, at forty-four, I finally decided to do something about my alcohol intake. I somehow knew that if I was going to succeed at anything in the future, I had to take care of this alcohol problem. And, I was truly *miserable*. The more I tried to control my drinking, the more I drank. And I had been trying to control my drinking for years. I was not trying to quit drinking. Just drink less. I thought that if I could drink only four nights out of the week, then I would not be considered an alcoholic. My latest solution was to quit trying to control it. So I woke up most mornings with a hangover, coupled with unbridled remorse, self-pity, and self-blame. "Shit, I did it again!" became my mantra.

I knew that I could not stop drinking on my own. I had tried for years. Hell, I couldn't even quit for five days. I finally came to the realization that I needed help. I thought, *Well, I cannot afford an inpatient alcoholic recovery center. Hey, I know, I will go to an ashram in India like Elizabeth Gilbert did. Since I can't drink there, I will get cured! Then I will be able to drink like a normal person.* So I did a bit of research, picked an ashram in the mountains with cool temperatures, and took off for India.

Again. My plan was to visit an ashram for a month, cure myself of alcoholism, then do a bit of sightseeing before returning.

My ashram experiences were memorable, spiritual, and enlightening. I had to leave the first ashram, called Tureya, after only two weeks, as a group of men were coming in. But I met a girl from South Africa there who told me of another ashram that she was heading to when she left Tureya. So I booked a stay there. Tureya is nestled in the mountains and has only ten shared rooms. I was lucky to get my own room during my stay. I quickly grew accustomed to our daily schedule. Prayer started at 6 a.m. and was a lovely chant with a catchy tune. By the time I left, I had it memorized. Chanting, like singing in choir, really did make me feel closer to God. Then yoga asana (at sunrise and on the roof, weather permitting), breakfast, break, chores, class, then yoga again with guided meditation. Fridays were a free day, and we drove into the nearby town and had fun.

Our yoga instructor, Aidan, was an adorable twenty-six-year-old all the way from Colorado with a PhD in sacred literature. Swami, the head and spiritual guru of the ashram, had been his professor at university in India. Aidan had been at the ashram for six years. The lady participants took turns helping in the kitchen with meals, which was a great opportunity to learn a bit about authentic Indian cuisine. I was anxious to talk to Swami. Gurus are skilled at seeing things in people.

I was very proud that I had weaned myself off my prescribed antidepressants before I left for India. I had not even brought them. I did, however, bring my sleeping pills. I was also proud that over the three plus weeks while at the ashrams, I drank not one drop of alcohol. And with our busy schedule, I barely even thought about drinking. I was cured. Or so I thought . . .

Here is my journal from India:

Monday, August 8, 2011

Day 1. After thirty-plus hours, I finally arrived at the Tureya Ashram in the southern state of Tamil Nadu. We are in the mountains at about 6,000 feet. This place is perfect. There is no need for AC. This was so important to escape the summer heat of Texas with 100°F plus temperatures. I chose this ashram also because I thought that the heat and mosquitos of other ashrams in India would dampen my attempts at meditation. I chose wisely. Perhaps I manifested this place, and experience. I met lovely ladies from Colorado, Miami, South Africa, France, Poland, Holland, and Singapore. I am anxious to talk to the swami here.

Tuesday, August 9, 2011

Day 2. We have class two days a week. Swami and Rudra, the ashram manager, both teach class. I am happy that our first class is on meditation. True meditation is a state where you are an observer of your thoughts from the outside. It is the process of expanding your awareness to reach enlightenment. If you are tense or upset, it is not good to meditate. Find some work instead.

The first step in one type of meditation is creating an awareness of sense perception. Perceive your smells right now, then after a time, forget them when the mind gets bored. Proceed through the rest of the senses. Step two is awareness of spontaneous thoughts. When a thought enters your mind, don't attach yourself to it or judge it. Observe it, like a bird singing in a tree. Step three is a conscious creation of thoughts. You have negative thoughts in your subconscious. Use them as bait, and then change the bait by burning that thought. This is a practice that cleanses the mind. Step four is awareness and disposal of spontaneous thoughts. Prevent the negative things from staying in your thoughts without finding a reason. Step five is the thoughtless stage, when you have no more spontaneous or negative thoughts. Step six is the emergence of a psychic symbol in your mind. This symbol will become your meditation focus.

Rudra, the ashram manager, told a story as a metaphor for the practice of meditation. Once, a crow fell asleep at the top of a tree as it started to rain. When he awoke the next morning, the entire area was flooded. The crow soon discovered that he was perched on the only tree that he could see for miles in every direction. Everything was water and sky. He panicked and flew off to find land and food. After several hours of flying, he became very tired. The crow knew that he would drown if he did not find land soon. When exhaustion almost overtook him, he finally spotted the same tree that he awoke on. He then knew that he needed to come up with a plan.

The next day, he used the placement of the sun to fly only in one direction. When he was tired, he turned around and flew back in the opposite direction to find his tree. He repeated this for the next several days, moving a few degrees in a clockwise direction each day. A week later, he discovered that he needed to fly farther in each direction to find land. Finally, weeks later and starving, he found land and food. He then had no need to fly back to his tree again. This is like practicing meditation. There is much practice needed, but once you find land, you will no longer need your tree.

Wednesday, ~~August~~ 10, 2011

Day 3. In class with Swami. He taught us that yoga is over 15,000 years old. Wow. Yoga is not just a series of postures that you practice for an hour, as we in the west believe. Yoga is an entire philosophy and way to live, based on prayer, compassion, selflessness and the understanding of higher consciousness. It is a detachment from ego. Asana, the physical postures, movements and exercise (and what we think of when we say yoga) is just a small part of the philosophy. Asana is better than a gym because it involves gradual cardio, which means that the heart is not stressed or strained. There are eighty-four asanas, or postures. Each posture triggers your chakras, and the practice eliminates toxins properly.

Swami explained that we tend to live in the past. He said that "if you harbor past traumas, that memory will become poison and manifest as a disease, and you will never progress in life." Boy, had I learned this the hard way! "We suppress bad thoughts because we don't know how to express them. Many people live in the past. They complain. They judge. They live artificial lives. Instead of thinking, "I can make this better if I . . . " they think, "why don't I have this . . . ," or "my ex-boyfriend did such and such . . . ." The negative can become strong inside of you. It can become your life." He said not to identify yourself as your failure, your pain, or your uselessness. Don't give excuses or look for sympathy. It weakens your mind. Don't say, "it could have been . . . "

We are teaching our children bitterness and hate. We must show children love and affection, and talk nicely to them. So that they will talk nicely with their children, Swami explained. Are you listening, Casey? "Fill your mind with love and affection, and the negative thoughts will pour out like oil in a bowl. Don't pour the oil out, fill the bowl with water instead and let the oil overflow. Control your mind. Listen to the good thoughts. When a criticism or negative thought comes, say, 'I shall not say these things.' Be authoritative with your mind. Contentment is being okay with whatever is there in life. Be thankful. Accept your past mistakes. Acknowledge them, and move on. Believe in your inner power." This man seems very wise.

Swami also held that we see sacrifice as a loss, when actually, it is sacrifice that strengthens our spirit. He said, "when you are young, you will carry thoughts; and when you are old, your thoughts will carry you." "If you do not apply effort and determination in every practice, you cannot achieve it." He said that every few years the way you see your life changes. That seemed to be true for me. I was finally seeing myself in a new light.

After class I was able to speak with Swami alone. He told me many useful things. He told me that I was angry with someone, maybe me, and that I must release that anger. He told me that I was keeping pain inside of me. Beyond my hot flashes, he said that my body was generating heat, that I don't sleep evenly, and that I was always thirsty. He said a diet change was in order: more yogurt, steamed rice, pasta and watermelon. He also told me to stop eating raw vegetables to curb my chronic diarrhea.

I asked him how I could gain self-confidence and strengthen my inner self. He said to know the truth about myself, to connect with who I am. Know how my mind, body and emotions work. Protect, clean and maneuver my heart and mind. He explained that confidence comes from sincerity, which is already innate within me. That confidence will come from achieving my life's work. He said that before I can help others, that I must stand solidly on two feet. Amen to that.

Thursday, August 11, 2011 — Cleansing Day

Day 4. Today started out as usual with prayer at 6:00 a.m. No tea or breakfast. Then, we all cleansed. Rudra boiled water and added one tablespoon of salt for every liter of water. Then, we drink it to cleanse our body. The minimum was six cups!

Rudra said it helps if you drink it fast. Else drank fifteen. I drank eight. Since I already have diarrhea issues, I was second on the toilet behind Else. I visited the toilet five or six times. Wow. Then we rest or take a short nap because it drained our energy. Lunch was at 1:00 p.m., then more rest until yoga at 4:00 p.m.

Aidan came up to my room to "register" me. He needed my forms, passport, visa, ashram fees, etc. I felt so goofy around him. I was someone else. I even wrote the wrong year on my form. The reason, of course, is that I am a student with a crush on the teacher. He is adorable, but my admiration and respect of his skills run ocean deep. His yoga classes are amazing. He has a beautiful voice in prayer. During free time, he plays on the piano in the Puja hall beneath my room. He says that he will probably never live in the States again.

His meditation class tonight was one of the most beautiful experiences of my life. We started standing and were guided to mentally root to the Earth. Hold white energy, then green energy in a ball, then back to white flowing all over our body. Then we were guided to lay down and feel the energy on every body part. Then, he sang to each chakra. I was tingly all over the entire hour. How lucky I am to cross paths with this soul.

Sunday, August 14, 2011

Day 7. Beautiful yoga class just after sunrise on the roof with the gorgeous views of the mountains. I got to skip class today so that Aidan could drive me to the city. I needed to get some cash so that I could pay the balance of my bill. Apparently, there is no way to pay with a credit card or on-line once you are here. It turned out to be good, though, because I got to talk with him one on one. He asked me about my past and future career, and gave me some pointers. He told me that he was offered a salary, but for six years he has donated it back to the Tureya foundation and children's programs. I told him that was admirable. I felt that we connected on a deeper level. I have so much love for him as a friend. I am trying to be more appropriate in my thoughts. No doubt, I am severely attracted to him. But I want more respect for him than to want sex. In fact, I don't really want sex with Aidan. I just want to lie next to him, feel his naked body next to mine and smell him.

I spent the better part of the day in the city, which was great because it was market day. Beautiful people were selling tons of fruits and vegetables on their tarps laid out on the ground. I got some great pictures. I bought some great Indian mangoes, the best on the planet, but I can't touch them because I am allergic to the skin. Turns out, they are in the same family as poison ivy. I hope someone back at the ashram can peel them for me.

When we returned to home base, there was some sad news. A couple of the girls were hiking in the mountains when they witnessed a Jeep hit the dog that lives here, Choktee. The driver saw the dog, but did not even slow down. As it impacted her body, it catapulted her over the side of the cliff where she disappeared. The Jeep stopped briefly, but kept on going. The girls were distraught and angry.

Aidan guided us through another meditation after dinner. How can he memorize it all? A pesky mosquito got a few bites of me. I moved my hand to scratch, and Aidan quickly nudged us to stop all body movement, "Say to yourself, I will not move the body. I will not move the body." Also, my injured wrist has been giving me some pain for quite some time. Aidan played a singing bowl and put on a recording of water flowing. We always start by mentally scanning the body. He guided us to begin building energy in the body to melt all negative feelings toward the self and the body. Then we pictured the green energy moving to the parts of the body that need it. The energy is then brought outside the body as a pink cloud envelops your body. The pink cloud is then broadened, raised above the body, then merged with the pink cloud energies of the adjacent girls. I could feel some of us, it was amazing. I felt tingling all over.

Aidan then had us bring up a person who has treated us badly recently. I immediately thought of James, my old boss, and all of the ways that he mistreated me. His disrespect towards me, mistrust, lack of communication, then forcing me to resign. One by one, he had us throw their bad qualities off a cliff. He then asked us to find their good qualities. Tears started streaming down my face. Well, he was a great father, and was even coach of his son's little league team. I was forced to realize that James is a good person, but has faults, just like I do. I also reminded myself that it was time for me to leave the non-profit world to pursue other things. Namely, starting my own company and writing. Aidan then asked us to reach out and hug this person. That was really hard! I had a full face of tears by this point, but I did it. I didn't know that I still harbored so much resentment towards James. I just wanted him out of my life, but I did not realize until then that I was still carrying all of that inside of me. How good for me that exercise was. Aidan is such a beautiful and talented person. How lucky I am to be here. After the meditation, one of the girls, Dina, could see that I was crying and touched my shoulder. I hugged her, and she did not let me go. Sweetie. We are going to meet up at another ashram in two weeks.

Okay, I have a dilemma and I don't know what to do. I cannot stop thinking about Aidan. When I am near him, I want him to notice me. I want to be special in his eyes, as he is in mine. I am sure that hundreds of women go through this place on a yearly basis. It must be difficult for him to date. But if I saw him with a date, or if he started to pay attention to either of the two younger girls here—teased them or looked at them in a certain way, I would be crushed. Which is ridiculous. And a problem for me. I am only hurting myself. I am 400 percent sure that he is not for me. So why do I toy with the idea of an affair? Why do I crave his attention? Why do I want to be near him? His guided meditations are like a drug for me. They are as intimate as touching. Well, almost. And he is just so damned cute, with baby blue eyes, and a smile that melts me completely. Not to mention a body that is perfect. Demeanor, skill, meaningful life work, in to everything spiritual that is my focus right now. Did God put him in my life as a challenge (in addition to the spiritual growth that he is guiding me through)? Why can't I just be professional and see him for his life's work? I feel like I have to avert my gaze whenever I am around him, lest he see the attraction in my eyes. Yoga class, meals. I am making this more difficult for myself. What do I do? How do I make myself not feel these feelings? When I am near him I want to run away from him, and when I am away from him, he fills my thoughts. I must deal with this. I either have to wallow in "hurt," or leave, which is not an option. I am part of this group with these beautiful ladies. I am on my very important spiritual journey with these gorgeous mountains, excellent hiking, great food, good accommodations and my own room. I am not leaving! So push him out of my mind. Consciously say I will not think about him. I will meditate.

    After meditation, I came to the conclusion that I have feelings for Aidan. But be realistic! Change your thoughts! I love myself. I have so much compassion for people and the Earth. I give so much of myself. Look at him differently. But how? Be strong, Della. ☺ He can see your distress. Don't let him see it. This is not his problem. It is better to avoid him. He is not the one. He is not the one. He is not! Leave your heart open. Look to the future, Della.

Monday, August 15, 2011

Day 8. In class, we learned the psychology of yoga. Finding, maintaining and expanding inner peace, inner clarity and balance of mind. Even when you find your balance, it is very difficult to maintain it. When you find happiness and peace, share it. If you do not forgive, you are keeping that memory inside your heart. When you have a chance to change your life, change it. When you bring a change, you will view life from a different angle. You will enter another dimension of life. You will be a different person.

How do you stay still in meditation? Shift your awareness by focusing on different parts of your body. Legs, trunk, head. Prolong by using all body parts. Imagine your body is like a tree. You are rooted. Feel strong. Don't move. We tried a walking meditation. Become completely aware of each movement. Your legs, your feet touching the ground, shift of weight. Lower your eyes. Look, but don't see. Watch the space between your nose and your foot. As you step, say "ohm." In a meditation lying down, find the pulse in your third eye. You can use this if you cannot fall asleep. We also tried meditation with a candle. Focus on the whole candle, then the things behind the candle, then the flame, the black part of the flame near the wick, then the blue part. You can also use the moon or a tree.

Tuesday, August 16, 2011

Day 9. Great news! Choktee, the dog, returned to the ashram! We were all so happy. She was banged up, limping and weak, but she was alive. It had taken her two days to crawl down and then back up our mountain to the ashram. They don't have vets here. Rudra put some turmeric, a spice used widely in India and elsewhere, known to have healing properties when ingested, directly onto her wounds. She seems very happy to be home.

So something amazing happened inside me yesterday. I was feeling so trapped with the feelings I was having for Aidan. I wrote the first part, meditated, then went to yoga class. At one point, we were both doing the same move, gliding our chests across the floor towards cobra, and his face came very close to mine. Mmmmm.

After yoga, three of us went for a hike in the mountains. Then, in class, my feelings for Aidan became so strong that my eyes actually welled with tears at the thought that I will never see him again. Then, something clicked inside my head. I think my angels may have adjusted my thoughts. *My God, I do not even know this person. And I am marrying him inside my head? Be real! He is a boy. He takes no salary. My future husband / mind-body-soul partner will be better suited for me. I know that my mate will be near my spiritual level. I will not let my silly feelings for this very young man get in the way of my life. My happiness and life's work are way too important!* Today, I could look at him and converse with him with very little of those silly feelings interrupting me. Thank you, my angels.

Wednesday, August 17, 2011

Day 10. I can't believe I have been here only ten days. It seems like much longer. Dina left today, but I will see her again at another ashram in Coimbatore. Four more ladies leave tomorrow, and I will miss them.

Today was a very good day. Prayer, tea, rooftop yoga. It was a bit cold, but there were eight participants, so we would not all fit in the Puja hall. A bit of hand-washing my laundry and breakfast. Then it began to rain during our free time. We waited a bit, then five of us decided to go ahead and walk to the nearby tiny village called Koval Patti, even though Swami had restricted us from going there. Ha! The villagers were very kind to us. They knew we were from the ashram. Everyone let us take their picture and no one asked us for money. Even the old ladies posed for us. It was a two-hour round trip and the scenery was absolutely breathtaking. Very good picture day.

Yoga at 4 p.m., quick shower and hair wash, prayer at 5:30 p.m. I am starting to memorize the prayer song. Then another great guided meditation with Aidan. Lying down, short breaths, eyes open, then feel your eyes get heavy. Bring awareness to the abdomen, this is where your connection to the universe lies. Fill it with white light, feel the energy. Move awareness to the throat. Imagine a channel linking it to the abdomen. Then, it started to rain hard, so Aidan incorporated the rain into our guided meditation. Imagine falling as a drop the mile from the cloud to the Earth. Land in a stream, then flow for miles to the ocean. Mix with the salt water and travel through the ocean. Then, leave the salt behind and evaporate back to the sky and start over. Awesome. Great dinner with much laughter, Aidan is a very funny guy. He made faces and put on a performance.

Friday, August 19, 2011

Day 12. Our day to break routine and go into town to Kodaikanal. Our weekend. Yesterday was very sad as four ladies left us, including the Dutch. We took lots of pics and gave them lots of hugs. Too many leaving on one day! Now, it is just the young French girl, the German girl and me. Breakfast was hysterical, the topic of conversation was urination. It started with the Indian toilet, basically a porcelain capped hole in the ground. Frenchie said that there are cups with tubes for ladies to pee while standing. I must find one, as this would be great for camping. I hate the splash on the feet. Aidan said that he had a girlfriend that peed in a bottle while a passenger on a road trip.

Lunch in town was so good. Then, I withdrew some cash, went shopping to buy fruit and other necessities, went to an Internet cafe to communicate with family and friends back home, then stopped for ice cream. Back at the ashram, we all shared our gifts, then I suggested that we lead ourselves through asana yoga.

I know now that yoga is a way of life, not just postures. I need to study my notes. But will this knowledge and practice really lead to a better Della? Do I have to give up my desires like sex, sweets and music? Or only if the quantity is too high? What the hell.

After dinner, I was feeling down. Suddenly, I remembered that I had not listened to my music since I arrived. That would definitely cheer me up. The stars were out, so I took my MP3 player and headphones to the rooftop and cranked Adam Lambert's *For Your Entertainment*. I immersed into each song, sang and danced on the roof until it hurt. I was aware that I was singing fairly loudly, and that the nearby farmers who stay awake to protect their crops from being eaten by feral hogs *could probably hear me. And I didn't care. Let them.*

His song, Aftermath, really moved me to tears. It was like Adam was talking directly to me. I have gone through so much pain in my life. And for so long. This song assures me that even after all the pain I have endured, everything will be alright in the end. And that maybe I need to change the way that I perceive the pain. It tells me to turn over a new leaf and live my life differently. I feel that this is a turning point in my life.

AFTERMATH

Songwriters: Alisan Porter / Ely Rise / Adam Lambert / Mahmoud Ferras

Have you lost your way?
Living in the shadow of the messes that you made
And so it goes
Everything inside your circle starts to overflow
Take a step before you leap
Into the colors that you seek
You get back what you give away
So don't look back on yesterday
Wanna scream out
No more hiding
Don't be afraid of what's inside
Gonna tell ya, you'll be all right
In the aftermath
Anytime anybody pulls you down
Anytime anybody says you're not allowed
Just remember you are not alone
In the aftermath
You feel the weight
Of lies and contradictions that you live with every day
And it's not too late

Think of what can be if you rewrite the role you play
Before you break you have to shed your armor
Take a trip and fall into the glitter
Tell a stranger that they're beautiful
So all you feel is love, love

When this album was over, I put on Phil Collins' *Hello, I Must Be Going*. Singing and dancing on the roof under the stars put me into a state of pure bliss. But I was still attracted to Aidan, and jealous of Frenchie. She pours herself on to him. And he catches it all. I am getting better, though. He deserves to be flirted with, I thought. He is twenty-six, beautiful, talented and spiritual. He deserves love, dammit. The other girls eventually joined me on the roof, and we had our first star show, as the sky was crystal clear. It was magical.

Sunday, ~~August~~ 21, 2011

Day 14. Must write fast. 6 a.m. puja (prayer) in half an hour. Yesterday, Frenchie drove me nuts in asana with her little mmm's after every position change. It was so obvious that it was a display for Aidan. Fine. But I don't want to be near it. She squealed with delight when Rudra told us that Aidan was going to join our class at the waterfall that we were hiking to. She is so blatant. But who can blame her. Thank goodness, he did not join us. The day was sunny and beautiful, perfect for a hike and dip in the river. Meditation on the rocks by the river was good, but a bit distracting with the leeches getting trapped in my Teva river sandals. On the way back, I got three . . . what . . . leech bites? Leech sucks? Frenchie and Rudra had to pull them off of my feet and ankles. I was grossed out. Plus, the thoughts of continued jealousy were a distraction. Then, after lunch (Aidan did not eat with us), he came to my room to finish my bill. I had gotten the last of the necessary cash to balance my bill, plus a small donation. I asked him if he was doing okay. He said he did not sleep well the night before. Then he opened up to me and we talked in my room for more than an hour. It was heavenly. Mostly about spirituality and how much better life can be with it. He told me that three years previous, he did not want to get out of bed. I can relate to that. He said that he works on his spirituality every day. I must too!

After class with Swami (it was a good one on happiness and enjoyment) it was my turn to make a meal. I was teaching Rudra my Daddy's suga recipe. I had purchased the ingredients in Kodaikanal and donated them. Dinner was running late, so Aidan got out his guitar and played for the two girls while I was still in the kitchen. The meal turned out pretty good. After dinner, I asked Aidan to play his guitar some more. He said something about it being easier to serenade one instead of three. But he played anyway. It was pure bliss. I love acoustic guitar. We had the USA connection, and sang the classics.

Then, he asked, "Do you want to hear a song that I wrote?" It was actually really good. It was something about one breath, one heart, and one smile. I asked him to repeat the lyrics. " . . . and, no, the song was not written about anyone in particular," he offered.

"You mean, no one inspired you to write that song?" I asked, surprised.

"Just a premonition of you."

I was so very touched. I wasn't sure why he was flirting with me in front of the other girls, but I didn't care. I felt the key turning the tumblers locking him in to my heart. Gazing into his eyes with that smile. Did I know him in a previous life? Did we meet on the other side? Our connection was so strong. Why does God challenge me so much? I have not felt this way in over two years. The other two girls were sitting there. I had to break the spell that I was under. "I did not bring my boots this evening" I said. He did not understand, so I offered, "It is best to wear boots when walking through shit." I felt it was a little harsh, but I did not want him to know how I truly felt. He did not like that comment, but continued to play. We sang Elvis, American Woman, and Macy Gray's "I try to say goodbye and I choke, try to walk away and I stumble, well I try to hide it, but It's clear, my world crumbles when you are not near . . . " At the end of the evening, we pass each other and Aidan whispers, "Sweet dreams." "Same to you" I reply. What are you doing to me???

Monday, August 22, 2011

Day 15. It is our last night at Tureya. A male retreat will begin in two days, so we all have to leave. Frenchie gave me a little guitar lesson in the puja hall on Aidan's guitar. I want to buy a used one, but it takes so much commitment to learn. My wrist is much better. I can put a lot more weight on it. Aidan says it will get better only by strengthening it and using it more. Since our cleanse, I have had two normal bowel movements. I am happy about that.

Tuesday, August 23, 2011

Day 16. Today is a very emotional day. I leave Tureya, and Aidan. Rudra taxied south, so the two girls took the cab with her. I am going north to an ashram near Coimbatore to meet Dina and take a course called "Inner Engineering." That left me alone with Aidan for one-and-a-half hours before my taxi arrived. As soon as their taxi took off, "Do you want some breakfast?" Aidan asks me. It was great because I thought I was getting an apple with some peanut butter. I stayed in the kitchen while Aidan sautéed onion, garlic, carrot, tomato and added some powdered ginger. He poured this over pasta. The conversation was God, religion downfalls, psychic power and energy (note to self to read the New Testament). I told him how, for me, finding God was bliss. But that I have negative feelings toward organized religion when they teach that ONLY THIS CHURCH is good, and only its members are going to heaven. But I am so fascinated by this man. Leaving him was so hard! Why couldn't Tureya have hired a female or ugly man for a yoga and spiritual instructor? I wish I knew if he knew the sadness I felt. Sometimes, I swear, he can read my mind. Once, in meditation, he described the exact dragon image I already had in my head. Another time, he added the singing bowl into our meditation after I had tried playing it just minutes before. He mentioned that sleeping pills are bad because they don't allow you to get to the super conscious during sleep. I must stop that shit, no matter how much sleep I lose. I have weaned down a lot.

It was finally time to leave. My taxi had arrived and we stood a few yards inside the gate. I gave him the last half of my dried wasabi edamame, some silver Mardi Gras beads, a Hot Wheels toy car, and a Texas key chain. And a card with a letter inside. The card read, "I want you to know, with the pink cloud and the singing bowl during your guided meditations, I felt an ecstasy from my own energy that I never knew existed. Thank you for that!" I hugged him tight. I could feel that he did not return the closeness. He opened his arms and said, "I am always here for you."

"This is not your destiny," I said.

"Why not?"

I then thought, *Who the heck are you to tell him this?!* I

smile and put my palm in the middle of his chest, turn and walk towards the gate. I get to the gate and turn around, "Maybe it is."

"One more hug," he says and rushes to me.

"Oh my God," I let slip. I dropped my bag as he wrapped his arms around me. I put my hand gently on the back of his head and pulled him close to me. He holds me tight this time. I can feel his heart pounding as hard as mine, and I knew that he had broken his rule about getting close to participants. For me. We part and he looks into my eyes. Those beautiful baby-blues.

"This relationship is symbiotic." He says to me.

I smile and reply, "synergistic!" Our connection was more than the two of us put together. He gives me that smile that says that I had one-upped him. I turn and walk up the hill to the taxi. I don't look back.

He was still standing there looking up when my taxi reached the second switch-back up the mountain. He gave a final wave goodbye. It was perfect. I finally got the answer that I did not want, that he felt for me too. Those songs he sang last night were for me. I put in my headphones and cried so much on the five-and-a-half-hour drive to Coimbatore that my eyes hurt. I felt that if he gives even the slightest effort to be with me, that I would drop everything in the US to be with him. Now, many hours later, I don't think so. Will I ever see him again? I just don't know. As of right now, thank God, he is unavailable with his life's work. I truly hope that he finds the love of a woman in his life. God isn't everything.

The ashram in Coimbatore and Inner Engineering course were very good. Our instructor was a tiny woman from Lebanon, her hair light brown, very long down her back and curly. She taught about the importance of living in the moment and being aware of every moment. And becoming more aware of your inner self and your surrounding environment. Some easy asanas were practiced every morning. We learned that if you take apart the word "responsibility," it means your "ability to respond." And that we can respond to the Earth, the air, the animals, the plants, and mostly, to our fellow human beings.

As soon as I started the sight-seeing portion of my India trip, I started drinking again. Ugh. So much for my theory. As Aristotle warned: "first you make your habits, then your habits make you." Too many bad habits to overcome. Where does it all end?

Chapter Twelve

THE VIOLATION

THE VIOLATION—1983

Less than one month after the final entry to the Fred diaries, in November of 1983, I drove to Marissa and Fred's apartment. I was sixteen years old. I had purchased my first car a few months earlier. Being able to drive myself around in my own car was a rite of passage in and of itself. It was an exciting time for me, and I was feeling more like an adult. Almost immediately after I arrived, Fred and I started making out, like we had so many times before. This time we were in the bedroom on the floor. Then, for only the second time, *all* our clothes came off. And Fred entered me.

But back to the beginning of our lives with Fred. As he began kissing and touching me in July of 1982, when I was fifteen, it opened up a whole new world of pure love for me, a love that was inescapable. I had never been sexually intimate with anyone before. He was my first love. At that time, he was paying a lot of attention to my sister too. This was very confusing and painful for me. Because I was so jealous of Marissa, and he knew it, Fred told me that he loved me more than my sister. And I believed him. It did not occur to me that he was telling her the same thing. I was so vulnerable and impressionable. And I had never experienced feelings so powerful. This was the beginning of his emotional manipulation and psychological assault, in combination with his physical molestation of me. This was the beginning of my trauma.

My sister and I became even worse enemies, and argued every day. Jealousy consumed us both. There were so many tears. We were young and caught up inside our first love, and we fought hard for Fred's attention and affection. This placed a huge emotional burden on both of us. It seemed our love for each other was gone when Fred was around.

After Fred was kicked out of our home, I desperately wanted him to be out of our lives *forever*. He had caused me and my family *so much pain*. But Marissa found out where he had moved to and began seeing him secretly. Mom found out and tried to stop her. Mom even threatened to call the cops. I wish she had. But Marissa was defiant and determined, and she yelled back. Mom then slapped Marissa across her face, the one and only time she ever did. That made Marissa's resolve to leave even stronger and she moved in with Fred that very day.

I was so devastated that I did not see or speak to Fred for over a year. I saw my sister occasionally. This was the hardest time I had ever gone through in my young life. So much pain, for so long. And my own sister now the enemy! Love had turned to hatred in me toward them both. He had come between me and my only sister. And my sister had torn the love of my life from my bleeding heart. I was broken to pieces.

It is important to acknowledge that Marissa truly has no blame for finding Fred, and making a life with him. She was in love with him, possibly even more than I was. From experience, I get that completely. It is clear from Fred's message to Dawn just after he was kicked out, to tell Marissa not to kill herself, that she was clearly in a state of deep emotional stress, and was considering suicide. Fred was her first love, too. In her mind, she could not lead a life without him. Fred had groomed her as well. He should have thwarted her advances from day one, and turned her away when she found him. He was the adult. But he instead chose to make a life with a seventeen-year-old girl.

After the painful, year plus separation from Fred, I gradually faced the fact that if I wanted any kind of relationship with my sister, I would have to mend things with Fred. I had no idea at the time that I was still in love with him. I thought that I hated him after causing me so much unbearable emotional pain. But how could my love for him have really changed? It hadn't.

Once we were speaking again, Fred told me that he did not want our relationship to end. I was shocked. He proceeded to tell me that he still loved me. I was completely elated at this news. So even though he was with my sister, I gradually let him back into my heart. And . . . my body. Hook, line, and sinker.

What I have to realize, and tell my middle-aged self over and over, is that as a sixteen-year-old girl inside of her first love, I didn't know any better. I had no idea at the time that he was just using my love, trust, and emotions to get what HE was after. At this point, he should have done the right thing and just LEFT ME ALONE. He already HAD MY SISTER! But I realize now that he is a very sick man. He *had* to have both of us. I hate him for that. Always will.

Dawn Too

I vaguely remember, at some point after Fred moved into our home, that my dearest friend, Dawn, had told me that she also felt like Fred had made a sexual advance toward her. Dawn recently explained to me what happened and how she felt at the time. The four of us were sitting on Mom's queen bed, listening to music and talking while Mom was at work. We had all just smoked a joint. Marissa and I had gone into Marissa's room to look for a record to play on the turntable. While they were alone, Fred took both of Dawn's hands into his and looked deeply into her eyes. He held her gaze for seconds. The message he was giving her was unmistakable: he was coming on to her, and testing out her reaction. Dawn internally freaked out and ran out of the room. Because of all the turmoil that she had gone through with her family, stemming from her father's involvement in criminal activities, she had become hypersensitive to the way that adults treated her. She recently told me that at that moment she felt queasy and icky. She felt like this was a terribly gross invasion of her space, and that she had just been violated. She felt strongly that he hoped to be intimate with her. No doubt, knowing him, he did.

Dawn told me that she had suspected that something was off with our relationships with Fred from the beginning. She felt that Marissa and I were just too close, too giggly, and too touchy with him. She somehow knew deep down that it was inappropriate for an adult male and two teenage girls to behave this way. I wonder now how it is that we did not have these thoughts? I think Mom taught us to yield to all male attention, like we saw her do. Dawn also felt that our feelings for him were intensely romantic. And the most important point was that he was doing it to both Marissa and me at the same time, keeping us both in the dark about the other. Of course, her suspicions were confirmed when the ugly shit came out. Marissa and I, both within a two-day period, had secretly told Dawn what was going on. She was the only one who knew the whole truth.

Fred was finally kicked out of our home only after Dawn's mother, Brenda, told my mother that Fred was having sex with Marissa and molesting me. Dawn shared that she had BEGGED her mother to tell my mother. She said that she felt guilty about it for years afterward. But ironically, things could have turned out worse if she had remained silent. I hate to think of how things may have turned out if Dawn had not violated our friendship and told on us. She did the right thing. But then, how could it have turned out worse than it did? Dawn also said that she had felt used, mainly because Marissa was using her to cover for her while she was secretly seeing Fred every day after school.

Dawn had been through some super tough family trauma herself. She is the oldest of three sisters. Her dad was rumored to be in the mafia, and so had a bodyguard. When Dawn was nine, her family was victim of a robbery when three masked gunmen invaded her home. Dawn, terrified by the invasion, had to untie her mother, father and bodyguard after the robbers left.

Her father, enraged by the robbery, went after the men. Dawn was even more terrified of what would happen if he found them.

When Dawn was twelve, that same bodyguard devised a plan to steal everything her father had. He and his gang of thugs came to her house, stole hidden money, took her dad, drugged him, and put him in the trunk of her dad's car. They drove to her father's jewelry store and robbed it too. The bodyguard did not want harm to come to Dawn's mom or her children, so he had called that day ahead of time and told her to take the children and leave the house immediately. When they returned home, her father was gone, and they were informed that his jewelry store had been robbed. Dawn found out about her father's murder a week later on the news, when his body was found buried at a remote site over a hundred miles away. She then felt a different type of violation than mine. Since it was on the news, she felt like her family was exposed. Like me, she buried her pain deep inside. We get each other. And we have never had a serious argument in almost forty years. Maybe that is why we have always been two peas in a pod, and I value her friendship to this day.

BACK TO THE VIOLATION

I was quite surprised at how much penetration hurt. I was totally freaking out, and my eyes were bulging wide open. I was looking for some comfort from Fred, but HIS eyes were closed. I could see the pleasure just oozing from his face. He cared only about his pleasure fucking yet another virgin half his age, and the sister of his live-in girlfriend, not for my obvious and overwhelming fear during this sacred rite of passage. He had been grooming me for over two years, and he was finally getting his "prize." Consumed by his unilateral sickness, he cared nothing for the vulnerable and frightened little girl that was experiencing so much emotional and physical pain underneath him. Disgusting, looking back . . .

I didn't know it at the time, but lurking beneath the physical pain and fear, I was also feeling incredible guilt and shame. Even though I was deep in love, I knew it was wrong. I was somehow getting Marissa back by having sex with her boyfriend. I still cling to much of that shame over thirty years later. It had become toxic within my body and grew for over three decades.

I do own the fact that I made a very poor decision at the age of sixteen. Still, it was not my fault. Fred did this TO me. And he put me in a terrible situation to make that adult decision while I was still a teenager. I am still trying to separate the adult woman that I am from that sixteen-year-old girl that I was. There was no physical force, but it was a clear violation. Statutory rape. Some would say that because he was living with my sister for some months prior to the rape, and soon became my brother-in-law, and was therefore related to me by marriage that this is a case of incest. There is no clear word for my abuse, but that does not change the suffering that I endured. He had groomed, molested and raped me over a three-year period, starting with a time when he was a member of our household. He had continued to influence and manipulate my youth, vulnerabilities, lack of emotional experience, and my overpowering love for him . . . until he finally got what he was after. Even though he was in a serious relationship with my only sister. Mission accomplished!

One unavoidable clue that he knew that what he was doing was inexcusably wrong: he had read my diary (up to the New Orleans trip) and had then had asked me to burn it! He had mumbled something about "evidence." I can't remember what my reply was at the time, but I do remember something deep inside my soul told me not to burn my diary, as he had asked. That these diaries would be very important someday. That little angel was right. And I hope that you, the reader, are able to listen when your angels speak to you. If you are going through or have gone through anything similar, it is not entirely your fault. Find your way out of the situation as quickly as possible. Tell someone. Anyone. I promise, it only gets worse if you keep it inside.

To this day, I still don't understand how my parents could have allowed the marriage of Marissa and Fred to happen, knowing that he had continuously molested me, *and* had regular sex with Marissa, while he was still living with us. I guess the unplanned pregnancy had a lot to do with it. And I still can't understand why no one thought to ask ME how I felt. How I was getting over my emotional trauma? My first love, who had intimate contact with me while also molesting my sister, was now marrying my sister! Did I, the younger sister, have any lasting emotional consequences? Was I okay? Yet, nothing. I felt like I was swept under the rug. I had to stuff all my feelings into my newly built dungeon. If I didn't, how was I to have a relationship with my sister? Or her husband? And subsequently, her children? Or myself?

It is clear to me in hindsight that Fred is a pedophile. He is a predator, my sister and I his easy prey. He spent years patiently manipulating and grooming our little minds. Make no mistake, if Fred had ever loved my sister or me at all, he would never have laid one finger on our little bodies! In my mind as a sixteen-year-old, having sex with Fred was "my" decision. This is where my shame begins. But I was a minor, barely fifteen, when he started to groom and molest me and my sister. We were both legally *incompetent to consent to sexual acts with an adult*. Fred was a thirty-year-old man. He knew better. We didn't.

Fred continued to have sex with me until January of 1985, while I was home on winter break from college. Although I had left for college the previous August, that period was over a year. I did not consider myself a victim of rape, or even realize the consequences of his three-year-long physical and psychological assault, until I was well into my forties, over three decades later. Rereading the Fred Diaries has caused me unbearable pain, as I came to know the truth as an adult of the devious manipulation I had undergone. In order for me to heal, I was forced to relive all of the raw emotions that I had gone through as a teenager. Yet, rereading the diaries also started me asking questions, along with uncovering the emotions that were trapped for so long in my self-constructed dungeon that Casey built. Those painful questions would eventually lead to my healing, heart-wrenching as it was, which has taken over three years of intense therapy. I am still in the healing process. It was back during that time of pain, jealousy, guilt and shame that Casey was born. The girl who criticized me for decades from her dungeon where she was trapped. That girl became mother to the woman of today, an emotional role reversal.

As is brutally apparent in the long and tortuous journey that I have stumbled through, my curse was the unjustified terror that was literally paralyzing me from doing what I needed to do to be redeemed. All those years of literally sacrificing myself to protect my sister, Fred, and her family by not telling a soul my horrible secret, all this mortal fear of confronting my personal demons, only served to deny me the love and support that was there and waiting all along.

Chapter Thirteen

MY JOURNEY TO SURVIVOR

SOBRIETY

After my return from India in September of 2011, I gave up sobriety and continued to drink... until I could take my misery no more. In March of 2012, I attempted to quit drinking again and started going to recovery program meetings. In May, I wrote that I knew that life would be brighter "on the other side." This is what I envisioned as being emotionally healed with no more misery, and at least a decrease in Casey's constant criticism. I knew that I had to confront my demons. I knew that I had to face the painful events of Fred from my childhood. Finally, I somehow *knew* that sobriety was the critical first step to getting there. It was the gateway to a normal life free from suffering. It was the only way.

" . . . Almost Della" had been my motto since childhood, because I perceived that I never quite got what I wanted out of life, always coming up short. Such self-pity. I knew that I had a ton of resentments of and for myself, because I blamed MYSELF for everything that had gone wrong in my life. Most critically, I blamed myself for my failure to find a life mate and have children of my own, which had been my dream since I was a child.

Almost three months into sobriety, I was working on my resentments list and questioning what turn my career should take. I had a particularly stressful interview for the very important position of director of a nonprofit. Five board members fired questions at me for over an hour. Although I did not feel that the interview was totally unsuccessful, deep down I knew that this type of job was not for me. Add on to that the feeling that I was not "director" material. I was not good enough. As is her method, Casey would not let up on her criticism and judgment of my interview performance. The demons inside of me were still so strong. To make matters worse, the various symptoms of menopause were still in full swing. So in desperation and need of escape, I bought a pint of dark rum on the way home, and drank most of it when I got there. I had been sober eighty-six days.

I tried to return to the program for a few weeks. Counterintuitively, I eventually convinced myself that I was NOT an alcoholic, and resumed drinking for another fifteen months. I knew that I had a problem with alcohol, but I did not consider that my life was unmanageable. I did not black out when I drank, ever. I had a good job that I loved and believed that my job was the only factor that defined my "success" in life. I believed that I was managing well in life, despite my misery with my drinking and my self-blame and shame.

But my vision of manageability had no sight of the emotional turmoil that I felt inside, or how it was affecting my life and my choices in life. I didn't yet realize that this was "unmanageability". I still had so many unanswered questions about myself: love, relationships, people, emotions, desire, injustice, and unfairness. Mostly I had questions about the impact that Fred had had on my current life. Suspicion had begun in 2010 when I reached out to my friend, Rosanna, for emotional help. It had been twenty-eight years since the abuse had begun, and questions began resurfacing in my mind about the consequences of the trauma I had been through as a teen. But this was only the very beginning of a very long journey of awareness and emotional healing. I was not yet ready to face my truth. I began drinking almost every day. I had to have it by 5 p.m. On Fridays, it was 3 p.m. I was physically and emotionally ill, and I still hated myself. Self-medication was in full bloom.

Intensive Outpatient Program

In September of 2013, I finally reached a point of utter and complete misery. I went back to my favorite meeting (a women's meeting) from fifteen months prior. I went to lunch with some ladies, and a member suggested a local recovery center. At that point, I was willing to try anything! I began eight weeks of an intensive outpatient program (IOP), significantly cheaper than an inpatient program. Thankfully, they worked with me on cost, adjusting it for my current income using donor funds. It was the perfect compromise. When that eight weeks was over, I was more than willing to do another eight weeks as recommended.

This time, I was willing and determined to earn my sobriety. I had finally completely surrendered. IOP met four nights per week, Monday through Thursday, for two to three hours. Two nights were spent in group therapy, one night was a class on the disease of alcoholism, and one night was a specialized class, which was determined through the long questionnaire given as an assessment. They put me in a class on co-dependency. Go figure. On Fridays, knowing that this was my norm for beginning my weekends of drinking, I signed up to be a volunteer at the local zoo and took a shift from 4 p.m. to 7 p.m.

To my surprise and relief, the recovery program also included working with an individual therapist specializing in addiction once per week, and a family therapist named Jasmine to work with me with my family members. I felt a special connection to Jasmine. She was beautiful, and I had a sense of comfort when I was with her that I had with no one else, including my individual therapist who was a fellow just out of school.

Therapy continued for a year after the IOP program ended. My assigned individual therapist left the center when my year was up. Thankfully, Jasmine agreed to become my individual therapist. I was so grateful that she squeezed me into her busy schedule. She eventually left the center, but I followed her into her private practice, and still see her on a regular basis today. Below are a few of my journal entries from this period of getting sober and the emotional healing that went with it. Here are my journal entries from that time period:

Tuesday, September 11, 2013

It has been fifteen months since I started drinking again after my first attempt to quit. Fifteen months of misery. I *finally* surrendered that I *cannot* get sober on my own. The last time I tried, I was sober for only three months. This WILL BE the greatest thing I have ever done! I will do greater things after, but none so important since. A fortune cookie I opened recently said that I "will be recognized and honored as a community leader." And I do believe that. But I knew that I must first help myself to be free from my self-imposed torture. Most importantly, confronting my alcoholism. I knew that I must begin to enjoy myself in life. To love Della . . . to love Della. Be present in life. I will stop drinking. I will not let this affliction run my life any longer. I will be happy and I will matter. I will help students and Mother Earth!

Monday, October 1, 2013

Day 9. Today I found a new sponsor, Maggie. We talked after the meeting today. I have really been enjoying my meetings, especially a women's meeting that I have decided to call my home group. So many wise words come from these women. So much love. So many trying to make their lives better. So many helping others to make their own lives better. It is the real magic in recovery.

I am lining up my tools to help me achieve the most important task I have ever done in my life: sobriety. I attend many different program meetings in my area, and I am meeting sober people who are fun. I am excited about my new life, and I am starting IOP tomorrow! I have been on cloud nine, they call it the pink cloud. I must be prepared for the hard times ahead—knowing that they will come.

The first year will be the hardest. Maggie gave me three instructions: Call her every day and call someone else in the program every day; pray to my Higher Power every morning to stay sober today and thank Him/Her every night for keeping me sober today; and think about and list all of the ways that I am powerless over alcohol and how my life is unmanageable. I know that if I go back and read this journal, I will find many examples. Here is what I came up with:

How I Am Powerless Over Alcohol

1. I love the way alcohol makes me feel. I cannot wait to get that buzz going.
2. Drinking is not a choice! I drink even on days that I have no desire to drink AND on days that I don't even want to drink.
3. I drink at home, alone, often.
4. Once I start drinking, I cannot stop until I go to bed, or sometimes I stop after dinner.
5. When I get home from work, I HAVE to drink a glass of wine BEFORE I walk my dog.
6. I have to drink before I go out drinking with friends.
7. I keep my wine glass partially full at all times so that I lose track of the number of glasses drunk in an evening.

8. I don't let myself drink until 5:00 p.m., on Fridays it's 3:00 p.m.
9. I will not give up drinking or my way of life for potential boyfriends who can't drink.
10. I could not take a break from alcohol to see if it increased the severity of my hot flashes from menopause.
11. My good friend, Lora, told me that she would quit drinking for two weeks, and I was amazed. I knew that I could not do that. I had tried!
12. At friends' parties, I would sneak a shot of the hard stuff in the kitchen while no one was looking.
13. I always had to know where my next drink was coming from. Do I have enough to last the evening?
14. Some nights I had a good reason not to drink, but I HAD to have it anyway. I was a slave to alcohol.
15. The more I tried to quit for any period of time, the more I wanted it.
16. So I quit quitting and trying to control my drinking
17. I remember vividly, drinking at home alone and pouring that third drink when I promised myself I would only have two, and then saying, "I don't care!"
18. After one of my failed attempts at the program, I remember saying, "Well all of these people can stop. But I can't stop. So I must not be an alcoholic." Stinking thinking, they call it.

How My Life is Unmanageable

1. I drive buzzed or over the legal limit and put myself and every other person on the road around me in danger.
2. Everything I do after work and on weekends revolves around alcohol.
3. I have a hangover every Saturday morning and many weekdays at work. I wake often with feelings of remorse and hopelessness.
4. I have to justify my drinking, usually by saying something good or bad that happened, or that I just had a hard day at work so I deserved it.
5. I count the number of drinks I have each night by marking them on my calendar. I tell myself I would not be alcoholic if I drank only four of seven nights per week.
6. So many times, when I had tried to say on a hangover-day or a Tuesday, "I will not drink tonight," I always end up going to the store to buy wine, and then drinking more than I would have if I had not tried to "control" my drinking.
7. My next solution to control my drinking was to QUIT controlling my drinking, so that I would drink less. Made sense to me!
8. When I wake in the morning, before I move an inch, I ask myself "Did I drink last night? How many drinks did I have? Is today going to be a bad hangover day?" This would result in an immediate frown if my head hurt. "I will make sure to DRINK LESS NEXT TIME." But I never did drink less next time. I drink too much, again and again, ad

nauseum. Yet, I would be so happy on the few occasions that I did not drink the night before!
9. I plan for hangovers and did not schedule things on weekend mornings.
10. I miss events that I really want to attend, and am unable to do the things I love to do because I was drinking, drunk or nursing a hangover: biking, yoga, going to movies, family time, work on my company of environmental education.
11. I do not exercise.
12. I am tired all the time, mostly due to hangovers.
13. I feel horrible, physically and emotionally.
14. I had to put a note on my fridge to remind myself that alcohol makes me physically ill.
15. I would not get a dog because it would interrupt my drinking by having to walk it. When I finally did get a dog, I have to drink a glass of wine before I took her for her afternoon walk.
16. Guilt, shame, remorse and misery were common. I am a bad person because I have to drink. I hate myself.
17. I feel that I cannot find a mate because of my drinking, so I am to blame for being alone.
18. I feel that I am lazy, because I am, being a blob on the couch.
19. I don't let myself feel—I cover my feelings with alcohol, especially the reasons behind my loneliness and grief. But I have plenty of self-pity.
20. I am miserable on the inside!!! And I admit it! Yet, I still drink!
21. Alcohol made me sad and depressed for years—clinically diagnosed.

22. My career stagnated and suffered because of alcohol.
23. I accomplished nothing outside of work—no personal goals, few hobbies, no play. I do the bare minimum and feel guilty for it.
24. I do not have the ambition to work at making my own company a success.
25. I isolate.
26. I allow men and friends to cross my boundaries.
27. I took a trip to India and stayed at an ashram for three weeks to be away from alcohol. I felt it would be easier and cheaper than an in-patient treatment.
28. My problems cause me to drink more, which causes my problems.
29. I feel an internal struggle because I want to protect all life, yet I abuse my own body with alcohol.

Wow! That is a lot!!! I had never seen all of these reasons written out together in one place. Now, when I walk my dog, Sicily, instead of worrying about my next glass of wine, I notice the beauty of the trees, the birds, the sky and the flowers. Thank you, God, for my sobriety today! And a very special thank you, God, for keeping me sober at my former neighbor's son's one-year-old birthday party last Saturday. I refused a shot of vanilla vodka that was shoved into my face. I didn't drink from a friend's drink before I handed it to her. And I spent some quality time with the birthday boy! He was my human connection that day. Time to start the second half of my new life! And my journey to "the other side."

Saturday, November 10, 2013

Day 14. We watched a fantastic documentary called *Pleasure Unwoven* in IOP class this week. It was made by a doctor named Kevin McCauley, an alcoholic in recovery, who studied the brain disease of addiction. It was so memorable and educational. It presents scientific evidence of how addiction is not a disease of choice, which was believed by most of society for so long. Alcoholism is, without a doubt, a physical disease. Dr. McCauley creates a metaphor of the brain using the topography in Utah, driving through the jagged mountains and canyons in a truck. I am going to attempt to describe this in layman's terms. Don't quote me! He demonstrates that craving is an unconscious process brought on by dopamine, a chemical produced by the body. Dopamine is produced in times of stress. It is also produced by using mind altering substances such as drugs and alcohol. When dopamine is made, it attaches to receptors in the brain. An addict's brain contains more of these receptors than a normal person from long-term substance abuse. When some of those receptors get filled with a little bit of dopamine, either from putting a substance in your body (like that first drink) or made by the body itself, the rest of the receptors cry out, "Hey! My neighbor got some dopamine. Where is mine?" This creates the overwhelming physical feeling of craving that addicts get when we have that first drink. Or first hit of marijuana. Or that first pill. Or get stressed out. Even intense joy can trigger the body to release dopamine.

God has a sense of humor. I have recently experienced this, twice! The night I went out for Halloween, I relapsed when I took two Ambien and stayed awake. I had been stressed out and ful of self-pity all evening, which caused dopamine to be produced in my brain and fill some of my receptors. Then, I loaded my body with nicotine, caffeine from three Red Bulls, and then the first Ambien. I could not stop myself from taking the second pill and increasing that buzz. My body was experiencing a physical craving caused by empty, screaming receptors in my brain, beginning with the stress I felt early in the evening. This also happened that Friday night before I began IOP when I took two puffs off a joint. I convinced myself that I was going to get high with pot so that I would not drink. Like I could substitute pot for alcohol, and that would "cure" my disease. Those hits filled some receptors. Then I had the worst craving of my life, so I bought a pint of rum and drank it in a cul-de-sac near my home. That shame of hiding that rum from my roommate was my bottom.

It was also stated in class that sixty percent of the disease of alcoholism can be hereditary. I mean, think about it, humans have been abusing alcohol since cavemen first discovered fermentation. Some families are more prone to the disease, depending on their ancestry. My father was an addict of caffeine and nicotine, and had to have his one glass of scotch every day. These revelations have completely removed the shame I feel for "allowing" myself to become an alcoholic. Since the disease is a symptom of an underlying emotional cause, now I can focus completely on the root of my disease, the demons inside of me. The elation I feel from the dissolution of that shame is indescribable.

Jasmine says that I have adapted to decreased communication because I come from a broken family. My communication skills are underdeveloped, especially as they relate to conflict. She says that I have become good at dealing with bad consequences instead of communicating that I need help. I have protected my parents, but they were not there for me in all ways. She says that I was vulnerable to child abuse at age fifteen because Fred was a father figure to me. He protected us from being alone. He was more available than Daddy. She said that I did *not stand up to Mom when she blamed ME for being intimate with Fred (after Brenda had told her what was happening in her own home). I never had resources to think differently. She said that Mom did not stand up for herself either. She said that it was all Mom knew, but it was not enough. I needed and deserved more. Genetically, and of course environmentally, it became clear that I was predisposed to dysfunction. I have come to accept that truth, and my shame is diminishing.*

Jasmine says that silence is an old coping mechanism, but it does not work for me anymore. She says to start using my voice and getting practice. It is possible to be in conflict without confrontation. When in a conflict, say, "This is important and I need to think, but my mind is cloudy right now." She says to rehearse with Dawn and to prepare ahead of time. What do I want to change? Ask for support and ideas.

LESSONS FOR US ALL

I hope that what I've shared from my long and winding road is somehow helpful to you. I've also learned that everybody has a different story, but in many respects, the stories are all the same. Whatever yours is, so be it. I hope and pray you find the strength and courage to change, and most importantly of all, to talk with someone. Seek out and *listen* to those trained to guide you back to sanity.

Chapter Fourteen

THE BIG REVEAL

PLANNING THE BIG REVEAL

Coming back around to the beginning of this memoir, it is important to take you through the events that led up to one of the most important days in my life: telling my mother and sister my deepest, darkest secrets, the ones that I had kept inside for so long. My truth. I had been debating whether to tell them for months, trying to clarify my exact reasons for doing something that would inevitably cause them pain. Would it tear them away from me? Would I lose their love? I had been keeping this truth silent for so long to protect Mom, Marissa, Joey, and Alex. I didn't want to transfer my pain to them. But in the process, I was punishing myself. Here are my journal entries:

Tuesday, December 16, 2015

Upon my return from Asia, I decided to let my employer know that I was not returning to my job. My income from the part-time job as Education and Accounts Manager of a recycling company wasn't a whole lot. It just felt wrong to continue to work for a boss that lies to me, is disrespectful to me and wears down my soul. Even so, as I have no clients scheduled with my own business (although two or three possibilities exist), I have not let go of the guilt from not having enough income. I have put a lot of hard work into my recovery and healing from my past. I have been making ends meet by living off of Daddy's inheritance, but I need time to write my book. I feel compelled to write my story, like I am getting a message from God. To help other women not to make the same mistakes that I have made. To tell them not to bury their shame, like I did. I should mention that even my financial advisor is totally supportive of my taking time off to write. He told me that even if I use $30,000 of my invested money to live on while I write, and the book is not successful, that I still need to do this for me. There must have been an angel in him that day. I am too worried about money, which takes away from the purpose and meaning of my book. So Jasmine asked me to journal about just that.

First and foremost, this book is for me. The process of reading my diaries and writing about my experiences has become an important part of my healing. It is a chance for me to connect to my soul. It is therapeutic, as I revisit and write about my various life traumas and experiences. Getting it out there helps, and although it is very painful, it is helping me to heal. And writing this book is gratifying on many fronts. I do this for the people of the world. I am hoping that my experiences will help others, especially teenagers and women who have been sexually or physically abused, to understand that any older man who tells a girl sixteen or younger that he loves her, while he is inappropriately touching her private parts, or is physically hurting her in any way, is lying! I want people to learn how to set boundaries to keep our emotional and physical bodies safe. I want people to understand that every human being is worth more than a planet full of gold, just because of our very existence!

You know that awkwardness that is felt so strongly as a teenager? Well, all successful adults felt awkward at that stage in life! That awkwardness is simply not a determinant of your future success. If you are feeling awkward, get out of yourself. The best way to do this is by helping others or volunteering. Find something you find fun and meaningful. Examples might be spending time with kids in the hospital, organizing a neighborhood event to clean up your park, or plant trees where needed. The possibilities are endless. Melinda Gates, one of the richest women in the world, recently shared her definition of success: "To know that one life has breathed easier because you live." Beautiful.

Wednesday, December 23, 2015

Session with Jasmine. She told me that it is not that I want Marissa and Mom to know my truth—all that Fred did to me and my experiences at that time—but that I NEED them to know. She also said that it is very important that I learn to trust myself. This part is agonizingly slow.

Monday, December 28, 2015

I had another Fred dream. It was very vivid. But first I want to back up just a bit. The first *sankhara* (forming intention or mental imprint) that showed itself to me during the Vipassana meditation retreat in Malaysia three months ago was a vision of me yelling at Fred for what he did to me at age fifteen through seventeen that undermined and messed up my future romantic life. What I did not realize, until now, is that I feel the need to tell him off face to face in order to free myself of this burden. I had always thought it was best to NEVER see him again. Well, you will see him at his kids' weddings. Now, I am thinking that perhaps never seeing him again is wrong.

In early December, Fred wrote a birthday message to me on Facebook. A few days later, he sent a check to me in a Christmas card. He is finally repaying me the money he owes me for bailing him out of jail two decades ago, for "alleged" underage molestation of his daughter's friend. I tore the birthday card to pieces, and blocked him on Facebook. Am I attracting him to send me these messages? Why am I dreaming about him? Does he know the anguish that I am now going through because of him? And of course, I did deposit the check.

On December 20th, my contractor hired to install my new granite countertops increased his fee AGAIN to a total of $600 over his "GUARANTEED low price." This is $600 over what I would have paid if I had hired the other contractor that I liked. But I was trying to save $200. I feel like I have been taken advantage of by him, and I start to cry. I call my friend, Crystal, and she helps me to see why I am so upset. He is just a "trigger." That little girl inside of me, Casey, is hurt. He brings up a vulnerability within me because I feel that he took advantage of me, just like Fred did. It is a lack of control, as I am not in charge of his arbitrary price increases. If I depend on someone else, they always seem to take advantage of me. Crystal said the universe sent this contractor to me so that I would be able to see more clearly. I must release this incessant pain. Until I do, the universe will continue to send people to take advantage of me. Learn this! I must shift my energy. How? Pray. Ask my angels for help. Crystal says that my angels want to help me. They are just like race horses waiting at the starting gate for me to ask for help. She said to tell them "I don't know what to do." Then, totally surrender and trust that they will show me the way forward. Be open to receive their messages. She also said to know that I am already whole and complete. Have trust and faith. Set in motion all that I want to change in my life. Let go, and let God.

That night, I meditated for thirty minutes, then went to my choir holiday party at the director's house. I have recently joined my church choir. I felt that my energy had shifted, and two people at the party told me that I was exuding light and positive energy. And I got asked out by a thirty-six-year-old who knew that I had just turned forty-eight! I had so much fun at that party. We sang carols by the piano, near a beautiful Christmas tree with sparkling white lights. We were joyfully expressive and we danced. I talked with fellow choir members and made new friends. It was magical. I felt like I was in a scene of an old Christmas movie.

Our choir sang at the three Christmas eve services. The songs were so beautiful. In the service, we each got a candle with a message wrapped around it. To reiterate what Crystal had told me, my messages were

1. God is in charge of my life. Every need is fulfilled easily
and completely.
2. The spirit of Christ within me fills my mind and body
with new life, new strength and new health.
3. God's will for me is complete peace and joy!

Now, to my dream last night. The last of a series. My very good friend Lora, Marissa, a bunch of friends and family, maybe Mom, were all at a long wooden table in a bar. Some are drinking beer. I am happy that I am not drinking. I glance across the table at Lora and she is not drinking either. Some people get up from the table, and suddenly I am alone with Fred. I rise in disgust and rush to the door. He follows me out, he wants to talk. I DO NOT. I turn to run, but he grabs my hand. I try to shake him off, but I can't. I look at my hand and realize there is some sort of metal tie around both of our hands. I cannot get away from him. Fear, anxiety and disgust rise within me. I then awoke, somewhat panicked.

I just cannot decide if it would be better for me if I DID confront Fred. Are my dreams sending me a message? Or are they just an echo of my ongoing indecision? I called a friend tonight, Stacey, to ask if she felt freer after she finally confronted her sexual abuser. She said yes, absolutely! I talked with Dawn about my dreams at the meditation retreat about yelling at Fred, Marissa and Mom. She said to talk with Fred only. That if I tell Marissa and Mom about what he did to me, that it would only hurt them. Have I been sent all of these messages to tell me that I must confront Fred? Eventually? Is it not enough to forgive him, in order to allow me to heal completely? Forgiving and writing a letter of my truth to Mom and Marissa was an important step. But do I have to confront him? And if I don't, will I ever be free of the burden that I have carried? Part of me is terrified that if I don't face him, I will continue to be trapped in this small room inside my soul filled with darkness, self-doubt and fear. My dungeon. The home that Casey built.

Tuesday, January 5, 2016

Another dream. I am romantically involved with someone that I do not love. We are sitting together. I tell him that I am going to leave him. He pulls out a gun and shoots me near my right arm pit. I should be bleeding a lot, but I realize that I am not. I look down and realize that it was just a bee bee gun. I feel no pain. Are guilt and shame still deep-rooted within me?

Wednesday, January 6, 2016

Today in a meeting at my home group, I felt resentment triggered by money and self-pity. Two ladies shared about their child rearing woes, but one had a nanny and the other had a driver. High-class problems, the fellowship calls it. Both of them certainly had valid issues. Still, I could not get off the feeling that they should not be complaining, because they both have children and money. I realized that I may never get either of those things. Victimhood. I let the tears flow during the meeting. Then, twice again during the same meeting. Good thing that recovery meetings are one place where tears can be expected. Visibly upset, my self-pity party starts and I get even more agitated. After the meeting, two lovely ladies who had noticed my tears approach me and comfort me. They get my cell number. I feel so honored by this. The love that happens in those meetings is so awesome, so real. Especially, for me, this sacred women's meeting. There is never any hesitation to help a fellow lady alcoholic. They text and call me over the next twenty-four hours. So sweet. I love the instinct in women to help others. And I want to be one of the women helpers. One day.

I feel this recent resentment has to do with my possible confrontation with Fred. I feel the need to talk with someone about it now. It can't be Marissa or Mom. Dawn and my sponsor, Daisy, don't answer their phone tonight. I call my friend Crystal, and thankfully she answers the phone. I explain the dream of December 28th. My intense fear of seeing and confronting Fred. My unrelenting fear that this is the path that MUST be taken in order to release my pain, shame, guilt and burden of my nightmare experiences as a teen. As I am explaining my pain that I experienced in the meeting, Crystal interrupts me. "Fred is just the schmuck who hurt you. It is Marissa and your mom that you love. It is them you need to face and tell your story to! Not Fred!" I feel my energy shift. It is almost a physical reaction. And the feeling of knowing this to be true flows over my mind like a warm, cozy blanket. I will reveal my truth to Mom and Marissa. Relief from my anxiety of confusion is palpable. I realize that my angels may be speaking through Crystal. She has the amazing ability to connect with them, more than most. She is a healer. Dawn was wrong. That is okay, she is not inside of me. I know what is best for me. And I must start trusting my intuition. Then, the relief that I never have to face Fred flows over me. I may never, ever see him again. And that is fine by me! I must have faith that the universe will let me know in time what is right. And I am comforted by that.

Crystal continues, "Make sure you speak with them in a safe place, your home. It may be separate, or together. Tell them that you must discuss something very important with them. Your mom will have a lot of guilt. Marissa will need some space to process. But know that you cannot control their reaction. That is theirs to own." I love Crystal. She was surely sent to me by God.

QUESTIONING THE REAL PURPOSE

Thursday, January 7, 2016

Talking with my sponsor Daisy this morning, I again begin to question whether I should confront Marissa and tell her the truth. "What will you gain?" Daisy asks. "Your mother did not protect you. But what did Marissa do? She will be changed forever, as well as her relationship with her kids' father." Ugh. Back to unsettling indecision. "Are you just unloading some of your backpack for your sister to carry?" Daisy asks. If this is true, then I should reassess whether or not to reveal my truth to her. What to do, what to do?

Session with Jasmine. "Why was that fifteen-year-old so vulnerable to be preyed upon?" Jasmine asks.

"Well, I was young and I didn't know any better. I was abandoned by my father at a very young age, the one man I love and trust most in the world. There is probably more."

"There is a lot more, Della. I want you to go home and make a list for next time. Think about this: a good-looking, older man enters your family's life. A family with an absent father. He kind of plays the role of a father. He wants to spend time with that fifteen-year-old misfit. He gets her alone by playing cards with her, and tells her that she is beautiful. And that he loves her. And that he loves her more than her sister. He is probably telling her sister the same thing. He continues to prey on you. Even after you shut him out of your life for over a year, as he is living with your sister. Because nothing has changed in him. He still wants to have sex with you." Jasmine says.

"And Marissa gets the prince, but no one acknowledges the pain, suffering and abuse that I endured!" I reply, then pause. "I now know why I must confront Mom and Marissa—

to finally get the compassion that I never got as a child. Or will they give it?

"I remember once crying out to my mother in the middle of the night when I was thirteen. Earlier that day, my cat was run over in the street right in front of our townhouse. A German lady neighbor knocked on our door. I answered. She very coldly said, 'Would you please remove your dead cat from the middle of the road?' I looked over her shoulder and saw the bloody remains of my beloved Lance on the road. I screamed in horror and slammed the door in her face. I was traumatized. That night, I just wanted my mother to be a mother. I just wanted her to hold me while I cried. I had been through a lot. At the minimum, I wanted her to hear my cries and comfort me to show me that she cared. Perhaps bring me a glass of water. She never came. The next day, I told her that I had a nightmare about my dead and bloody cat. Mom replied, 'I heard you cry out.' My heart broke. She had heard me, and she chose not to come to my bedside. She must not love me enough to console me when I had just gone through the trauma of seeing the bloody remains of my dead cat." Hard to fathom, especially for a thirteen-year-old.

I continued my train of thought to Jasmine, "Then, when Dawn's mother told Mom that Fred was sexually abusing both of her daughters, Mom blamed me! 'I can't believe you would do that to me! After all of the money that I spent on you at the expensive hotel last month.' She said that it was my fault that Fred did that to me." I cried silently on Jasmine's couch. "Perhaps Marissa will forgive me for what I have done?

"I know that I am still processing this, but I still feel shame and guilt for having an affair with him. While he was engaged to Marissa, and even after she discovered that she was pregnant. But I must ask for the forgiveness that I deserve. I must lay the foundation so that I can forgive myself.

To eradicate the shame that I have been carrying for so long. For over thirty years."

Jasmine replied, "She may not forgive you right away. Be prepared for that."

My mind began to race. After thirty years, my conscious mind was finally aware that that fifteen-year-old version of me, Casey, was indeed innocent. I was a victim of sexual abuse. I am a survivor! But subconsciously, I still feel so much guilt and shame. And that part of my mind has sought opportunities to work out this issue. It led me into bad relationships and situations where I could bring that guilt, shame and fear into my awareness, the inevitable consequences be damned!

Throughout my adult life, I have allowed fifteen boyfriends to treat me like crap. I could not accept my innocence, so I found opportunities to beat myself up. Instead of facing my guilt, I have buried it deep down, and numbed the pain with alcohol. Because of this, I have attracted relationships with men who have verbally criticized me and emotionally hurt me, triggering this backlash of guilt. I have NEVER known true love or a healthy relationship. Guilt and shame have been constant, yet unacknowledged emotions inside of me. And I have never forgiven myself. Ever—until now.

Deep down, I do not love myself. So I have never felt completely at peace with myself. And I certainly have never trusted myself. I would not allow myself to feel that I was good enough to deserve a good man. I was far less than perfect. I subconsciously perpetuated a pattern in the men that I chose to have a relationship with. Daddy tried to tell me this in his letter. The pattern to continue to experience the pain. Over and over. I need to completely appreciate all that I truly am. I must.

I thought again about revealing my truth to my mother and sister. "If Marissa begins to blame me for what he did to me, I must say, 'Stop. You are allowed to feel what you feel, but you are not allowed to talk to me like that.' I am grateful for you and the women in my life that support me."

Jasmine says, "This is an exciting time in your life right now. Each week, you are piling on the experiences of talking about your past with your support group. Dawn, Crystal, Daisy and other women are helping you through your healing." *Exciting* is not a word I would have used. But I guess she is right.

Sunday, January 10, 2016

As I was reading in a program book, I looked at my bookmark which reads, "You will know the truth, and the truth shall set you free." I am caught in anguish between the walls of wanting Marissa and Mom to know my truth, and NEEDING them to know my truth. I don't want to hurt them, or risk losing the love they have for me. I feel like I need to protect them from the truth. I think of the bookmark again, *"Set me free?" How? Am I locked up?* And it hits me, Yes! Casey was locked in a dungeon deep within me when I hid the secret that Fred was repeatedly touching me on my virgin private parts while we were playing cards in the living room. It was too easy for him living with us. My mother did not protect us. I threw the key away when, in New Orleans, I first discovered that he was having sex with Marissa as well. That was the worst moment of my life. He had told me that he loved me! But how could he love me, and have sex with my sister? Sex became something different for me before I even had a chance to experience it! I was warped, very early on.

I am so nervous. I have set the date with Marissa and Mom to come over so that I can read them "The Letter of My Truth" on February 13th. Now, I just need to write it!

Tuesday, February 9, 2016

Session with Jasmine did not go as planned. And now my level of certainty about telling Mom and Marissa my truth has lessened . . . again. I finally wrote the letter of my truth, and read it to Jasmine as a role-playing exercise. Before I read it, I expressed my high levels of fear and anxiety that, after reading my letter, my sister would take away our loving relationship of sisterhood and friendship. I was so nervous reading it, that my mouth and throat felt like a desert.

After I finished the letter of my truth, Jasmine asked, "How do you feel?"

"I am scared."

"I am scared too. Put the letter down." She paused in thought. "It feels like you still have some unresolved questions about your part in what happened to you." Jasmine said. I did not say anything. "Do you have any empathy for the way Marissa will feel?" This question threw me into a spiral of guilt. I said nothing. "Are you trying to seek revenge for the way she treated you? Or for the fact that she got her prince?" Jasmine asked me. I stared at the floor frowning like a child who was being punished. I tried desperately to think. "Why do you tell her that Fred told you that he loved you more than her?"

I was shocked. This had never consciously entered my mind. I thought that I was trying to prove that he was a liar. But subconsciously, I realized that in a way, I did want to hurt her. Perhaps in the same way that I told her at the Cheesecake Factory a few months before that Fred had messed with me too. I remembered the jealousy that I felt as a teenager when Marissa grabbed Fred's private parts in the swimming pool right in front of me. And Mom was there too! Although it was dark, and he was facing away from us, the way that he laughed, I knew exactly what she had done. She knew that I was watching.

I felt like that was an emotional bullet for me, directly from Marissa's hateful gun. And it triggered a heck of a lot of tears for me. When I later asked Fred about the pool incident, he laughed and said, "Yes, she grabbed my dick." He laughed at the situation! He had no regard for my feelings! When I look back on the conversation that I later had with Fred, telling him how much his reaction had hurt me, I realize that he had then told me just what I wanted to hear. He said that he was sorry, when it is clear now that he was not. He was manipulating Marissa and me the whole time! But we were so young. He was the inappropriate adult. He was the deviant, not her. How many other examples were there? Too many. He made us jealous enough to hurt each other so often. I hate him for that. Marissa and I already argued too much before he came into our lives.

Through it all, it wasn't just that she ended up marrying Fred. I didn't want him (or so I tried to delude myself.) Was the letter just my way of getting her back for being so evil to me during our childhood and adolescence? It seemed like she was somehow jealous of me, just because I was alive. Always. And so, she bullied me. For so long. So yes, perhaps I slept with Fred to pay her back! I was so tired of getting shat upon. She deserved it! But oh the pain and guilt that I feel now for that revenge. I love Marissa so much now.

In rereading my diary, I discovered that Fred and I started having sex near the end of the fall semester of my senior year of high school. I was sixteen. In my last semester of high school, we probably had sex only a handful of times. I honestly don't remember. I have repressed most of those memories. Another coping mechanism, I am sure. But that same spring, they announced that Marissa was pregnant. And that they were getting married. Another dagger in my bleeding, broken heart.

I distinctly remember the very last time that Fred and I had sex. I had come home for winter break from my freshman year of college. I had just turned eighteen. We were on the floor in the hallway of their townhome. The same townhome that was my home for seven years, but where Fred and Marissa now lived. We were only feet away from the place on the floor in the living room where Fred had first molested me. I will never forget, after my orgasm, I burst into tears. I told Fred that I wished that the baby was mine. I was so torn and hurt! Marissa had won his love, affection, attention, and now marriage and a baby on the way! Even though I did not want to marry Fred, she had gotten someone to love. And now they were having a child. When I wanted him out of my life—out of my family's lives forever, he fucking got her pregnant! He took the control completely away from me! I realized that it was revenge in my mind. Yes, I was in love with him, but maybe I also slept with him for revenge. God, he caused us so much pain, and ruined our lives! Perhaps that is why I never told a soul. That is the REAL shame I feel. The acid drip in the dungeon, slowly eating Casey (and me) away. My shame had caused me so much pain. It needed to end, one way or another.

Okay. I take ownership of my insensitive actions and poor choices. Even though he put me in the position to make those choices, he was the predator! So now my part is clear. There it is. Can I forgive myself? Am I seeking forgiveness from Marissa for what I need to forgive myself? Jasmine asked, "If you feel that Marissa's forgiveness will absolve the forgiveness that you need from yourself, then aren't you just repeating the pattern? Aren't you continuing to seek from others that which you cannot give to yourself? And if so, aren't you giving Marissa YOUR power by doing that?" Damn, Jasmine was good! Damn it all to hell!

I continued to stare at the floor. The tears were flowing. I searched my thoughts. I must give myself that power! That is the only way to love myself completely! I see that now! So how do I forgive myself? It must come from within.

Jasmine says, "This is all very complex. Remember to stay compassionate with yourself."

"I am so impatient! I am doing everything that I can to heal. But I want it all resolved now!"

Jasmine had thrown a wrench into my "reveal" plans. I cancelled the reading of the letter of my truth with Mom and Marissa. I must resolve my own issues first. Am I trying to get Marissa back? Seek revenge? Hurt her for hurting me? As for my part, at sixteen years old: did I feel that I was getting her back by sleeping with Fred? Yes, that is a big part of my shame. If I give Marissa my power, won't she then be able to hurt me? Good questions, no doubt.

I feel like I have come to a stand-still. Again. This may be why I hate coming to a stand-still while sitting in traffic. Hmmmm. But I *am* moving forward. I am working on my healing, even though it seems like I am at a halt. I must feel right with Marissa. At best, I should feel more love for myself first. The letter should come from a place of love, not from a place of spite or revenge. Maybe there is a gentler way to do this. The letter may be too harsh the way it is currently written. I must ask God how to get in touch with my heart. Crystal says that I am going to get there. I must muddle through a lot more, but I will get there. How much longer must I endure this bitter torment?

Thursday, February 11, 2016

In my effort to forgive myself, I thought it would be a good idea to google statutory rape. I was sixteen, which is below the age of eighteen, the legal age in Texas to consent to sex. Therefore, I was a minor. This means that I could not *legally consent to sex with an adult, and that I was therefore coerced into having sex with Fred. Meaning that Fred used my vulnerabilities and love for him to convince me to have sex with him. He was fourteen years older than me! I was incapable of consenting, which makes it non-consensual. It WAS rape! That word just seems so harsh. (Or am I still minimizing what happened to me?) I had always felt that it was my fault because I had consented. But he was the adult. He was the predator. This is a lot to take in. Regardless, it is also a foundation that I can use to begin to forgive myself.*

So why am I telling Marissa and Mom my truth?

1. *I need to tell them my story face to face. I need to tell them my truth. I need for them to know! The silence is killing me emotionally and physically.*
2. *So that they can finally understand what I went through and how I was injured emotionally.*
3. *For my personal survival. I have been through depression, addiction and was even suicidal for a short period. I am at the end of my rope.*
4. *Even though I was coerced, I still must ask Marissa for her forgiveness. It is okay if it takes her a while. I should not expect it right away, if ever.*
5. *So that I can stop punishing myself.*
6. *So that I can attract a good man. I can only attract a man as good as the good that I feel about myself. That is something so important that I have learned in my healing.*
7. *So that I can break the cycle. Stop my pattern of poor choices in men.*
8. *To help me heal so that I can move past it. Once and for all!*

I now realize that my level of fear and anxiety while I was reading Jasmine the letter of my truth, as well as the dryness of my mouth and throat, were clues that something was wrong. I still needed to work on the guilt within myself. Ugh.

Monday, February 15, 2016

Yesterday, Crystal invited me to do the I-Fly with her. I-Fly is a place where you step into a vertical tube of air blowing upward incredibly fast, and float on it. It is supposed to mimic jumping out of a plane, and sky divers use it for training. But anyone can do it. I was a natural! I screamed for joy the entire minute. Even though we had learned hand signs, our trainer did not need to use any of them with me. He released his hold on me within ten seconds, and I was on my own! I got to fly three times, because Crystal was having shoulder pain after her first fly. It was exhilarating. And, like scuba diving, it made me feel brave and self-confident. I was stepping out into the unknown. I was capable of facing my fears . . .

The Cabin

Wednesday, March 2, 2016

Tim, my masseuse and healer, told me after my last massage that it was important to spend more time in nature while I am going through this confusion. And to create some art. So I bought a sketch tablet and some paints and rented a cabin on the water. I also brought a book that Jasmine had suggested for me to read. It is a guide for sexual abuse survivors called *The Courage to Heal*. As I began reading it, I remembered three other times I was sexually abused. First, I must have been three or four at my Nana's house (Daddy's mother), I was forced to lie down on the bathroom counter and she inserted a tube into my anus and turned the water on. I thought I was being punished. I think she did the same to Marissa, but I am not sure. I distinctly remember Marissa talking to me through the locked bathroom door because I was crying. She was concerned. Then, when I was around eight, a guy that my mom had been dating for a while stuck his tongue in my mouth while holding me when Mom was in another room. The third time was at my first gynecological appointment. I must have been fourteen. The perverted asshole doctor put his finger inside my anus. The pain was very real, and like nothing I had ever experienced. I was so mad and full of rage. I do not know why I did not tell Mom. Instead, I took it out on her. We went directly to K-Mart after, and I refused to speak to her. My future pattern of self-implosion emerged very early on.

Thursday, March 3, 2016

Reading *The Courage to Heal*, I was, quite simply, amazed. It is like one light bulb after another was turning on. Now, my whole house was lit. As a rape survivor, I suffered despair, depression, anxiety attacks, and addiction, because I was susceptible to these things! These are a direct consequence of my sexual abuse. I got involved with people who were inappropriate, unavailable, and who abused me. I didn't know who to trust. Or worse, I trusted too many people too readily. I frequently felt betrayed and taken advantage of. And this was because of my abuse. I have always had good friends, but I struggled in sexual relationships. This is freaking amazing. Wait, it gets better, "When abuse is coupled with affection, the need for nurturing can become linked with sex." And "I need to control everything about sex to feel safe." No wonder I could not separate love from sex! I tried so hard! I failed. Clearly.

The book also talked about how survivors coped, and what they did to survive the trauma of being sexually abused. And they advise honoring what I did to survive! Really? Honor these disgusting things? The following represent my own coping mechanisms for my personal abuse:

1. This man that I love and trust, and a father figure, is kissing and touching me. I did not fight off his advances because I needed his attention and closeness. It felt so good. And I adored my abuser!
2. I denied that I was sexually abused for over three decades. I never considered that I was a victim, and completely innocent. I thought that I had consented to sex with Fred, that it was my choice too. Denial is a coping mechanism. But sixteen-year-olds are too young to consent to sex with adults. He was almost twice my age. Plus, there was a ton of added guilt and shame for having sex with my sister's boyfriend, which may have been worse than the abuse itself, considering the subsequent self-torture I put myself through.
3. I thought that if I just ignored the shame long enough, that I would get over it. Oddly enough, I have no recollection of sex with Fred apart from the first and last times. Forgetting or repressing is also a coping mechanism. Over time, and trauma, the power of my grief, guilt and shame only grew.
4. I minimized, and somehow even forgot, how painful that time-period was. I thought that since there was no "force" involved, that it wasn't that bad. It

wasn't until I reread my diaries that I remembered the intense emotional trauma that I went through. But even then, I felt that women who were force-raped had it so much worse than me.

5. I blocked out these memories by abusing alcohol. Numb and mute the pain. This was a coping mechanism! I had no one safe to turn to. No one knew my dark secret. I could not handle my grief, shame and guilt. So I had to repress my anger and rage with alcohol and drugs. My first love married my sister!

6. I had sex with a lot of men in college, and the first few years after. I lost count. I have blocked a lot of that out. It baffles me that there were so many. Looking back, my emotional development was warped by an older man at a time when my sexuality was budding. I was using sex to get close to men. Casey was trying so hard to fill that hole. Perhaps I was promiscuous because I drowned those evenings with alcohol. My lifestyle was facilitated by alcohol. Sex goes with a good buzz. All coping mechanisms. Denial dominated.

7. To achieve control and remain safe, I forced relationships that were not meant to be. Ray played by the rules, but in the end, I did not love him. I married a man who was emotionally stable, who wouldn't leave me, and who was a high achiever. Harry was my rock. That said, I was not IN love with him. I gave myself hell for that stupid decision for years. When I closed my eyes, I could see Casey shaking her head at me for marrying him, and then letting him go. Through therapy, I now realize that I was coping with my sexual abuse. Fred warped my

conception of a normal relationship by having sex with me while he was with my sister, telling me that he would never marry Marissa, and then doing just that, all while I was still in love with him.
8. I escape by watching too much TV so that I can avoid or ignore my feelings. I still give myself hell for this. I had no idea that I was coping by escaping myself.
9. Since I have been in sobriety, I regularly eat sweets at night. This is another form of addiction, and hence, another coping mechanism.
10. I still smoke cigarettes, about a pack every five days.
11. I exhibit excessive "busy-ness." I always feel like I must be doing something to avoid feeling lazy. I am always rushing. I must achieve to feel like I am a good and successful person. Maybe it is to avoid feeling at all?
12. I padded my expenses from a previous employer, to a total of around $150. I have since repaid this by making a donation to the organization. But this book says that theft is a way to create a distraction, which is yet another coping mechanism.
13. Now I am avoiding sex and men completely. In 2009, Levi was my last real boyfriend.

I gave myself so many excuses to hate myself so that I could feel guilty. I held myself especially shameful because I allowed Fred to touch me and have sex with me while he was also being intimate with my sister. In all honesty, I forgot that I wanted so much to be close to him. Because of my vulnerabilities, I needed his attention and affection. I adored my abuser. In no world could I have fought off his sexual advances. I was not wrong. I was not to blame. I was very *vulnerable, and he was very perceptive—all of this makes sense now. What a relief!*

Jasmine talks a lot about the healing process. She says to take care of myself, eat right, get enough sleep (check, this one I definitely do) and to do things that I enjoy. As I sit here writing at the cabin, I am listening to a red-bellied woodpecker sing. This is a form of bliss for me (I go especially crazy for the Pileated Woodpecker, such a fantastic creature). Jasmine also says to be patient with myself and not to rush the healing process. If I force it, that action will delay the healing. She says to feel my feelings and not to stuff the hurt any longer. She warned me that healing is hard work. It will bring up some tough stuff and will cause me much pain and sadness. That has certainly been true. Some of this has been excruciating.

THE LETTER TO MARISSA

March 2016

Just as I was wondering <u>if</u> I would ever reveal my truth to Marissa and Mom, an opportunity came out of the blue. I believe it was a sign from God. It was time. Marissa had invited Fred to a planned family lunch while my niece, Alex, was in town for a family wedding. When I inadvertently found out during a conversation with Marissa, I froze in terror. I knew that I could not face him at this delicate stage in my healing. Marissa noticed my hesitation, and I had no choice but to uninvite myself. In a panic, I was able to talk with Jasmine, who told me to tell Marissa a portion of the truth. She knew some of it already, of course. She knew why Fred was kicked out of our home all those years ago, when we were teenagers—that he had become sexual with both of us. At that time, he had not had actual intercourse with me (yet). In fact, our pants had never come off. I did not have to mention that sex had occurred a year later between Fred and I, after they were an official couple. Instead of the ten-page letter, I rewrote a one-page letter.

The next day, she came over to color my hair for my cousin's wedding. I was so nervous with anticipation as she applied the color to my hair. As we were waiting for my hair color to set, my heart pounding, I asked Marissa if we could sit on the couch and talk. I read her the letter.

Dear Marissa,

Do you remember when Fred was kicked out of our home? Do you remember why? It was because he was touching both of us sexually. Do you remember how you felt when he was kicked out of our home? [Let her answer.] Well, I felt that pain too. I thought I loved him.

"That must have been hard for you," she replied. I melted a little at her immediate compassion, but continued reading.

Remember when you found him again, and began seeing him secretly? And then Mom found out. And then Daddy was summoned from New Orleans, because Mom could not handle the situation by herself? And how Daddy sent us to therapy? Remember how the stupid therapist played cards with us?

But eventually you moved in with Fred. Do you remember that I did not see or speak to him for over a year after that? And then, you got pregnant, and a wedding date was set. But at seventeen, the pain was still there, as he became my brother-in-law. So I just buried the pain . . . for thirty years. I pretended it did not exist. I pretended that nothing was wrong inside of me. I thought that if I ignored the pain long enough, that it would just go away. I remembered recently that the therapist we saw as teens told me then to seek therapy before I tried to have a normal relationship with a man. But I never did. At the time, I could not understand why I would need therapy.

But I am learning now that my silence and buried pain has affected my entire life. Shortly after I left for college, I was sexually molested by my employer.

"That must have been terrible for you! I can't believe this," she replied, again with clear and sincere compassion.

I have been in therapy as part of my recovery from alcoholism for two and a half years. I am now, finally, working through that pain. And so, I cannot see Fred during this delicate phase of my healing. And that is why I cannot go to lunch with you and Alex, since Fred will be there.

Marissa's reaction was full of understanding, love and compassion, "Why didn't you tell me sooner?"
"Because I did not want to lose you."
"You are my family! And Fred is a PERVERT!" Marissa blurted out.
I cannot describe the incredible relief and love that I felt for her at that moment! Thirty years of fear of losing my sister if she knew the truth, because I thought that she would blame me, melted away in that single instant. Jasmine said later that hearing Marissa describe Fred as a pervert allowed me to finally look at that man from the outside—a place that I had never been to before.
The timer went off. As we walked to my kitchen sink so she could wash the color out of my hair, Marissa said, "I kind of already knew that you had sex with Fred. Alice had said something to me years ago. But I didn't want to believe it."
What? I was shocked. Marissa had asked Fred for a divorce only seven years after they were married. He then married another young girl, which only lasted a short time. Fred then married Alice, a woman his same age, who is his current wife. After Fred had been sent to jail for alleged child molestation with a nine-year-old friend of his daughter, Alex, the child's

mother forced him to leave town. Fred had apparently told Alice everything. Even the fact that he had sex with me too, the sister of his then girlfriend. Then, unbeknownst to Fred, Alice had pulled Marissa aside and told her, "You know, he had sex with your sister too!" This was many years ago. I kind of remembered this, because Marissa had said something vague to me at the time: "I know something about you and Fred." But when I asked Fred about it the next day, he said that Marissa did not know that we had slept together. And I believed him. So I blew off her comment, and forgot about it. More denial.

Since she already knew, I validated this truth, "Yes, Fred and I did have sex." Another huge weight lifted off my shoulders.

As Marissa turned on the kitchen faucet and felt it to see if it was warm, she asked, "After we were together?" Yikes! There it was, again! The whole truth was coming out, and I was not controlling it. I had sex with my sister's boyfriend after they were living together. I had not anticipated this question! I was planning to leave this part out, per Jasmine's suggestion. But I knew that I had to be truthful to Marissa. Yet somehow, I could not verbalize. It was just too ugly. There was too much shame and guilt surrounding it. So with sticky color in my hair, and watching Marissa with her hand under the kitchen faucet waiting for the water to warm, I simply nodded in affirmation. And it was DONE!

But shockingly, she did not blame me! After the color was rinsed out and I was seated back in the chair, we began the long conversation. I told her of my unending pattern of choosing bad men to have relationships with. While she was getting the tangles out of my curly hair, she said that she felt bad about all the emotional and physical abuse that I had endured from men for the past thirty years.

When I was through with my story, I said, "Marissa, I was wrong for sleeping with Fred after you were together with him. I am so sorry. Do you hate me?"

"You didn't do anything wrong! It was not your fault!" she blurted out.

My sister continued to love me! My worst fears were not coming true! My sponsor Daisy, Dawn, and the psychic had been wrong! I see now that Marissa inviting Fred to our family lunch with Alex was meant to be. It had to happen that way. My relationship with Marissa changed that day. My unspeakable secret was out, and I had not lost my only sister. And in fact, we had become closer in those moments of my revelation. She finally knew my truth. I was beyond elation.

I told Marissa that I had recently written the full story in a letter to her and Mom, and I asked her if it would be okay for me to read it to her and Mom together. She agreed, and we set a time to get together with Mom in two days.

Chapter Fifteen

THE LETTER OF MY TRUTH

March 12, 2016

Dear Marissa and Mom,

The next step in my healing is to talk to both of you about something very important to me about my past. I have been hiding my truth from both of you for over three decades. It has taken two and a half years of recovery and therapy for me to have this conversation with you and finally reveal my truth.

Most alcoholics and addicts are addicts due to events that happened in their past. It has taken me over thirty years to finally shed my tears and relieve my pain. Pain which has been locked in a dungeon deep within me. My guilt and shame were never brought to the surface until recently, yet they have impacted and shaped my entire adult life. My silence has kept my heart bound. I anticipate that my heart will be set free when we can talk about this.

This is the most difficult thing I have ever done. There is a part of me that is terrified that I will be rejected by you both for telling you my truth now. I hope that the opposite is true, and that we can become closer. Some of the things I am going to say are going to hurt. But I am not doing this to hurt either of you. I am doing this because it is the only way for me to heal. I ask that you listen with an open heart. And I ask you both not to say anything until I am finished.

I want to take you back to a time when Marissa and I were adolescents. Why the fifteen-year-old version of me was so vulnerable:

Marissa and I were abandoned by our father at the ages of three and four—the one man I loved and trusted most in the world.

Our father then moves to another state. This is devastating to us both.

Our father always lives with another man and never dates women, a bit confusing.

Our father has hurt you, Mom, very much, and this hurts me. But none of us ever talks about the pain you were feeling.

You are raising two girls alone.

You work very hard, and most nights, you come home from work angry and yelling at us.

We never tell you how bad that makes us feel.

Marissa and I argue on a daily basis, and she bullies me for fifteen years. I believe a lot of the criticisms that she throws my way.

I was very young and not very wise.

I had no male role model.

I had never witnessed a healthy relationship between a man and a woman.

As are all adolescents, I was going through puberty. My hormones were surfacing inside of me, causing unpredictable swings of joy and rage for no apparent reason. And the beginnings of feelings of sexual desire arise within me that are uncontrollable. Confusion is a new friend.

I was bullied by the boys in school because I did not develop breasts while in high school. This teasing by my male peers was truly devastating, and I can remember it vividly to this day.

I really tried to be successful in school. Because grades were important to me, I was bullied at school for being too smart and a "goodie goodie."

I did not fit into any clique at school, not even the misfits.

I was betrayed by many of my friends at school. My junior and senior year, I had no close friends to eat lunch with.

I feel like my status at school is very low. I feel like a nobody.

In high school, only one boy asked me out on a date.

I kept all of this inside of me. For all of these reasons, I am filled with the feeling of not being good enough, and I unknowingly punish myself for it on a daily basis in my head.

At the age of fifteen, a good looking, twenty-nine-year-old man enters our family's life through a neighbor friend. He wants to spend a lot of time with our family. But who would want to spend time with this fifteen-year-old misfit? Because of the way I was treated by some boys in school, I was thrilled and excited that any male person would want to spend time with me. He was filling a hole that was inside my heart. He became sort-of a father figure to me. He made me feel good about myself. He made me feel wanted.

Then, he moves in to our home. He plays cards with me in the living room on most nights. Eventually, he tells me that I am beautiful. And he tells me that he loves me. As time goes on, he tells me that my tiny little boobies are pretty. He starts touching them. And kissing them, and kissing me. This is my very first intimate experience with a male.

But he is paying a lot of attention to Marissa too. This is very confusing to me. I tell him that I am jealous. I write him letters, and we discuss it. Again, he tells me that he loves me very much. That our relationship is important to him. And I believe him.

I will never forget the moment in New Orleans (while visiting Daddy), on the sofa bed on Burgundy Street, when you, Marissa, tell me that he is having sex with you. This is a crushing blow, and it felt like my heart died right then! I felt so much betrayal from the man I thought loved me. The man that I loved more than anyone at that time. But for reasons that I still do not understand, I do not tell you that he is touching me too. Probably because my self-esteem was zero. And, I somehow wanted to protect you, Marissa, even though I am feeling a devastating pain that I have never felt before. First loves are always the strongest.

When I return from New Orleans alone, I am thrown into a depression, and I avoid him. My best friend, Dawn, knows that something is wrong with me. She eventually gets the truth out of me, that he is touching me and having sex with you. Unbeknownst to me, Dawn tells her mother, who correctly identifies this man as an abuser. And she is compelled to tell you, Mom. Of course, you immediately kick Fred out of our home. When Marissa returns from New Orleans, Mom tells her that she knows that Fred is sleeping with her and molesting me. Marissa has an emotional break-down.

Despite everything, Marissa finds Fred, and they begin seeing each other secretly. Mom eventually catches Marissa in a lie about where she had been. They have a heated argument, and Mom slaps her across her face. So a defiant Marissa moves in with Fred, telling Mom that she "cannot stop her." Daddy is summoned from New Orleans, and he sends us to therapy for a very brief period. I remember that the therapist told me then to seek therapy before I try to have a normal relationship with a man. I never did.

Marissa and Fred go on to live happily ever after. But no one acknowledges the pain and suffering that continue to fester inside of me. I hate Fred with a vengeance. So I shut him out of my life, for a full year. And I see Marissa very little during that year. I felt like I had lost you, Marissa.

Unavoidably, Fred is to become part of my family. If I want to spend time with my sister, I have no choice but to accept this. So eventually, Fred and I begin to speak again. He slowly lies his way back into my heart. That little girl, now sixteen, is still so very vulnerable and full of pain. Over time, he continues to prey on me just where he left off. He tells me that he does not want our relationship to end. And so, he convinces me to have sex with him. He assures me, and I believe him, that you, Marissa will eventually grow tired of him and leave him. Why couldn't he have just left me alone? Part of me feels that he had to finish what he started with me. He had groomed me for so long. He had to have his prize. He had to have both of us. So he stole my virginity too.

At sixteen, I made a very poor choice to continue intimacy with him while he was with you, Marissa. I own this, and I am so very sorry. But I was the child, and he was the adult, twice my age. It was his responsibility as an adult to protect us children. Instead, he preyed upon us. And I was already in love with him. He had already been intimate with me before. I had already endured so much pain for so long.

So I suppressed my feelings of loneliness and shame that I felt for having sex with Fred. And for getting Marissa back, hurting her with a very callous act. And then I hated myself for being so mean. Just like I hated you, Marissa, for being so mean to me growing up. Revenge hurts the revenger more, I was slowly finding out.

Undeniably, that thirty-year-old man, who was with my sister, put me in that position to make that poor choice. He knew how I felt about him, and he took advantage of it. He used my vulnerability and love for him to convince me to have sex with him. As a minor, I could not legally consent to sex.

Thankfully, I soon left for college. And soon after that, our relationship was finally over for good. I had no idea at the time that the pain, shame, suffering and guilt that I felt for having sex with him in total secrecy would shape my life for the next thirty years. I stuffed all of these emotions deep within me.

So I buried the pain. I was unaware that I was doing it, but I threw that little girl into a dungeon, and buried her very deep inside of me, sentenced to a life in prison. Guilt and shame were thrown into the cage with her, and like an acid drip, slowly ate away at my self-worth. I criticized and yelled at myself in my head for thirty years. I was completely unaware that I was unable to love myself with that part of me imprisoned in shame.

I was forced to forget that she was locked away in my heart, as my first lover became my brother-in-law. Then, Marissa becomes pregnant, and your two beautiful children enter our lives. I was unable to tell my unbearable secret to any other person on Earth. Even my best friend, Dawn. I really can't remember when or how I forgave Fred. But we were amicable.

Why have I never told you this before? To protect you both from the truth. And to protect you both from the hurt that the truth would undoubtedly cause. As we were growing up, it was just us three. I felt that I had to protect that bond. And Mom, I did not want you to feel guilty for not protecting us. But mostly, I remained silent to protect the love that you both have for me. I knew that you both would reject me forever if you knew the truth. Even though you and Fred divorced only seven years after your marriage, I still felt that I had to protect *my nephew and niece, Joey and Alex. And so, I felt that I had no choice but to remain silent. I truly believed that I would take this unspeakable secret to my grave. But as Paul Simon writes, "silence, like a cancer, grows". In protecting you both, Joey and Alex, and even Fred, I subconsciously locked my heart up in shame and guilt inside that dungeon.*

Instead of facing my guilt and shame, I subconsciously buried it deep down inside me with that sixteen-year-old girl. And for thirty years, I numbed that pain with alcohol. Because I did not face my fears, I attracted and entered relationships with men who triggered this guilt and shame, which was unacknowledged inside of me. These relationships never ended well. And eventually, I became an alcoholic.

I did not accept that I was a victim of sexual abuse until two years ago, when I began therapy as part of my recovery from alcoholism. Over the next thirty years, I continued to beat myself up. I subconsciously perpetuated a pattern in the men I chose to have relationships with. I continued to experience the pain over and over to punish myself through bad relationships, sexual and emotional abuse. Throughout my long dating career, I have had fifteen boyfriends who have treated me very badly. Or I entered relationships with men who were either unavailable or whom I was not in love with. My only criteria for a boyfriend was that they wanted to have sex with me. I never knew how to set boundaries to protect myself. I was incapable of separating sex from healthy love. And I was unaware of this. I was broken.

For so many years I allowed men to criticize me, to hurt me, and to take advantage of me physically and emotionally. Sometimes I had sex with men when I really didn't want to. Subconsciously, I felt that I was less than, or that I somehow deserved the pain. I only knew punishment, because I punished myself. I believed that I was the guilty party. So I have never felt completely at peace with myself. I would not allow myself to feel that I was good enough. So I attracted men who verbally, emotionally and sexually abused me. It is known that you attract and manifest whatever corresponds to your inner state of how you feel about yourself. I could attract someone only able to love me as much as I loved myself. Or, as little. As I said, I was broken. Of the fifteen debilitating heartbreaks in three decades, four were unavailable, two were con artists who ended up in prison, and six were cruel and disrespectful to me. Many were also alcoholics.

My sophomore year of college I was sexually abused by my employer over a six-month period. He would molest and have oral sex with me in exchange for extra cash. Several years later, I entered into a two-year relationship with a married man, Leo. I had a serious relationship with a con man, Dick, who stole a car and my friend's antique guns. With help from a friend, I put him in prison. At thirty-seven, I was engaged to Jeff, an abrasive and hostile man who finally admitted that he had seven prior DUI's. I happily waited fourteen months for him to get out of prison, so he could continue our abrasive relationship. Really? Who does that? As I said, I never learned how to set boundaries. I never even knew they existed.

At nearly fifty years old, I have never known true love or a healthy emotional and sexual relationship with a man. Through recovery, therapy and a lot of hard work over the past two and a half years, I have attempted to forgive Fred in my heart so that I could finally heal. But I have never forgiven myself. I want and need to completely love and appreciate all that I am. All that I can give. I have finally come to know that that fifteen-year-old girl was in reality a victim of sexual abuse, preyed upon by a man twice her age with lies and deception. I was taken advantage of. Manipulated again and again over three years, using my vulnerability and my love for him. Of course, no fifteen-year-old knows what love is. And this set the stage for me to believe myself unworthy, so I could continue to choose unhealthy relationships.

By telling you both, I am asking the two most important people in my life for validation, compassion and forgiveness. I am telling you so that you both can understand what I went through and how I was injured. I need to lay the foundation so that I can begin to heal and forgive myself. I need to eradicate the shame that I have been carrying for thirty years. This is not an easy task. I am asking you to help me heal. I need your forgiveness so that I can be free to forgive myself. To love myself completely, free from guilt, shame and punishment. Once set free, I can attract and love a man who is worthy of my love. One who will treat me with honesty and respect.

And, if I don't get this monster that is inside of me out, I will never fully love myself. And I will surely drink alcohol again. I have suffered four relapses since I began recovery, and I was very close to another relapse this past October while in Malaysia.

This is my reality. This is my truth. I love you both very, very much. I will always be here for you. As I said, you two are the two most important people in my life. I ask that you both keep this confidential between us. I am open to hearing your thoughts and feelings. Now, or at any time in the future.

Love you both so much, Della

Well, after thirty years, my truth was finally known by the most important people in my life, my sister and mother. After I read the letter, we actually had our first conversation about everything! Mom was shocked, but not overly reactive. She kept saying, "I didn't know." When I told Mom that she had blamed me when Brenda told her that Fred was sexually active with both of her daughters, she replied that she did not recall doing that.

Denial is a universal phenomenon. Mom did tell me that she had once walked in on us lying together on the living room floor, but she never said anything. She said that our clothes were on, and she just thought we were hugging. I immediately thought, *Still inappropriate! If only she would have questioned us that night, things may have turned out so differently.* We will never know, that's for sure.

Then Marissa dropped a bomb. My niece, Alex, had figured out the truth about her father. "I tried to explain why Della would not be at the family lunch, because Fred was invited. And she figured it out."

"What! She knows that we had sex? And she doesn't hate me?" I asked.

"She knows that her dad is a pervert. She knew that I was only eighteen when he married me. She watched him flirt with her friends' mothers. And his marriage right after me was with another girl half his age."

I couldn't believe it. Another gift from the universe. Yet another huge weight was lifted from my shoulders. I had been protecting everyone in my family from my truth for so long, to the detriment of myself. I felt a relief that I had never known before. The shame I had been carrying, that unbelievable burden I harbored within me for thirty years WAS LIFTED. My inner adolescent, Casey, was finally set free from her dungeon of shame. Or so I thought.

I realized that night why I allowed emotional abuse from men to continue for so long. No! *Allowed* is the wrong word. Fred had *stolen* my virginity under a sky of guilt and shame for my own sister. I became attached to him because I was vulnerable. What I thought was love—my first act of sexual intimacy—held hands with guilt and shame. I needed to be punished for my acts. So the subsequent times that I loved, or thought I loved a man, sex continued to be attached to guilt and shame. Abuse, infidelity, molestation—they all equaled love in my warped mind. They went together like peas in a pod. Sex became a currency, a necessary payment for love. I felt that I deserved this bad treatment from assholes, for I *was* guilt and shame. I finally owned my pain.

Chapter Sixteen

LOVE YOU ALL

My Life in Review

Catharsis is defined as the process of releasing, and thereby providing release from, strong or repressed emotions. I feel like in the past three years of my recovery and healing, this has happened to me. Every day I tap deeper into a love that I have found for myself. I am not only "good enough," but I am magnificent! And . . . I promise, so are you! Just because you exist.

Throughout the dating years in my life, I let myself fall so hard for men that each breakup was excruciating. And I blamed myself for trying so hard to make horrible relationships work, just so that I could be *in* a relationship. I was completely oblivious as to the cause, and continuation, of failure. Nor did I have any skills to find a good man. Fred had taught me that abnormal was normal. I did not allow myself to realize the blame I put on myself. Or if I did think about it, I just covered that thought with alcohol. So, how did I get here? Let's review:

My father left my loving household when I was just three. This left my mother devastated. It is not surprising that growing up, she was not there for me at a few critical times when I was in pain or my heart was breaking. When I needed her to just be a mom.

When I was thirteen, she chose not to come to my bed to comfort me as I called out during the night after my cat had been tragically hit by a car in front of my home. After telling her about the separation from my husband, instead of comforting me, she let me know how much she had spent on my wedding. It felt like the money she "wasted" on my wedding was more important than the pain that I was feeling for my impending divorce from yet another bad decision. And then, the unthinkable, when she found out from Dawn's mother that Fred was molesting me (and having sex with Marissa) she blamed me. *The Courage to Heal* states, "The way the abuse was handled when you were a child has a lot to do with subsequent impact. If a child's disclosure [to family] is met with compassion and effective intervention, the healing begins immediately. But if no one noticed or responded to your pain, you were left feeling abandoned and alone. If you were blamed, were not believed, or suffered further trauma, the damage was compounded. And the ways you coped with the abuse might have created further problems." When my mother blamed me, I really thought it was my fault. This could partially explain why I had intimacy issues later in life.

I don't want to imply that Mom was a bad mother. She showered us with love most of the time. She was there for us every day, raising us all on her own. I am so very grateful for the very close relationship that we have shared in my life, and we are closer now than ever. We still go to rock concerts together, and Mom is seventy-four. Mom was always very open with us. I felt like I could talk to her about anything. Except for Fred, of course. And I cannot forget that she was inside her own struggle and emotional pain. It was all she could manage to put a roof over our heads and food on our table in her own time of great sorrow from her divorce. A separation she believed she was the cause of.

Mom taught us good morals. She did not tolerate racism in our house, and quickly corrected us as young girls when we repeated the "n" word, a word that her parents used at times. And, perhaps, Mom had intimacy or neglect issues with her own mother. That is not for me to judge.

I barely dated boys during my high school years, especially after I met Fred. The few dates I had were awful, paling in comparison to my "first love." I accelerated my alcohol intake immediately after I entered college, binging and then vomiting almost every weekend. The fiasco with Fred was still so new, but I had no idea the affect it was having on my emotions.

Then, a blessing and miracle, I witnessed the birth of Joey. I was an aunt! Yet it is now clear to me that his birth drove me farther into the hole that Casey was digging, because he was the result of the love of my sister and first love! Ray, my first true boyfriend, was just an attempt to settle with someone to be with someone. He wanted to marry me, but I was not in love with him. I thought that I needed to have a boyfriend to fit into society, and I loved being in the military community with girlfriends. I also needed his undying affection. But in the end, his love was suffocating me, or so Casey had me believe. Aaron was a complete shithead. He broke up with me on my birthday, then the SOB started spreading untrue rumors about me. He was truly an asshole of the first degree.

My relationship with Ricky was the longest thus far. It was really intimate, and a seemingly healthy relationship. When we were first declared exclusive, I told Ricky that I needed him in my life. I believed that he completed me, that I was not whole without him. I now know that this is a red flag for myself! One and one do not make one, they make two. But as was my pattern, I used the long distance-New Jersey issue as an excuse to terminate us.

I now know that a healthy relationship must include unconditional self-love, individual hobbies, and some healthy time spent apart. I must love myself first before I can attract and be capable of loving another. Somehow, on some level, I have always known this, but I have never applied it. Or else I just deluded myself that I loved me, while Casey continued to bash me relentlessly. A daily vicious cycle of self-loathing. Such self-torture.

The Casey cycle was becoming very apparent by the end of my undergraduate college years. It was a repetitious pattern of *always* becoming too close, too soon—with the outcome somehow never in doubt. Rejection, on my part or mostly theirs, became my never-ending downward spiral. The theme recurred in graduate school, with a commanding attraction to an older, seemingly mature man. I just could not escape from that "in love" feeling. But Leo was married, and our future was doomed from the start. As is evident from my diary, I had warned myself so many times to stay away from him. But, I persisted and caused myself unbearable pain over a two-year period.

Of course, I always blindly accepted that a successful relationship was the key to happiness. It is, right? So, I blamed myself for "choosing to stay" in relationships of disrespect and cruelty. I expected too much from them, and I expected them to be what they were not and never could be. And I enabled their bad behavior.

Europe was a great way for me to escape all my relationship failures of college. But there was no geographical escape. Diego, David, and Dario proved to be more chain links in a recurring pattern that brought me so much pain and grief. Looking back, I am really surprised that I allowed Diego to speak to me the way that he did. Perhaps the constant cut-downs in the past by my bullying sister allowed me to accept his sharp tongue, along with the accumulated damage of abusive relationships, and of course, Casey inside my own head.

After attempting a fresh start with a move to California, I dragged along and entered into a doomed relationship with a con artist from Texas. Of course, I again blamed myself for this very poor decision. I later put him in prison for auto and property theft. Following that meltdown and the abortion of our child, I was distraught and very vulnerable.

On the rebound from immense emotional pain from the fiasco of Dick, I entered into a loveless and very short-lived marriage: an ill-fated union with a good man who was determined to marry me. I told myself that I deserved Harry because he was financially stable. That his devout love for me was enough for both of us. How ridiculous is that? When the marriage ended so quickly, I of course blamed myself for getting married to a man that I "loved," but with whom I was not in love.

Then there was the failed relationship with the young and immature Cristiano from Paris. The romance and European appeal was just too good to pass up. I know, Daddy, I know. Of course, I saw the pattern, but I didn't know then how to fix it. I only knew that I was to blame.

After what seemed like a lifetime of unending pain and shame, I could not deal with the death of my father, the one man that I loved most in the world. It was the worst time of my life. I felt that I was a complete failure, and Daddy's words of repeating my pattern rang true to my feelings of self-blame. I had failed to ever have a healthy relationship and give him a grandchild before his death.

So I coped by increasing my alcohol intake and entering yet another horrible relationship with a liar and alcoholic, Jeff. Of course, I did not admit to my own disease until years later. I even waited fourteen months for him to get out of prison for seven DUI's before I became engaged to him. Who does that?

Levi was my last attempt at a romantic relationship. Again, I dove in and fell in love too quick. To be fair, he did too. But, Levi was bipolar and had to end the relationship because he knew that he could not be in one. His meds were really affecting his emotions. But, he continued to contact me for over two months, which kept my hopes up. So it took twice as long to end the relationship as it had lasted. I truly believed that I could heal Levi! How sick is that? But again, I only saw my own failure.

But I had a few years left to have a baby. Or so I thought. Menopause at forty-three hit me like a slap in the face. It was like God's cruel answer to that question. Dealing with hormonal imbalance, hot flashes, night sweats, unspeakable shame, self-blame, self-torture, anxiety attacks, hives, losing my cat of fifteen years, and then being fired, I entered a deep and dark depression with suicidal thoughts. Looking back, I just could not understand how much I allowed myself to be hurt. What was wrong with me?

My disease was becoming more progressive, and I drank to self-medicate. Little did I know that it was virtually impossible for me to find a good man, because I hated myself so much. I had no self-worth, confidence, or self-esteem. I spent so many days on my couch recovering from hangovers, unable to spend the time to attend healthy activities or search for a good man. I was dishonest with myself. I was selfish, self-seeking, and sometimes inconsiderate toward others. I had worked so hard to force serious romantic relationships with men, as well as friendships with women. I blamed myself for repeatedly allowing men to hurt and disrespect me.

This all led to the shame and blame of myself for everything bad that had ever happened in my life. The shame that led to the feeling that I was not deserving of true love. The shame that led to choosing men who could not love me the way that I wanted. I finally saw that my only option left was sobriety.

It has taken over three long years of recovery and therapy to get to this point. In brutal retrospect, it all makes sense. Through the prism of therapy, this all shocks me. I now see the unbearable shame that that warped first relationship with Fred created within me. Fred established a lifelong pattern by sexually and emotionally abusing me at such a young age, and right as my sexual identity was emerging. He taught me that sex was for pleasure, not a mutual love and respect for a partner. He taught me that sex was a commodity, not a sacred gift, which led to my periods of promiscuity and using men. I was groomed and manipulated by a sophisticated pedophile. He knew his stuff. Part of my healing now is continued suffering, because I can see with my diary how he groomed me for so long. And it makes me nauseous. But I am finally realizing that it was *not my fault*. He stole my innocent teenage love with his eyes, and then he sealed the deal with his touch. For his own fucking pleasure. And it affected the rest of my life. Until now.

The Courage to Heal

Studying the book, *The Courage to Heal* that Jasmine recommended has allowed me to free some guilt that I felt, based on assumptions that were not true. And it allowed me to clearly see the coping mechanisms I created to help ease the trauma that I endured and its subsequent effects on my life.

I have learned that addiction is a form of self-punishment as well as a coping mechanism. When I first entered recovery from alcoholism, I truly felt that the fault was mine for everything that had happened with Fred. I did not see that I was a victim of sexual abuse for decades. One of the steps to recovery is to write down an inventory of flaws and character defects. What was my part in past events? Where I was to blame?

In 2013, I wrote that I *allowed* Fred to touch me on my private parts when he moved into our home. I *allowed* myself to love him, and to fall in love with him. It was *my fault* that I was so jealous of the relationship that he had with Marissa at the same time. I *chose* to stay with him. And later, when Marissa moved in with him, it was *my fault* that I had sex with my sister's boyfriend.

But *he* had lied and wormed his way back in to my life, after I had not spoken to him for fourteen months. *He* had told me that he still loved me, and that he did not want our relationship to end! *He* resumed his advances toward me. But, I refused to place any of the blame on him and placed it solely on me, even though I was only fifteen years old when the sick relationship began. I not only carried my shame, I carried his too. He was the thirty-year-old adult. He *had* to know that having sex with two teenage sisters at the same time was wrong! He knew it was statutory rape; otherwise, why would he have asked me to burn my diary? It was written proof of his crime. Yes, he knew.

After that unbearable three-year ordeal, I craved intimacy and love, and sought it from men. Of course, I mistook sex for intimacy. Fred had taught me that. Not only was I abandoned by my father, whom I adored, but I felt abandoned by Daddy again and again every year when our visits across state lines were over for another four to six months. Few and far between. My therapist felt that this must have been very significant in my need for affection. Fred filled my daddy hole. At the ashram with Aidan, more than sex, I really just wanted to lay next to him. For so long, I craved intimacy and love from men, a closeness that I so rarely got. So when I did get it, I tended to latch on and smother. Or lie to myself about my true feelings (or lack of feelings) for the man giving me intimacy.

Even though my experience of abuse at age fifteen through seventeen was confusing and devastating (since Fred was also having sex with my sister, which made me jealous as hell), I did experience sexual pleasure and orgasms. For me, this was very difficult to deal with. It does not mean that I was responsible in any way. These are natural bodily reactions, and I had no control over them. Puberty is nearly impossible to understand, especially when you are going through it.

As I mentioned, since I was a teenager, I had a very difficult time accepting that having sex with Fred was not my fault. I was, after all, sixteen. That seems a little old to be coerced into sex. But abuse is abuse! Age does not matter. Fred groomed and manipulated me, knowing that I adored him. Of course, he was fully aware, having read my diary. He once laughed as he shared that his friend told him, "Well, you got them both, didn't you," referring to me and my sister. How very inappropriate to share this with me, the sixteen-year-old that had just been "got." Fred was the adult, so *he* is the only one to blame. "It is unfair to expect children or even teenagers to be able to protect themselves. Teenagers and young adults do not have the same power and perspective of older people. Nor do they have the experience to help them confront such a devastating situation . . . It is always the responsibility of the adults to behave with respect toward children." Saying "no" was simply not something I could have done, because I thought that I loved him. I was just beginning to test my own limits and attitudes. It was my responsibility to discover my world. And, even though Marissa made advances toward Fred while the family was sleeping, *he* is still to blame. It was his responsibility to say "no!" Marissa must have felt guilt, yet she was physically and emotionally abused too. That truth is beyond dispute.

Continued abuse is not uncommon. In my case, the abuse continued well into my forties, just with different men. I was nineteen, a sophomore in college when my employer sexually abused me. I was twenty-four when I allowed a married man into my bed, which lead to heart-wrenching emotional abuse. I was thirty-six when Jeff abused me with his rage and fear. But I was still responding from the perspective of a young, powerless fifteen-year-old. Casey, my inner child, ran my life for so very long because she was so intensely hurt by Fred. Unbelievable, when I think about it.

But I never learned any differently. Until now. My boundaries had always been violated, because I never drew them. The term "personal boundaries" did not even enter my vocabulary until I entered therapy in my forties. So it is unfair to expect myself to be able to see them all of a sudden. I did not become assertive just because I grew up and left home. That was something only time and experience could teach my troubled soul.

What I have finally realized through therapy is that I was choosing men with the same characteristics I saw in myself. I now see that I could not choose good men, because I could allow someone else to love me *only* as much as I loved myself. I could not attract a man who was capable of more love than I was able to give to myself. I thought that I was a bad person, so I chose bad people with whom to form relationships. It seemed like my only criteria for jumping in to bed with men was simply that they wanted to jump in bed with me. I did not say yes all the time. Mostly, I did so only when I thought there could be a chance of a happy marriage. I thought society would accept me only if I was in a successful relationship, like all my friends. And like my parents expected. I did not realize until therapy that the shame rightfully rested on my molester, Fred, and not me. And that I am completely innocent of what happened to me, given my age when the grooming started. What a huge burden of shame to keep inside of myself for so long. It was this shame that allowed Casey to blame me for continuing the pattern of choosing bad or unavailable men. She would not allow me to see Fred's impact on my life. But she kept repeating it.

For most of my life up to this point, the dreams I would have while sleeping would always follow an underlying theme: FAILURE! I was given a task, mostly with a group of people, but something stopped me from achieving it. I always failed at it or disappointed someone in some way. I seemed to be frozen and could not move when the danger was very close, or there were cracks in the floor stopping the hair I am trying to sweep, or there was water coming through the holes in the wall. Someone I was attracted to would not let me ride the yellow swings hanging from the trees. Rosanna was helping me to complete my part of a task because I cannot complete it myself. In many dreams, it was Daddy I had disappointed, but sometimes it would be my work colleagues or my boss. Or my colleagues would rudely ignore me when I spoke directly to them. So high school! Now I love it when Daddy appears in my dreams. Sometimes we hug, and it feels so real. I wake up feeling like I just hugged my Daddy. But there is always a sense of urgency because he is dying, our time together running out.

What was the meaning of all these dreams? I did not trust myself. I was very disappointed in myself. I was not performing my best. I was a slacker. I was just not good enough in my own eyes. By whatever or whomever's yardstick, I just did not measure up.

Still in therapy, I am continuing to peel the layers of my onion of shame. Rereading my diary from the years of sexual abuse with Fred, I had to relive all the raw emotions that I had gone through all those years ago. Every failed relationship and drunken embarrassment was a layer being peeled away. They say the only way to the "other side" is through. I have certainly experienced that, and I believe it wholeheartedly. The pain, the anger, the nausea, the shame, and the fear are still inside of me, but have mostly diminished. Every therapy session, and the work I put into them, exposes that pain, so I can release it. Then, I can peel away and lessen the hatred for myself. Bit by bit, I am becoming whole again.

It's not the poison and the hate that kill you, it is keeping secrets shaped by shame that are so emotionally toxic. Because I lived in fear that my family would find out about my sexual relationship with Fred and hate me, my secrets were destroying me. Speak the truth and "the truth shall set you free." That is the way it really is. When I finally allowed my mother and sister to know my truth, there were no more secrets left to kill me. Casey is finally breaking free from her dungeon. Rather than kill me, sharing my secrets healed me. And it can heal you too.

THE COURAGE TO LOVE ME

I finally see that I can change! I can make better choices and make a better life. This is the first step, and the next is to completely forgive myself. Knowing what I have been through—feeling so many years of pain—I did the very best that I could under impossible circumstances of repeated sexual and emotional abuse and poor choices. I coped. I can now see that I have a right to a decent relationship with a man who will honor me as a woman. I get to be seen, acknowledged, and respected.

I forgive myself. It was not my fault. I have no reason to be ashamed. I am a survivor! And, damn it, I have earned that name. I have the power to make positive changes in my life. From a place of self-acceptance and self-love. I will do so. I love you, my Della. This is so powerful. And I am so grateful for my friends and my therapist, Jasmine. And to my Higher Power. And to me!

The starting point of my healing was sobriety. It removed the blanket that was hiding my authentic self so that I could discover all that love. Today, I am doing well. I don't blame myself any longer. I am working through the shame. I have good friends in recovery, and I even helped two of my best friends to join the recovery program. Now, I am happy to say that we hang out together and have a ton of fun, clean and sober. I *never* would have believed that I could have so much fun without alcohol or drugs. I had to experience it for myself. I have been to rock concerts, weddings and parties and danced my ass off; and was literally inside joy. And I never have to worry about getting to the bar for my next drink! I proved myself wrong! I *can* live a happy life without alcohol. That seems so absurd to say. But I love life. I really do! Sure, there are still ups and downs. But I can do things that I love (without any hangovers), and continue to work on myself. I am cultivating a love for myself that I never thought I would have. And I am continuing to grow emotionally. I would never have been able to write this book if I was still drinking or using.

One of the cornerstones of my foundation that allowed me to heal was the compassion and forgiveness that my beloved sister, Marissa, showed me the day that she was coloring my hair and I confessed my deepest, darkest secrets about Fred and me. I shared my secrets with the most important human that needed to know. The secrets that I had originally planned to take to my grave so that I could keep her love and protect her family. The secrets that housed the toxic shame that were poisoning me from the inside. The secrets that were preventing me from loving myself. My secrets had become my silence, and silence had become my longtime nemesis.

My sister's reaction to my truth was so far from what I had expected. It was one of the most heartwarming moments of relief in my life. In the span of less than five minutes, Marissa lifted my cross, that ugly burden, from my soul. She told me that Fred was a pervert, and that I had done nothing wrong. It was a precious gift from her, one that finally allowed me to let go of all that guilt and shame I had been holding for thirty-five years. My love for my sister grew exponentially that day. Over the next few days, she repeatedly asked why I had taken so long to tell her. For so long I believed that I would lose her love if she knew my truth, but just the opposite happened.

I want to stress to you, my readers, to find the courage and take the risk to share your secrets. You never know how people will react. I want to give you permission to face your demons, especially the number one, called denial, and to share your story. Tell anyone. If that person does not validate your truth, then find someone else. Please do not keep your shame buried in the dungeon of your soul for as long as I did. It is a senseless waste of this gift called life.

I have also learned that happiness cannot come from some nifty little recipe that society has taught us: get married, get a house, have kids. It also cannot come from any mind-altering substance. Or money. Happiness is not the same as pleasure, such as the feeling we get from riding a roller coaster or receiving flowers from a mate. Happiness especially cannot come only from a spouse, 2.5 children, and that white picket fence. Don't believe me? Ask any of your married friends. Happiness will not magically appear as soon as I find Mr. Right, or if I get that job and become "successful."

To me, real success is found in discovering my most authentic self. In fact, I believe that happiness cannot come from another individual at all. It must come from within. To me, happiness is the satisfaction I felt while moving toward my potential. It is the look on my students' faces when they finally got the algebra concept I was trying to explain. Or when they found a love for some part of science that I was showing them that day. Or when they realized that they want to do their part to protect our little planet. For me, it was also finally seeing the light at the end of the long tunnel in my process of healing. It was finally being able to see my true, authentic self as the healing process began to define who I truly am. Now, success for me is feeling truly aligned with my life work.

I used to be so in love with being in love, or what I thought was love. I used to say that being in love with a man was the most powerful feeling on Earth. I yearned for that irresistible giddiness so much that I would do anything to get it. Casey gave me hell for that, and the failures that were the results, for decades. And alcohol allowed me to numb the pain. I now know that the truest form of love is the love that you cultivate for yourself. All the rest, such as success and love from a partner, will come only after that is achieved.

"Almost Della" is a reference to my relentless yearning for happiness (or what I thought was happiness) and my "almost" finding it, but never quite getting there. In a way, it was the constant nagging voice of my inner adolescent, Casey. She kept my awful truth buried in her dungeon, yet she constantly criticized me for it at the same time. She kept me in victimhood. As I wrote at the top of the Acropolis in Athens, Greece in December of 1993: *I must love every part of me. All of me. Even the bad emotions. And deal with them as best I can. When I am in times of hurt, I must go all the way through the pain. Let it live its course. Get in touch with it, know it, and try to understand it instead of pushing it away.*

I wish that I had really listened to that twenty-seven-year-old self in Greece. But incredibly, it would take over two decades to take root in my mind. I have completely changed my perspective on the way that I should think about myself. And writing this book has offered me the opportunity to remember what happened to me. To reveal and release Casey from her bondage, so that she can be more respectful to and of me. I have risen above victimhood, and learned that I cannot teach from an empty cup. And I have reconciled with Casey. I am filling back up. Whenever I feel Casey criticizing me, I remember the beautiful words my friend Crystal told me, "Love her." I picture adult Della holding Casey and filling her with the love that I have nurtured for both of us.

I have learned that all of those lost "loves" were not wasted time, because each one of them helped me grow. They became part of who I am. The pain provided what I needed to know. All my "failures" were in fact opportunities to learn to do it differently. I also realized that in each relationship, I taught "him" as well. Perhaps he chose me for a reason. Who knows?

I have come a long way. I have stopped trying to make "Almost Della" whole, because I finally see that I already *am* whole. I have realized a new love for myself. I no longer expect a guy to do that for me. I am now proactively pursuing good habits. I have healthy dietary habits (well, mostly: I do love my cookies!). I volunteer at schools, I am on the board of a local nonprofit, I practice yoga (asana) and meditation on a regular basis, and I have joined the choir at a church I love, Unity Church. I continue to indulge my love for the spirit. I continue to invigorate the love I have for traveling, reviving myself by immersing in the amazing cultures of others. And I continue to attend and enjoy recovery meetings. I listen and learn from others' experience, strength and hope. And I share mine and help others too.

The other day I had a dream that began the same as all the others: I am given some task and must perform it in front of a crowd of "judgers." But for the first time that I can remember, on the third try of this task, I succeeded! I performed the task, and I enjoyed it. And I wanted to do it again and again. I was so proud of myself when I woke. I was, and finally am, just . . . Della.

According to the National Sexual Violence Resource Center, 55% of women report molestation in their lifetime, 20% will be raped, and 35% of rape cases will go unreported. And 25% of girls will be sexually abused before they turn eighteen. Most victims will experience some sort of emotional stress that surfaces later in life. For me, my rape and subsequent shame manifested in physical pain such as addiction, anxiety and hives. In others, it may manifest as a disease or cancer. Make no mistake: it will surface in some way.

My Gift is You

My hope is that I have touched a pain in your life that you will consider healing. Of course, cultivating a love and forgiving myself was the ultimate gift for me. And believe me, I am still working on it. But, having an audience with whom I can share my experiences with makes all this pain worthwhile.

My gift is you. And I hope that I get to meet some of you in future speaking engagements and workshops. Being able to share how I became a survivor and began my healing, knowing that it may help even one person, is the ultimate gift in life. Remember Melinda Gates' definition of success? *"To know that one life has breathed easier because you live."*

You may ask me, how can you get so personal with your story? How can you write and talk about all of this for the public eyes to see? The only answer that I have is that it is truly a gift from my Higher Power. I *want* to share my story with you. I don't want you to go through the length of suffering that I have. I feel that deep inside my heart. And the only explanation for that is that this is my life purpose. This is my life work. This is what I was put on this Earth to do. I truly feel that I am aligning with my destiny. That is the only way I can explain the way I feel.

I write this book in the hopes that if you have any similarities with my life, that you might become aware of the reason behind some of the choices you have made or may be making at present. I have hope that you become aware, so that you can embrace life-changing rebirth as I am. Stop beating yourself up. Learn from my mistakes. Learn from your own. But above all, do not bury your shame. If it is already buried, acknowledge it, and let's dig it up! When you judge someone else, see it as an opportunity for growth. Know that every human being has some good within them. And that *everyone* has bad days. And then do a little search within yourself to discover if you are judging others for what you secretly judge in yourself. I sure did. What an eye-opener that was.

With sobriety, recovery, and healing, I am taking the steps to empower my life and build a love for myself. Only then will I be able to freely love others. I am reaching a freedom that I have never known. I am peeling my onion. I am flowing from abuse victim to survivor. I now look for validation from within myself. I no longer give away my power by searching for praise from others. It is my parting wish that you are blessed with these profound realizations as well. I am with you, and I love you all.

Epilogue

FOR YEARS, I suffered terribly, continuously struggling with my own heart and mind. Ceaselessly searching for Mr. Right to fulfill my own happiness, and then forcing relationships when I thought that I had found "him." On top of that, I abused alcohol to cope with my emotional pain, which caused even greater suffering. I never realized that the "forcing" was my heart telling me, "This is NOT it!" True happiness is never a struggle. It should flow like a stream. Sure, there will be rocks, and sometimes boulders obstructing the way. But the stream will always flow to the ocean without force. The ocean of happiness and your Higher Power. If your stream dries up, go back to the fork, and try again. I now know that the suffering of going down the wrong path again and again were actually achievements on my journey to eventual enlightenment.

Perhaps my long-term suffering grew from a conflict between what I thought was the reason for my existence and my true inner reason for existence, which was unknown to my conscious self. For so long, I felt like I had no inherent instinct to guide me to happiness. So I listened to, and followed, what other people did. But mostly I did what my parents wished me to do: find Mr. Right, marry him, and make a family. That will lead to happiness. (And, by the way, grandchildren for them.) The drumbeat of this supposed wisdom was relentless. Mom made her obvious judgement after I told her that I was getting a divorce, and Daddy chimed in with "You are breaking up with Cristiano? Do you see a pattern here?" This was especially painful because Cristiano was my next failed relationship after my divorce. My parents' definition of happiness, a successful marriage, became my own at a very young age. I interpreted my life's task as coming from my parents and society, not from what my own subconscious voice was trying to tell me. Hence, suffering.

For so long I thought humans existed to find a spouse and procreate. To give love to a spouse and child, and receive their love in return. But perhaps the reason we exist is to find a love for ourselves, and then to nurture that love, so that we can then give it freely. To accept and embrace who we truly are. To disregard what society says will make us "happy" and learn to trust our own feelings. To truly trust ourselves. Society's standard of happiness proved to be a vicious lie for me, which made finding it extremely difficult. I put it before listening to my own heart. I paid dearly for that mistake.

It was my constant search for my perfect life mate that tore me down. After thirty years and fifteen failed relationships, I became keenly aware of the lack of solid content in my life. And my lack of contentment. This became increasingly true on weekends, with the realization that weekend after weekend, I had no one special to go to events with. Where was my plus-one? When I awoke with a hangover and spent the day alone on the couch for the thousandth time, the long-term void within me was too much to bear.

It took almost three decades of failed searching, then over three years of "failed-search recovery" to find a true love for myself. Even though my career was somewhat successful, the tension between what I had achieved and what I still HAD to accomplish (finding Mr. Right and bearing our children) drove me ever downward, into mind-numbing addiction and suicidal depression. I was broken. After years of recovery with therapy, I finally began to turn my life around. I began to see the love and acceptance that I was tirelessly searching for from a mate needed to come from my very own heart. My involvement at Unity Church and a lot of *Super Soul Sunday* episodes certainly helped. But it was therapy with Jasmine, some group therapy, and the twelve-step recovery program with its fellowship that truly got me there. It took over three years and a strong determination to make meaning out of my life! Another important part of my work on myself was being with myself. I did not date during this period. And I certainly did not have sex. Celibacy can have its advantages while healing.

My despair from all those years stemmed from my perceived lack of worthiness and importance of my life while on this Earth. I did not see a reason for my existence. I did not matter. These perceptions grew so strongly that I developed ways to cope with these perceived failures. In order to live with that monster attached to me, I had to bury her within me. So I locked her up and threw away the key. When that did not keep her silent, I numbed her constant nagging by pouring more and more alcohol into our shared body, which turned into an evil twin monster: addiction.

But every pain, every fight to force the wrong person to fit into my puzzle of perceived importance, was in fact a light shining on the edge of the puzzle of my heart, exposing its true shape. Outlining the beautiful design of my true soul. The deeply hidden meaning of my true existence. Shoving puzzle piece after puzzle piece into the light of my heart, I finally found that my true love had been right there all along. My true love *is* the light and love of my heart! Without my suffering, growing from my search for what I thought was my true life meaning, I never would have found my true life meaning. The Della I almost lost. I now see clearly that my purpose in life is much broader than a spouse and 2.5 children. My true life meaning includes sharing my suffering with you!

Through it all, even if I was unaware of it much of the time, I now realize that I *was* growing, as a person and a soul. They say that inside every wound lies a jewel. With the passing of time, and the grasping of wisdom, I came to accept an eternal truth: try as we may—and Lord knows, I tried—inner peace can never be found without, only within. No Mr. Right could ever fix what was wrong inside of me. Only I can achieve that. I am. I truly hope these words provide some inspiration to my readers struggling with your own journeys. To find, you must begin seeking. My next book will chronicle my expedition to healing and self-love. Until then, namaste.

Always remember that you are not alone! Confidential help is available for free!

The 24-hour National Sexual Assault Hotline is 1-800-656-4673.

I strongly encourage you to get to the internet and do some searching. Put the word "rape" or "domestic violence" into the browser bar with your local city or area. Find local domestic violence or rape crisis hotlines, online chats and other helpful links. They will put you in touch with someone nearby who can get you out of immediate danger and build an action plan with you. They can also set up housing and counseling. In Houston, we have the Houston Area Women's Center and The Council on Recovery (which saved my life), among others.

You are invited to check out my blog on my website where I will be sharing more of my experiences at dellabarbato.com. I am also in the process of creating some music that will accompany this memoir, so keep an eye out for that on my website as well.

Acknowledgments

I AM IN deep gratitude to the women in my recovery community who have been indispensable to my recovery. You have been with me through all my tears, shares, and steps over the years as I went through the most difficult times in my recovery and healing. My Gratitude Gals, you know who you are. And especially to my sponsor and MWF home group, you know who you are.

To my best friend of almost forty years, Dawn, you helped me through the most difficult times in my life. More times than I can count. To my good friend, Alora, you taught me what a good relationship should feel like, and what it shouldn't. We had so much fun on weekends for so many years, and we still do! And you have invited me into your family of little ones when I didn't have my own. To my various former roommates and friends in college and after: Camille, Cindy, Lisa, Terry, Julie N., Julie G., Kathleen, you were there when I laughed in joy and cried in grief. To my Choir Goddesses: Ellen, Susan, and Donna, you sing with me in joy and provide me with such valuable friendship.

To my therapist, Jasmine, working with you for these several years was often excruciating, but from every tear came an opportunity to find a way through the pain to the "other side." You saved my life.

To Mom, who was my support and my rock. And so many times when I was alone on a weekend night, you were my friend. Daddy, there are no words. Your love is with me always. To my niece and nephew, you mean the world to me and you are like my own children. Your love is unconditional. To every single person in my extended family, I am so lucky to have you all in my life. I am blessed and I absolutely love family time! I don't know how we escaped, but we have no bad apples in our bunch.

To my sister, your love and compassion has done more for me than you will ever know.

And to my Higher Power, none of this would have been possible without You.

www.ingramcontent.com/pod-product-compliance
Lightning Source LLC
Chambersburg PA
CBHW070045080526
44586CB00013B/919